Gothic Arches, Latin Crosses

Gothic Arches, Latin Crosses

ANTI-CATHOLICISM AND
AMERICAN CHURCH DESIGNS IN
THE NINETEENTH CENTURY

Ryan K. Smith

The University of North Carolina Press
Chapel Hill

Designed by Kimberly Bryant
Set in ITC Galliard by
Tseng Information Systems, Inc.

The paper in this book meets the guidelines for permanence
and durability of the Committee on Production Guidelines
for Book Longevity of the Council on Library Resources.

Library of Congress Cataloging-in-Publication Data
Smith, Ryan K.
Gothic arches, Latin crosses : anti-Catholicism and American church
designs in the nineteenth century / Ryan K. Smith.
p. cm.
Includes bibliographical references and index.
ISBN-13: 978-0-8078-3025-3 (cloth : alk. paper)
ISBN-10: 0-8078-3025-9 (cloth : alk. paper)
ISBN-13: 978-0-8078-5689-5 (pbk. : alk. paper)
ISBN-10: 0-8078-5689-4 (pbk. : alk. paper)
1. Anti-Catholicism—United States—History—19th century. 2. United
States—Church history—19th century. 3. Church buildings—United
States—Design and construction. 4. Church architecture—United States.
5. Architecture, Gothic—United States. I. Title.
BX1766.S59 2006
246'.9097309034—dc22
2005034947

cloth   10 09 08 07 06   5 4 3 2 1
paper   10 09 08 07 06   5 4 3 2 1

For Todd

Contents

Illustrations

Photographs

Table

Acknowledgments

Writing this book has been a lively pursuit, and it is a unique pleasure to be able to thank those individuals and institutions that have made it possible. My mentor Christine Leigh Heyrman helped start the chase, and she assisted me at every step along the way. Her counsel lifted me, and her style inspired me. I cannot imagine this project without her. Bernard Herman was also involved and inspiring from the beginning. He offered constant aid, and I hope that I have been able to make at least some small use of his considerable expertise.

Many others played key roles. Ritchie Garrison and Gretchen Buggeln consistently broadened my views. Anne Boylan and Richard Bushman stepped in at a critical time and provided valuable readings, as did Peter Williams and an anonymous reader for the University of North Carolina Press. John Davis, Grant Wacker, Chandos Brown, Joseph Bendersky, Louis Nelson, Lyn Causey, Pat Anderson, Jalynn Olsen, Becky Martin, Ann Kirschner, Brooke Hunter, Tracey Birdwell, Angeline Robertson, and Jennifer Bandas assisted in countless ways. Paul and Ann Jerome Croce taught me creative lessons that I continue to draw from to this day. Gerald Stamler and Tom Smith made extraordinary trips for my illustrations. And Pat Orendorf relieved many administrative burdens with skill and good cheer.

I have depended on the resources of many institutions for this study, and there are a few I would like to single out. The University of Delaware granted me funds for research and writing, and the university's Special Collections Department at Morris Library facilitated my work. The Library Company of Philadelphia expertly handled many of my special requests. The staff of the Union Theological Seminary and Presbyterian School of Christian Education, particularly Jeff Keezel, provided special assistance with my illustrations, and the seminary's Morton Library served as a delightful resource. Other repositories that were particularly helpful include the Winterthur Library, the Associated Archives at St. Mary's Seminary and University, the Maryland State Archives, the Library of Virginia, Swem Library at the College of William and Mary, and the Cabell Library at Virginia Commonwealth University. The McNeil Center for Early American Studies offered a useful forum to discuss the work in progress. And I thank the journal *Church History* for permission to reprint an article in revised form for Chapter 3.

The staff of the University of North Carolina Press has welcomed this project warmly and professionally. I am greatly indebted to the staff's skill and hard work. Elaine Maisner, in particular, guided the manuscript with great steadiness and care. Mary Caviness copyedited the manuscript with precision and helped me clarify my thoughts.

Finally, my family and my wife's family provided many levels of support and encouragement. In particular, my parents, Kenneth and Lorraine Smith, helped develop my appreciation for old books and old buildings. And like family, Patrick and Marianne Fugeman offered shelter and uplift. But my largest debt is to my wife, Andrea. She challenged me to take on the project from the beginning, and she has seen it through to the end. She has infused it and my own life with a sense of balance that they would not have had without her. My dearest thanks go to her.

Gothic Arches, Latin Crosses

I

Introductions

On the evening of May 8, 1844, a mob marched toward St. Augustine's Catholic Church in Philadelphia. Two days earlier, thousands of anti-Catholic rioters had stormed immigrant neighborhoods in the northern suburb of Kensington, clashing with Irish residents and destroying dozens of homes and shops. A fight at a political meeting had sparked the riots, but ethnic and religious tensions had long been simmering. By the third day of rioting, the city's militia had yet to restore order, and the mob turned its attention to the nearby Catholic churches and seminaries. Rumors circulated that these structures housed arms, but the buildings also held symbolic importance, representing what nativist leaders called the "bloody hand of the Pope." In the afternoon, a crowd set fire to St. Michael's Catholic Church and prevented interference from area firemen. One reporter observed that as this "beautiful gothic struc- ture" burned, "the mob continued to shout, and when the cross at the peak of the roof fell, they gave three cheers." Militia units then scrambled to post defenses around other Catholic targets as rioters left Kensington for St. Augustine's Church, a proud old sanctu- ary within the city proper.[1]

Philadelphia's mayor hurried to the spot.

Speaking from the steps of the large brick church, he attempted to calm the hostile crowds and assured them that the building was unarmed. His words had little effect, and the masses continued to swell. The city's troops held a thin line until nightfall, when rioters finally overcame them and charged on the structure with a battering ram. Shortly thereafter, flames burst from the windows and began climbing to the high belfry. An onlooker watched the flames spread up the church walls to "at last reach the cross"—a primary symbol of Roman Catholicism—which "soon fell in, and thousands of throats yelled applause." Firemen prevented the blaze from spreading to nearby houses, and the mob finally began to disperse. The next day, authorities imposed a shaky peace on the sobered city, even as new threats were made on other Catholic churches. The tension in the city smoldered until two months later when riots broke out again and soldiers were forced to guard the Church of Saint Philip de Neri in the face of cannon shots. The governor himself managed to restore order shortly thereafter. Respectable voices deplored the violence, but the city's Protestant establishment nevertheless continued to foster long-standing and widespread anti-Catholic feelings. Philadelphia's Grand Jury later blamed the riots on "a band of lawless" immigrants and hardly acknowledged the destruction of Catholic property.[2]

About three years after the Grand Jury concluded its investigations, a group of wealthy Episcopalians constructed a new church on the outskirts of Philadelphia. The chief patron, merchant Robert Ralston, had selected a distinguished set of plans. The plans were given to him by a clergyman friend from Connecticut, who in turn had received them from England's Cambridge Camden Society, an Anglican reform group. These plans were precise, measured drawings of an actual thirteenth-century parish church still standing in Cambridgeshire, and Ralston's group followed them meticulously. The resulting church, known as St. James-the-Less, stood as a near replica of the original stone building. It featured an asymmetrical plan, steep vertical lines, a prominent altar, crosses atop the gables and bell cote, stained-glass windows, and other characteristic features of Gothic architecture built by medieval Roman Catholics. The vestrymen of St.

Street scene showing the burning of St. Augustine's Catholic Church, Philadelphia, on the evening of May 8, 1844. This engraving highlights the scale of the blaze, which was seen for miles. The cross on the belfry is shown engulfed in flames, moments before its symbolic crash. The uniform mass of onlookers in top hats belies the chaos of the event. From *Full Particulars of the Late Riots*, 21. Courtesy of the Library Company of Philadelphia.

Church of St. James-the-Less, Philadelphia (1849). Photo by James E.
McClees, 1855. Image (5)2526.F.10b, Library Company of Philadelphia.
Courtesy of the Library Company of Philadelphia.

James-the-Less shared the Cambridge Camden Society's belief that
this historic style had sprung from a more devout Christian society,
and they hoped that its forms would enable the parish to worship
with greater ritual and mystery. St. James-the-Less inspired widespread admiration and imitation, bolstering the spread of medieval

symbolism across the churches of other denominations, including Philadelphia's own Green Hill Presbyterian Church, Calvary Presbyterian Church, Broad Street Baptist Church, and Fourth Universalist Church, all Gothicized by the early 1850s. So even as anti-Catholic rioters directed much of their wrath at buildings that represented the city's Catholic presence, many of Philadelphia's Protestant congregations began investing their own identities in sharply Catholic forms.[3]

Neither of these two contrasting movements was unique to Philadelphia. Beyond the city, a broad "Protestant Crusade" against the Roman Catholic Church was under way, led by prominent ministers and members of the laity. Anti-Catholicism, always latent in Anglo-America, erupted in the 1820s in response to Catholic growth and quickly peaked by midcentury. Church relations were not uniformly poor; for example, individual Protestants commonly contributed funds to help Catholics rebuild facilities destroyed by mobs. And anti-Catholicism often channeled nonreligious concerns, including fears among the working classes that Catholic immigrants would take their jobs, fears among city leaders that impoverished newcomers would strain public relief efforts, and concerns that Catholic bloc voting would subvert the political process. Yet America's largest Protestant denominations took up the crusade with such intensity that they would come to be defined by their opposition to the Catholic institutions in their midst. At the same time, a remarkable transformation was taking place in church buildings. There had always been a wide spectrum of church finishes, from fancy to plain, but Protestant congregations throughout the country were beginning to add entirely novel elements, ones recognizably derived from Roman Catholic rivals. These consisted of a class of items and practices often derided as "priestcraft" or "popery," representing customary Catholic approaches to the sacred through the senses. Beyond an enthusiasm for Gothic architecture, one Protestant congregation after another broke with tradition to employ symbolic crosses, to decorate sanctuaries with flowers and candles, to worship with robed choirs, and to celebrate regular feasts and festivals. The move, though gradual and difficult, would initiate a new religious landscape.

Thus we have a puzzle. Why, when Protestant and Roman Catholic relations were at their most troubled point in the nation's history, did denominations recast their church environments in the image of a longtime rival? Why, when the stakes seemed so high, did congregations suddenly risk placing such controversial symbols atop their own places of worship? One Presbyterian from Virginia asked simply, "Why do we abuse the papists, and then imitate them?"[4]

It is sometimes difficult for modern Christians to imagine how daring these changes could be. Crosses, stained glass, robed choirs, and Easter flowers are now commonplace ingredients found in almost any church. But for centuries, generations of Protestants had proudly maintained traditions intended to be free of such "popish superstitions." The sides were first drawn after German monk Martin Luther's famed attacks on Catholic corruption in 1517. In the ensuing Reformation, a multitude of differing reformers and reformed churches identified themselves as "Protestant," but almost all affirmed Luther's main message—that God and his scripture, not the church and its sacraments, were the sources of salvation and grace. In practice, this meant that believers should read the Bible for themselves and nurture their own relationship with God. As a result, the art and celebrations previously used to sanctify church sacraments became suspect, since they could interfere with an individual's focus on scripture or imply a need for priestly intercession. A few reformers, including Luther himself, cautiously retained the use of some churchly devices such as altars, crosses, holidays, and vestments, in the belief that traditional art was an aid to faith. This perspective found support in the reformed churches of Germany and, for a time, England. In contrast, other European countries became much less hospitable to the older designs. Protestants in Scotland, the Netherlands, and areas of England looked to Switzerland, where influential theologians like John Calvin denied the propriety of Catholic symbolism in worship altogether. These reformers argued that erecting crosses, statues, and the like violated the second commandment prohibiting false idols. And they rejected the notion that any unique Godly presence appeared at Communion, thereby dismissing the need for any special dress or decor. So in varying ways, Protestants began exploring new means to properly celebrate God—by writing new creeds, singing new hymns, resetting the Communion table, and rearranging church plans.

Early Protestant hostilities toward Roman Catholic practices had another, nontheological edge. After the Reformation, a series of religious conflicts engulfed much of Europe, as leaders with differing faiths struggled for power. On the ground, this meant that participants attacked church property, as well as rival believers. In England, France, the Netherlands, and elsewhere, Protestants and Catholics smashed and torched their rivals' sanctuaries not merely because of theological details but because of their actual associations with the literal enemy. Once Reformation battle lines began to settle in the seventeenth century, lingering hostilities colored each side's view of the other's physical presence. The echoes of all these theological and militant objections to Catholic symbolism could be heard in America's Protestant churches into the early nineteenth century, when nearly any observer could discern the rare Catholic "mass-house" and its ceremonies at a glance.

Historians have rarely offered answers for the ensuing puzzle, since they have tended to treat the era's anti-Catholicism and church design changes separately. Architectural historians have not identified "Catholic" features in Protestant churches. Rather, they have viewed most of the artistic changes as part of the broader Gothic Revival, described as a picturesque "episode in taste" that broke from earlier Enlightenment preferences for classical lines and forms. In turn, religious historians have tended to study Protestantism and Catholicism in isolation. Historians of Roman Catholicism portray the church as a refuge for urban immigrants—one that had little direct influence on the nation's ascendant evangelical denominations. And evangelicals are portrayed as resourceful combatants whose primary challenges lay elsewhere. When describing worship changes, scholars attribute most of their findings to the peculiar heritage and personalities within their own subject denominations.[5]

But several studies do offer more direct clues. First, we know that ambivalence has long marked Protestant/Catholic relations. For example, at the start of the American Revolution, New Englanders publicly mocked the pope and Roman Catholicism even as they solicited the assistance of devout French troops. In the young republic, Protestant tourists flocked to the Vatican and other Catholic landmarks but returned home with their religious hostilities intact. By midcentury, American Protestants had developed a deeply mixed fascination for Roman Catholic worship, as nunneries, monasteries, chapels, and cathedrals served as popular settings for numerous tales and paintings. And civic leaders in northern cities such as Buffalo characterized the Catholic Church as a danger to republican liberty while actively praising the church's ability to ease the chaos and upheaval associated with working-class immigrants. Further, the Know-Nothing political party of the 1850s attacked what it saw as Catholic conspiracies by becoming something of a secret society itself. And by the century's end, many privileged Protestants would view Catholicism's fervent rituals as a welcome antidote to the hurried, corporate structure of modern life. Evidence for ambivalence on the part of Catholics abounds as well, suggesting that paradoxical religious borrowings may have been the rule rather than the exception.[6]

Additionally, we know that many factors encouraged American Christians to adopt more colorful art and ceremonies in the decades leading up to the 1840s. Perhaps most important, throughout the country during the early part of the century, charismatic preachers led sweeping revivals, in which attendants made emotional, public displays of their renewed faith. The revivals prompted the recognition that certain atmospheres helped stir the work of the Lord within human souls, so congregations became more open to adding melodious pipe organs and other evocative trimmings to their sanctuaries. Just before the revivals, Protestants of all stripes had been making sharper distinctions between "sacred" and "secular" activities, often by moving their worship from multipurpose public meetinghouses to formal churches. New embellishments like spires and elaborate entranceways helped define these distinctly religious spaces. And nonreligious developments bolstered these changes. In particular, the ideals of refinement and gentility gained prominence in the early republic, motivating upwardly mobile Americans to dress up their activities at home and in public. The spontaneous, Bible-verse-based worship that had once taken place in plain buildings began to seem out of place in a world of comfortable middle-class homes, elegant stores, and cultured diversions. Churches, jostling for a place in an increasingly market-based society, began to experiment with more theatrical touches. Corresponding forces shaped congregations across the Atlantic, lending an air of international authority to these "temples of grace."[7]

As churches became more distinctive and refined, it was by no means clear that Protestant/Catholic differences would play into the changes. Protestants might have continued on their well-worn path, with the Gothic and its highly charged accoutrements offering minor options among many others. Instead, designs once disparaged as exclusively "popish" became central. The activities of Lyman Beecher, a clergyman of old Puritan stock, epitomized the puzzle. Why, for example, would Beecher help his Boston congregation erect a medieval-themed sanctuary in 1831, complete with rows of pointed, colored windows and a musical program that ventured movements from traditional Catholic masses, just before he gained nationwide fame for his heated anti-Catholic sermons?

The answer appears to lie with the Catholic Church itself. The rise of intense anti-Catholicism alongside the Gothic Revival throughout antebellum America reveals their shared origins—the perception and appropriation of Roman Catholic power. Both movements came to the fore just as the Catholic Church was gaining significant ground. From 1820 to 1850, the Catholic Church grew from about 195,000 members—less than four percent of the nation's total number of Christians—to 1.75 million, becoming the largest religious body in the United States. Incoming waves of Catholic immigrants prompted the spread of new schools, parishes, and missions throughout the country, introducing this faith into countless communities for the first time. The surprising growth challenged an innate sense of Protestant destiny, and despite the role of immigration in the church's

Threat led to similation.

expansion, Protestants themselves acknowledged that Catholics employed impressive appeals and resources. Shortly after the shift in momentum began, a number of high-profile, widely publicized conversions to Catholicism appeared, further fueling Protestant fears of losing ground to Rome.[8]

Enthralled with the Catholic "threat," Protestant denominations adopted one of its most potent, yet seemingly most superficial, components—its imposing physical presence. Recently constructed Catholic chapels and cathedrals presented a host of new worship options that glittered in the eyes of observers. Congregations began employing symbolic crosses, investing in Gothic atmospheres, and sanctifying altars with flowers and colors, hoping to provide a more vibrant worship experience, project a more "churchly" appearance, and defuse some of the peculiar attractions of the Roman Catholic Church. Near the end of nineteenth century, the appropriation reached a successful conclusion, as crosses, stained glass, robed choirs, Easter flowers, and the like lost their exclusive Catholic associations and became synonymous with church worship in America.

Fashion, refinement, changes in theology, and other factors continued to shape church designs. Yet these would not dim the challenge Catholicism presented to ambitious American Protestants in the 1840s and 1850s. For Catholic worship, in its expressive art and its emphasis on tangible access to the sacred, seems to have been well-suited for the era's romanticism and market-based materialism. Far from being the exclusive concern of the urban refugees, the successful Roman Church animated Protestant denominations in ways that ethnic and economic tensions did not. Fashion and church wealth fail to account for the number of evangelical churches that placed a Catholic-inspired cross atop a Catholic-inspired gable or gathered to hear Catholic-inspired music on Catholic holidays. In these departures, congregations selected from recent design trends and Catholic models to fashion a material response to Catholic growth. This strategy was more effective at gaining and retaining members than the low and, for most, unacceptable alternative of anti-Catholic violence. But it pushed Protestant worship beyond a basic evolution in ritual and sacred space by challenging the assumptions upon which that worship was based. And it illustrated that beneath the hard surface of religious conflict there existed a surprising fluidity.

Not everyone endorsed the departures. The introduction of Catholic art into Protestant communions was a jagged, spontaneous process involving selective features. It divided congregations, and it racked denominations. Typically, the earliest and most enthusiastic support came from congregations in the North and the West, both urban and rural. Cities housed the most grandiose designs, but churches in the countryside and on the frontier competed for religious ground just as keenly. Protestant proponents of Catholic art often targeted rural areas, and it did not cost much to place a wooden cross atop a bell tower or brighten services with decorative candles. Still, Catholic art aroused the most passion among wealthy congregations, whose members could remain abreast of design changes and spend a bit more on patronage. Particularly susceptible to Catholic conversion, this class of Protestants also proved the most apprehensive of rioting and unrest. Within such churches, clergymen often led the Gothic charge, but these innovators depended upon sympathetic vestries and parishioners to sustain architectural and liturgical changes. Men occupied the most public roles, though women, who made up the majority of actual members, frequently participated in the appropriations through traditional channels. In all cases, youth seems to have been a dynamic factor, as advocates consistently faced the objections of "old citizens" who, in the words of one magazine, wished "to defend the 'old style' of church-building." And though issues of race rarely appeared in denominational debates over Catholicism, white congregations consistently showed more concern for Protestant/Catholic distinctions than their black counterparts.[9]

In terms of denominations, the vast majority of English-speaking American Protestants at the time belonged to one of five groups: the Episcopal, Congregational, Presbyterian, Baptist, and Methodist churches. Each had a tradition of strict opposition to the Roman Catholic Church, and each joined in the appropriations. The Episcopal Church, known for its wealth and Anglican heritage, became the leading proponent of artistic changes, but this may have had as much to do with its early "high church" elements as with its means. The Congregational Church, mostly localized in the Northeast and Midwest, operated without a centralized hierarchy, and it traditionally emphasized individual repentance over structured rituals. Presbyterians shared these evangelical characteristics, but they enjoyed a wider distribution across America. The Baptists were even more numerous. They were given to intense public rituals, but these centered on individual conversions, and the various independent associations showed a wide diversity in practice. The rapidly growing Methodist Church mixed evangelical and high church elements; members advocated simple, passionate worship and lay participation, but clergymen were tightly organized under regional bishops. These Protestant variations ensured that the adoption of Catholic art would not be a blanket process. In general, the movement of churches and denominations toward Catholic art resembled a shift—with each church "shifting" one notch closer to Catholic practices relative to their earlier stance. Churches that had the most affinities with Roman Catholicism before appropriation, like the Episcopalians, adopted the most extensive, controversial features, whereas churches that had the fewest similarities with Catholic practices, like the Baptists, stopped with the most basic, well-accepted features.

Conflict among and within all five denominations was frequent. Various subjects aroused heated disputes, and debates over slavery eventually split the Methodist, Baptist, and Presbyterian churches into rival sectional organizations before the Civil War. Arguments over the use of Catholic art became particularly complex, since what was controversial one year could quickly become the norm the next. Conservative efforts to halt the spread of inappropriate rituals threatened to tear individual denominations apart and sever ties between denominations. But opposition to Rome did help Episcopalians, Congregationalists, Presbyterians, Baptists, and Methodists accept one another as Protestant allies. As explained by one New England editor, "The Methodist, the Baptist, the Congregationalist or Presbyterian, and the Episcopalian, can treat each other kindly; and while they differ in various degrees on certain points of doctrine and of ecclesiastical regulation . . . they can feel toward each other as neighbors and friends." This was in stark contrast to "the Roman Catholics," who "do not seem to enjoy, in some quarters, the full benefit of this tolerant disposition," since, in this editor's view, "their religion is in every relation hostile to every other form of Christianity" and its difference was "such as admits no compromise." The editor wrote in idealized terms, but his or her words illustrate how antagonism to Roman Catholicism could encourage a common sense of purpose among otherwise divided churches.[10]

Lutheranism in America presented a special case. The Protestant loyalties of this German-based faith were beyond reproach, but its artistic and liturgical conventions remained closer to those of Catholicism than other American denominations. Some Lutheran congregations upheld the controversial belief that the real body and blood of Jesus Christ became present in ritual Communion. And as early as the mid-eighteenth century, Lutherans freely decorated their American churches with crosses and statues of saints, Lutheran choirs sang regular hymns with musical accompaniment, and German congregations celebrated numerous traditional holidays. Apart from the gradual spread of holiday customs, these peculiarities had few effects upon other Protestants. Lutheran churches were relatively modest in number, and they maintained close associations with German-speaking communities. One prominent Lutheran writer acknowledged in 1852 that "the English [speaking] community has remained comparatively unacquainted with the precise doctrines and forms of worship" of his denomination. And the publications of other denominations, which commonly described and compared Catholic and Protestant customs, rarely commented on Lutheran practices. The use of the cross and other elements of traditional Christian art remained "popish" customs and Lutheran curiosities until new pressures emerged in the mid-nineteenth century.[11]

So the adoption of Catholic architecture, symbolism, and pageantry involved many different factors—denominational background, region, youth, and wealth, among others. But many of the Protestant participants treated Catholicism itself as monolithic. Outside observers could attribute all sorts of adjectives to Catholicism as a whole, such as oppressive, feminine, idolatrous, and beautiful, but they rarely conceded its diversity. In truth, Roman Catholicism was a sprawling, global institution that encompassed many differing communities and customs. In America alone, beyond the Irish, some Germans, and some old-stock Americans, there were French, Spanish, English, and a small number of Belgian and Italian members, all before 1830. Ethnic communities tended to congregate separately and maintain their own church traditions, and immigration from other ports increased this complexity throughout the nineteenth century. The Catholic Church did have a comparatively tight hierarchy, with well-defined channels of authority descending from the pope in Rome to archbishops, bishops, and priests. And members of the American hierarchy themselves, increasingly dominated by the Irish contingent, often encouraged a static view of their faith, stressing Catholicism's universal claims and its uniform doctrines. But they faced frequent challenges from congregations claiming ownership of church property and attempting to select their own priests. Further, the church officially provided for a certain amount of leeway through its diverse orders and organizations, to say nothing of individual interpretive differences. These features translated into material differences. Catholic sanctuaries might have commonly hosted altars, crosses, and bells, but architectural styles, sizes, plans, and furnishings varied from congregation to congregation, as did patron saints and celebrations.[12]

Despite their tendency to generalize Catholicism, Protestants typically were not ignorant of these variations. After the 1820s, detailed descriptions of Catholic churches began appearing throughout Protestant literature, and many curious folks attended Catholic ceremonies at home and abroad. Their visits included long pilgrimages throughout Europe, modest vacation stops around American cities, and simple neighborhood visits to services, lectures, or funerals. Spectators could see ethnic differences within Catholicism firsthand, especially after touring cities like St. Augustine, Florida; New Orleans, Louisiana; or even Philadelphia, Pennsylvania. Protestants also took note of changes in Catholicism over time. Some architectural revivalists spent years categorizing and classifying the development of the medieval church, and critics bemoaned the modern church's adaptations "to the popular taste" in the United States.[13]

Protestants tended to generalize Catholicism because that was how the age-old debate was framed. And behind the differing saints, celebrations, and assemblages present in Catholic parishes, Protestants recognized a common Catholic assumption that art, as perceived through the senses, could offer legitimate avenues to God. Though all Protestant congregations engaged the world of art at some level as well, they generally resisted any art with "sacred" connotations. So Protestants characterized the Catholic Church's approach and its Vatican trademarks with a vocabulary that glossed over individual variations. Offensive though it may be, this vocabulary demonstrates the depths and breadths of Protestant passions. The most popular term might have been "popery," but others included "mummery," "trumpery," "frippery," "priestcraft," and even "solemn enchantments." In 1841, one Episcopal bishop outlined the scope of these terms as he mocked "the sweeping charge of Popery" leveled at his own activities. He asked rhetorically, "Do they use a liturgy? Popery! Popery is a form of prayer. Do they make the sign of the cross in baptism? Popery! Popery is a gesture. Do they kneel in the communion? Popery! Popery is a posture. Do they wear a surplice? Popery! Popery is a garment. Do they erect a cross upon a church, or a private dwelling? Sheer Popery! A bit of wood is Popery!" Thus whether or not all American Catholics worshipped in Gothic buildings or whether or not all Catholics bowed before the cross became unimportant. Generalizing epithets such as "popery" and "Romanism" served not only as verbal grenades lobbed at Catholic rivals but also as shorthand for the inviting yet threatening tradition of material-based worship.[14]

American Protestants adopted from this tradition selectively. The chapters that follow trace the selections of Episcopalians, Congregationalists, Presbyterians, Baptists, and Methodists and explore their effects. Chapter 2 describes the basic engine driving Protestant appropriations, in terms of the new Catholic growth in America, the extent of Protestant exposure to Catholic art, and the nature of conversions to Catholicism. The remaining chapters turn to the borrowings themselves, which can be divided into three categories. Chapter 3 focuses on church symbolism, specifically the transformation of the Latin cross from Catholic emblem to universal Christian ornament. The battles fought over the use of this symbol reveal the intensity of the Protestant/Catholic conflict and the religious weight of simple decorations. Chapter 4 broadens to consider architectural style. It explains how the newly popular Gothic, and, to a lesser degree, Romanesque, revivals provided indirect Catholic channels through which Protestants softened and sanctified the atmosphere of their churches. Chapter 5 describes the rise of Catholic-based customs in Protestant devotions, including the spread of candles, flowers, robed choirs, and holy festivals. Closely tied with architecture and symbolism, these innovations helped put the newfound designs in motion and offered churches a means by which to engage modern prosperity. The result was a rich blend of improvisation and Christian imagery that addressed observers' sentiments and co-opted the most alluring aspects of Catholicism. The innumerable aspects that were not appropriated —Latin-language services, holy water fonts, visual veneration of the Virgin Mary and other saints, foreign-based hierarchies, confessional chambers, the use of high altars, and the doctrine of Christ's body and blood in the Eucharist, to name a few—highlighted remaining Protestant distinctions.

Such changes took place amidst the nation's great transformation from a rural republic into an advanced industrial state. During the era spanned by this study, settlers poured westward from the Mississippi to the Pacific, the political process became more boisterous, the marketplace became more sophisticated, and civil war racked the citizenry and ultimately abolished slavery. Such developments necessarily played into the religious world of crosses, stained glass, and flowers. For example, in the movement west, Protestant church designs became an important component of "civilizing" the land and preventing Catholic dominance in the region. In the rough campaigns of popular democracy, both Catholic and Protestant organizations directly shaped the party system, blurring political and religious issues. And while new church designs carved out a distinctly religious presence on the landscape, the nation's courts and civic governments attempted to settle relations between church and state. Similarly, American women became increasingly defined by their attachments to the home, even as church decorations, music, and festivals depended on their skills and support. And the Civil War marked a watershed moment; though Protestant/Catholic tensions illustrated a significant issue that cut across sectional lines, the war's drama and death only stirred the need for satisfying spiritual atmospheres. One writer explained after the war that "the war-period made it natural for many people to remember with special fervor" the spring Easter festival and its resurrection-themed flowers. But perhaps the most relevant development was the "market revolution," the expanding network of suppliers, retailers, advertisers, and consumers that came to dominate American life in the late nineteenth century. This revolution helped usher in a world of increasing beauty and refinement, one in which Protestants could not allow Roman Catholics to retain such an admittedly potent edge. All of these changes played across the lives of churchgoers, whose faiths navigated their own rhythms. Yet on the denominational level, the unexpected rise of Roman Catholicism helped Protestant churches as a whole find their footing in this new world.[15]

Anti-Catholicism, then, became the seed of Protestant adaptation. "No question of mere clothes, candlesticks, and artificial flowers," explained one editor in 1875, "could excite so deeply so large and intelligent and sensible countries in the world as the subject of ritualism has plainly done." The desire to secure members brought the material environment of churches onto the same polemical platform as sermons, revivals, prayers, and pamphlets. Today's legacy of crosses, stained glass, vestments, and festivals may obscure these origins with a familiar grace, but an older generation of churchgoers saw plainly the challenge behind such articles. In 1849, only five years after the

Philadelphia riots, Boston's monthly *Christian Examiner* set forth the religious dilemma with perfect clarity. An essay on the renewed public interest in "the Church of the Middle Ages" acknowledged that there existed a number of men and women of "each Protestant communion" who could become "easy converts to the Roman Church." The author, a minister and later divinity professor at Harvard University, noted the growing popularity of Catholicism, described various motivations for conversions, and concluded that the church's artistic appeals had been the most efficient. In its "bewitching charm," Catholicism "has most powerful influences to address to the eye, the imagination, and the feelings," and it is "richly furnished" with attractions that are "akin to the religious sentiment in very many breasts." In terms of architecture alone, the author conceded that the Catholic Church "invented what is certainly the most impressive style of architecture," the "so-called Gothic style." But the problem of these seductions revealed its own solution, for "Protestantism may minister too exclusively to the intellect," and its houses of worship may be comparably inadequate. "But," the author proposed, "when Protestantism is fully aware of any mistake of this kind which she may commit, she has the means of rectifying it." Protestantism "may share" the use of Christian art and symbolism with the Roman Catholic Church— the "star, the cross, the cup, and the candlestick, may serve with us as sacred emblems." That this "sharing" eventually faded from memory is little wonder. Rather, we are left to consider how such artistry emerged from such bitter conflict.[16]

2 Catholic Churches

From 1820 to 1850, American Catholics built over one thousand new churches throughout the country. Before this construction boom, the material presence of Catholicism in the United States had been slight. From the Atlantic coast to the Mississippi River, only about 124 Catholic churches could be found after three centuries of European settlement. And these churches generally clustered around Baltimore and New Orleans—Maryland and Louisiana held almost half of the nation's total number. In the whole of New England, there were only six. The state of New York held only five, including two in New York City. Pennsylvania, Kentucky, and Missouri claimed the bulk of the rest. Catholic institutions and schools added a bit more visibility, but as late as 1820, many of the nation's 195,000 Catholics conducted their lives beyond the shadow of a consecrated chapel. In contrast, American Baptists and Methodists each occupied about 2,700 meetinghouses, distributed across the country. Even the modest Quakers held 350 meetinghouses, more than doubling Catholic holdings.[1]

But after 1820, Roman Catholic construction activities began to outpace those of every other denomination. With the arrival of large numbers of European immigrants, and with the strengthening of the church's organizational base, Catholic chapels were erected for the first time in thousands of communities. In New Jersey, where only two Catholic churches appeared in 1820, twenty-one more dotted the landscape by 1850. The handful of early Catholic congregations in Ohio grew to include 130 church buildings by midcentury. And New England's six Catholic churches increased to at least eighty-two, with the Boston area accounting for only about nine of these. Southerners were the only group to see little of this activity, as large portions of such states as Tennessee and North Carolina remained devoid of Catholic chapels. Still, the church established new dioceses in Richmond, Natchez, Mobile, and Savannah, and at least 120 new buildings were raised south of Maryland and Kentucky by 1850. In all, the number of Catholic churches in the United States increased 885 percent between 1820 and 1850, and the total number then doubled in ten years, becoming 2,550 by 1860. In comparison, this growth rate was about three times that of the Methodist churches, the nearest competitor, and well over six times

TABLE 1   Church Construction in the United States

Denomination	Churches in 1820	Churches in 1850	Churches in 1860	Percent Increase 1820–60
Baptist	2,700	9,375	12,150	350
Congregational	1,100	1,706	2,234	103
Episcopal	600	1,459	2,145	258
Lutheran	800	1,217	2,128	166
Methodist	2,700	13,280	19,883	636
Presbyterian	1,700	4,824	6,406	277
Quaker	350	726	726	107
Roman Catholic	124	1,221	2,550	1,956

Source: Adapted from Gaustad, *Historical Atlas of Religion in America*, 43. Used with permission of the author.

that of smaller denominations like the Presbyterians and the Episcopalians. In terms of sheer numbers, Catholic churches still lagged far behind the Methodist and Baptist denominations as late as 1860. And the new buildings still left some of the nation's Catholics, numbering three million by 1860, without the comforts of a nearby church. But the buildings sheltered many young congregations, they publicized Catholicism's expanding presence on a local level, and they easily accommodated interested spectators.[2]

This new proximity would have profound effects on Protestant churches. On one level, it kindled competitive passions, raising concern among Episcopalians, Congregationalists, Presbyterians, Baptists, Methodists, and others over losing religious "ground" to Catholics. But on a deeper level, the very fabric of Catholic chapels themselves challenged Protestant conceptions of church architecture. For even the humblest Catholic churches differed from those of Protestants in their appearances and in their claims. American Catholics, though diverse, consistently employed traditional art and symbolism in worship, and they consecrated their churches as sites for miraculous communion with God and the saints. When facing these mysteries, American Protestants displayed a characteristic ambivalence, as countless observers disparaged Catholic beliefs while acknowledging their appeal. And with the proliferation of Catholic churches, opportunities for these encounters grew. It no longer required a grand tour of Europe to experience the seductive allure of Catholic architecture, nor even did it require braving the immigrant quarters of America's largest cities. Beyond New York, Philadelphia, Baltimore, and New Orleans, Catholic churches increasingly appeared on the same public stage as those of Protestant denominations. As Catholic membership surpassed that of the largest denominations, a surge underscored by sensational public conversions, the Protestant fascination for Catholic worship gained significance that could not be dismissed. Thus the ready availability of Catholic churches presented both a motive and a means for congregations to reinvigorate their worship spaces.

In 1847, the official newspaper of New England's Methodist conferences, *Zion's Herald and Wesleyan Journal*, featured an article titled "Progress of Popery." Its author addressed "the popular alarm on account of the progress of Romanism in this country." Attributing the advance of Catholicism to priestly "meddling," "craft," and "oppression," the author warned readers not to become overly alarmed, for such fear and alarm would only lend Catholicism strength.[3]

This article addressed a familiar subject among Protestant audiences of the mid-nineteenth century. For many other publicists observed the "progress of popery" in the United States, illustrating a broad awareness of Catholicism's expansion. In articles, books, and lectures, Protestants surveyed the rising number of Catholic communicants, clergy, dioceses, convents, seminaries, and church buildings, making these developments a matter of common knowledge. Their surveys served a variety of purposes, from arousing missionary zeal, to encouraging donations for Protestant schools, to inspiring political action. And though *Zion's Herald* instructed its readers "not to be alarmed," such works sounded distinct notes of apprehension.

A handful of activists provided the most colorful examples. In the 1830s, two evangelicals from New England, Samuel F. B. Morse and Lyman Beecher, gained a measure of fame by "exposing" fantastic Catholic designs for mastery in America. Beecher focused on schools, while Morse focused on politics, but both men outlined in general terms the supposed Roman Catholic hostility toward republican institutions. In contrast, many other sensationalists based their accounts on actual figures taken from Catholic publications. In 1845, the American Protestant Association, an interdenominational organization based in Philadelphia, published a study titled "Progress of Popery in the United States" in its quarterly review. It cited statistics taken from the Catholic *Religious Cabinet*, outlining the nation's new dioceses, priests, religious orders, churches, and schools. Likewise, the Baptist preacher John Dowling published his popular *History of Romanism* that same year, drawing from the *Metropolitan Catholic*

Almanac and Laity's Directory to produce extensive statistical tables charting Catholic growth, diocese by diocese. A smaller work, *Popery in the United States*, written by a Presbyterian minister in 1848, detailed the nation's Catholic churches, clergy, and schools using the same Catholic directory. A Congregational pastor from New Hampshire published another representative book that same decade, asserting that "vigorous, extensive and skilful [*sic*] efforts" were being made "by the friends of popery to establish among us the supremacy of their system." He then defended his concerns by counting the recent increase in the number of Catholic bishops, priests, communicants, and churches throughout America. The pastor regretfully concluded his listings with the "melancholy truth, that, in many sections of the land, popery has of late years advanced more rapidly than Protestantism," and he plainly stated that "Catholic churches have multiplied faster" and "their schools have been more prosperous" than their Protestant counterparts. A particularly provocative example came from an ex-priest, who published *A Synopsis of Popery* in 1845. After similarly tracing recent Catholic growth in the United States, the author then projected these figures to an unhappy end: "Should the said church go on increasing for the next thirty years as she has done for the last eight years, the Papists would be a majority of the population of the United States, and the Pope our supreme temporal ruler." Though their views were clouded by anxiety, all of these authors recognized that Catholic expansion was not exclusively the concern of large cities like Baltimore and New York City. The American Protestant Association seconded a Boston newspaper's observation that "almost every manufacturing village has its 'church and parsonage'" where popery" was working to establish itself "in our 'protestant' country."[4]

The announcements of Catholic growth that appeared in established religious journals took on a more measured tone. Yet their findings could be equally striking. In 1833, the *Episcopal Watchman* of Hartford, Connecticut, detailed what it referred to as the "Progress of the Roman Catholics in the United States." The editor explained that in 1788, American Catholicism "was almost entirely confined to the state of Maryland, and to a few scattered districts of Pennsylvania." But by 1814, "the face of things had greatly changed" with the addition of new dioceses, schools, convents, and priests. And for the years following 1814, the editor found "the increase of the Catholics in this country" to be "astonishing." Again enumerating new dioceses, schools, convents, and priests, in addition to churches, congregations, and total communicants, the editor conceded that these numbers gave "that denomination a greater number of communicants than are attached to any other denomination in the country." Similar expositions could be found in the *Christian Examiner* and the *Church Review*, in addition to *Zion's Herald* and others.[5]

The Protestant press also alerted Americans to a comparable resurgence of Roman Catholicism in Great Britain. Parliament had passed a Catholic Emancipation Act in 1829, which brought to culmination decades of new freedoms for Roman Catholics in that country. The move triggered a corresponding rise in anti-Catholic activities similar to those taking shape in America. By highlighting the impressive "Progress of Popery in Great Britain," publicists deepened the implications of Catholic expansion in America. For example, one piece published in the Presbyterian *New York Observer* in 1833 found the recent "increase of Popery" in England and Scotland to be "rapid" and "startling." The article outlined rates of increase in communicants, schools, and chapels that resembled those seen in America, and it went beyond London and Glasgow to chart Catholic growth in several small towns. Other articles on this subject appeared as late as 1862, when the Methodist *Christian Recorder* surveyed the categories of Catholicism's "startling" growth in the United Kingdom. Such transatlantic figures marked a substantial trend that raised doubts about Protestantism's comparative vigor.[6]

In addition to these generalized reviews, American Protestants followed the spread of Catholicism through specific reports on the church's construction projects. Brief posts from around the country informed readers of ambitious cathedral plans, remote parish construction efforts, or remarkable new churches. Most appeared as miscellaneous news items in Protestant periodicals, where editors acknowledged the beauties of the new Catholic buildings while betraying a sense of rivalry. The editors' detailed descriptions fed popular interest in the nature of Catholic architecture and ceremony. A fine example appeared in an 1845 issue of the *American Protestant Magazine*, with the description of a new church being built by the "Romanists" in Southport, Wisconsin. "Designed to be the handsomest building in the Territory," the brick building measured eighty by fifty feet and employed "the Gothic style." This substantial structure was "to be adorned with a steeple one hundred and eighty feet high." After reviewing its features and commenting on the number of other Catholic chapels in the area, the editor exclaimed, "Who will help our missionaries and their infant churches in that region, so that they too may arise and build a church in every settlement? The combat thickens!" Other papers affirmed that the "combat" involved an impressive, tangible foe. In 1846, the *New York Observer* described a Catholic church project in Washington, D.C., as "magnificent," and in 1849, *Zion's Herald* announced a sizable construction project in Cincinnati. In 1868, the Episcopal *Spirit of Missions* presented a stirring portrait of Catholic resources in tiny Palatka, Florida. The state's Episcopal bishop explained that though local Catholics were few in number, their ambitious sanctuary, school, and programs demonstrated that "nothing is wanting on the part of the Romanists, while others are paralyzed by poverty and discouragement."[7]

Not every reader appreciated these posts. In 1836, one crank complained about an announcement on the pages of the *New York Observer*: "What should I see, in taking up the Observer of January 3d, but an article headed 'Cathedral at St. Louis?' Then followed a description taken, be it known, not from any scandalous Protestant paper, but from the Catholic Telegraph, printed at Cincinnati, of the building, altar, &c." Despite this reader's frustration, such descriptions put a public face on the abstract Catholic growth followed by the same press. At the same time, the descriptions tended to downplay the uniqueness of various Roman Catholic expressions by attributing them all to a forceful, seemingly unified "Romanism." Comparable posts also publicized Protestant church plans and figures, but the frequency and character of Catholic reports marked a unique vigilance. From the number of communicants and priests to the appearance of scattered church buildings, American Protestants were no strangers to the rising presence of Catholicism.[8]

"Churches in which the Christian feels the presence of his God"

Even more visible to American Protestants than published reports were the Catholic chapels next door. For the rapid diffusion of churches across the North, West, and coastal South brought the material presence of Catholicism into Protestants' daily lives. Offering new and varied windows into Catholic worship, these churches presented scenes distinctly different from those found in most Protestant churches.

According to one prominent Catholic bishop, the root of these distinctions lay in conceptions of church "Sanctity." By "Sanctity," Martin Spalding of the Diocese of Louisville, Kentucky, meant an inherent holiness. In a lecture beneath the vaulted roof of his city's new cathedral, shortly after its dedication in 1852, Spalding guided his mixed audience through a basic Protestant and Catholic comparison. He began by noting the lack of sanctity attributed to Protestant church space, where "the magnificent Christian temple has dwindled down to a mere lecture-room." This jibe had nothing to do with expense or fashionable taste; rather, it pointed to an essential assumption behind Protestant worship—that God was no more and no less present in church than anywhere else. In contrast, Catholics viewed their churches as literal houses of God, "in which Christ is really present in the Holy Eucharist, and is always ready to receive the homage of His people, and to shower His choicest blessings on their heads." These two assumptions directed the worship environments of the respective traditions. Protestant churches tended to center on "*preaching*" and on personal redemption within a community of believers, while Catholic churches emphasized the divine authority of Roman Catholicism, the material respect "due to the house of God," and the "reverent awe" produced by communion with God.[9]

Spalding illustrated these characteristics through a series of rhetorical examples. "Enter, for a moment," he said, "into one of our *fashionable* Protestant Churches." "Is there any religious symbol, to remind you of heavenly things? Is there an altar, before which you may bend down in reverent awe and devotion? . . . Is there any fragrant incense, filling the house of God with its sweet odor, and curling up to heaven, a fit emblem of the Christian's prayer?" Likely, there was not, for Christ's "real presence in the holy sacrament has been denied" and Protestants had "banished" most examples of explicitly devotional art. Without such objects, Spalding found it difficult to imagine worship at all. Pushing his portrait to an extreme, he exclaimed, "Unlighted altars, or rather no altars at all, unstoled priests, undecorated walls, total barrenness of all religious association . . . these are the things that freeze your very soul." Spalding then reviewed a few related Protestant distinctions. Churches were "generally kept locked during the six days of the week, and opened for worship only on the *Sabbath*," moving private devotions elsewhere. Public worship consisted mostly of hymns, prayers, and sermons, with the observance of "only two sacraments,—Baptism and the Lord's Supper," neither of which were "viewed as channels of grace, as instruments of the divine presence and assistance." And Protestants respected the examples of "moral, edifying Christians" but did not honor them as "*saints* properly so called." From Spalding's perspective, these Protestant disavowals of church sanctity and ecclesiastic authority thus composed a material worship tradition in which "the spirit of reverence and religious awe is gone for ever."[10]

Naturally, the bishop's opinions of Catholic architecture proved more favorable. The construction of Catholic worship space as "God's holy temple," where his presence was simultaneously revealed and honored, left no shortage of religious awe. "Here we have an altar, as Christians had in the days of St. Paul; a daily sacrifice; churches always open to worshipers, . . . churches decorated with all the ornaments of the fine arts, and filled with beautiful and appropriate symbols that raise the heart to heavenly things and to God." These objects served as essential aids to individual and communal devotion, and they signified Roman Catholicism's divine sanction. Spalding gloried in this material representation of sanctity; he boasted of "churches in which the Christian *feels* the presence of his God, and bends down in lowly reverence and awe before Him; . . . churches, in a word, to which respect is shown which is due to the house of God, in which He delights to dwell in the midst of His children." Further, Catholic churches demanded rigorous religious exercise. Believers attended to seven sacraments "containing substantial graces," observed numerous feasts and fasts, acknowledged a community of historic saints, and generally looked to "the voice of the Church as to that of Christ Himself." In church consecration ceremonies, Catholics celebrated the construction of a unique instrument of God's will.[11]

Bishop Spalding could be forgiven a little bias, for his words echoed down the wide aisles of an imposing new cathedral. And the building's design and use reflected many of his observations on material sanctity. Financed primarily by the local community, the Cathedral of the Assumption had been erected "under the name and patronage of the most holy and Immaculate Virgin Mary," one of the most revered saints among American Catholics. Upon the cathedral's substantial completion in October 1852, two archbishops and eight bishops met amid great ceremony and celebration to consecrate the structure and to dedicate its use to the service of God. Built of brick, it measured 187 feet long and 90 feet wide. Its tower and steeple were finished six years later, raising a cross 287 feet above the city's central district. Mostly Gothic in style, the cathedral featured pointed arches, steep lines, and a ribbed, vaulted ceiling. The rectangular plan was divided between a nave and a chancel. In the nave, closed wooden pews held seats for about 1,300 worshippers, a baptistry stood ready to receive new members, and a loft on the rear wall housed a pipe organ. At the opposite end, the chancel formed a sacred sanctuary, dominated by a gray marble altar for the Eucharist. Elaborate candlesticks lit the altar and its tabernacle, which reserved the blessed sacrament of bread and wine. Nearby sat the cathedra, the literal chair representing the bishop's symbolic authority in his diocese. Directly beneath the altar, a crypt was built, and the remains of Kentucky's first

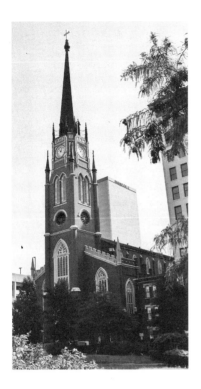

Cathedral of the Assumption, Louisville, Kentucky (1852). Photo by Gerald R. Stamler, 2005.

bishop, Benedict Flaget, were given the place of honor. On the ceiling above the altar, a fresco of Mary looked down upon the scene. Other images appeared throughout the interior: a brass representation of the *Agnus Dei*, the lamb of God; a statue of the Virgin with clasped hands; assorted paintings of saints; and medallions showing papal and episcopal symbols. From where Bishop Spalding's audience sat, one could view the grand sweep. The bishop's words filled a space that blended emblems of church authority, like the cathedra and the protected sanctuary, with ornaments intended for uplift and homage, like the ceiling fresco and the pipe organ. This space was distinctive, and with its attendant ceremonies and dedications it emanated a deliberate sense of sanctity.[12]

Though it reinforced many of Spalding's assertions, the cathedral

A view down the center aisle to the high altar of Bishop Martin Spalding's cathedral. "Interior of the Cathedral of the Assumption, Louisville, Ky.," postcard, circa 1900–1920. In author's possession.

did not offer a simple model of Catholic architecture in America. Indeed, there was no such thing. With Hispanic and Native American church traditions in the West, German traditions in midwestern towns, French Catholicism along the Mississippi, and growing Irish establishments in the East, important differences existed within the practice of American Catholicism. Even in Louisville itself, Catholic believers divided among three parishes and other institutions. The French element laid the city's Catholic foundations with the diocese's first bishop, Benedict Flaget, and an initial parish named St. Louis. Soon German-speaking Catholics erected two churches—St. Boniface's and Immaculate Conception, as Irish and older-stock Americans helped construct a new building for St. Louis and outlying French residents formed Our Lady's parish. Each congregation heard services in Latin, but these were led by their own German-, English-, or French-speaking priests, and each maintained separate decorative and devotional practices. A scholarly Jesuit school and a benevolent Sisters of Charity of Nazareth house added further color to the city's

Catholic presence. The Cathedral of the Assumption also differed from other nearby cathedrals. It presented a more domesticated sight than its French-inspired predecessor, St. Joseph's, erected in 1819 at Bardstown, Kentucky, and its Gothic lines contrasted with the neo-classicism seen in the nearby Diocese of Cincinnati's structure, the Cathedral of St. Peter in Chains. And beneath Bishop Spalding's abstract claims for Catholic authority and universality lay a simmering debate between his nation's hierarchy and scattered congregations claiming sole ownership and prerogative over their church facilities.[13]

Amidst these divisions, there were unifying forces operating on Catholic art and worship. First, the church prescribed the same dogma and sacraments for every congregation, regardless of ethnicity or location. Second, it enforced a few minimum design rules for every chapel, including the use of a properly consecrated and dressed high altar. Third, Catholics of all backgrounds demonstrated widespread support for the use of devotional art in their churches. Fourth, the nation's single hierarchy became increasingly dominated by an effective Irish contingent throughout the nineteenth century. And the Irish emphasized a Rome-centered approach known as "post-Tridentine Catholicism," which had developed out of the Counter-Reformation and which focused on the Mass and the fulfillment of religious duties. In the preceding centuries, this approach had dramatically reduced the number of regionalisms that had once characterized the church's worship. Finally, though many Catholic congregations employed architects from different backgrounds, the denomination tended to award commissions to the relatively small number of Catholic architects working in America. This pattern was exemplified most dramatically in the ubiquitous career of Brooklyn's Patrick Keely, who designed most of the Northeast's cathedrals in the nineteenth century, as well as hundreds of smaller parish churches throughout the country. All of these forces encouraged the development of familiar parish church designs. In 1869, architect Charles Sholl published a detailed pattern book titled *Working Designs for Ten Catholic Churches* that gained the approbations of five bishops and archbishops throughout North America. Sholl's first and simplest design, for a wooden

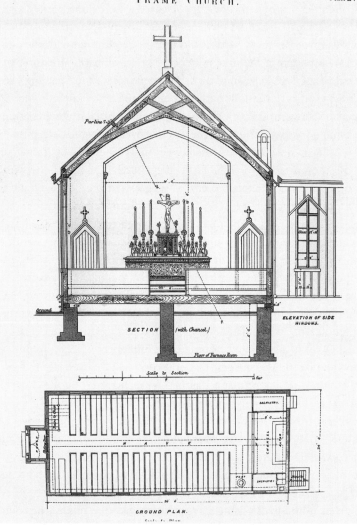

Designs for a "Frame Church," from a Catholic church pattern book.
From Sholl, *Working Designs for Ten Catholic Churches*, Design A, plate 2.
Courtesy of the University of Delaware Library, Newark, Delaware.

"Frame Church," featured a high, open ceiling; a rectangular plan split into chancel and nave; regular pews; a choir loft; a high altar and tabernacle decorated with candles, flowers, and a crucifix; symbolic crosses throughout the structure; and even pointed arches—all of which could also be found in Louisville's cathedral. Other plans in Sholl's book offered different styles, sizes, and levels of finish, but they employed similar tools for sanctifying worship space. Surely the congregations building such structures in the mid-nineteenth century would bring their own personalities to the prescribed plans, but they drew from a common architectural vocabulary, reflecting Spalding's basic assertions. And in the eyes of Protestant visitors, these commonalities carried great weight. Unifying forces did not fully mute the several developing dialects within Catholic worship, but they could bond diverse parishes in the face of opposition.[14]

Bishop Spalding's assessment of Protestant art proved less durable. For beyond the doors of his cathedral, the sharp distinctions he drew between Catholic and Protestant art were already losing their edge. Contemporary changes taking place in Protestant architecture and worship would prove that a "spirit of reverence and religious awe" was not "gone for ever." And the primary engine of these changes sat in the pews before him.

Attending "one of our principal shows"

Protestants and other non-Catholics regularly explored America's new Catholic churches. "Magnificent" cathedrals like those of Louisville, Kentucky, and St. Louis, Missouri, received most of the fanfare, but a host of parish churches opened their doors in communities of every size. For many visitors, the structures' blends of form and spirit affirmed the potency implied by Catholic growth.

Several factors drew such visitors into the new churches. Simple curiosity provided a general motivation. As Catholic facilities entered some areas for the first time, local citizens stopped by for a look. In dedication ceremonies and holiday celebrations, curious onlookers found opportunities to participate in popular civic events. Occasionally, Protestant residents actually contributed money to Catholic construction projects and so wished to view the outcome of their benevolence. For less generous Protestants, Catholic churches offered chances to test religious claims and personally evaluate the subjects of so much controversy. The spectacular stories circulating in anti-Catholic propaganda, such as those regarding lewd behavior in confessionals, fortified dungeons beneath worshippers' feet, and semi-pagan idolatry, heightened public interest. Under the shadow of cross-crowned steeples, non-Catholics felt the tug of novelty and mystery.

Other factors were less specific to Catholicism. Mid-nineteenth-century Americans customarily sampled the services of different denominations, whether or not they were interested in membership. Visits from notable speakers often prompted denominational mingling, as did special requests or occasions among friends. Thus the inspection of Catholic churches typically did not require the disruption of social routines. Similarly, when tourists journeyed across North America, they frequently visited various churches on their path. And when travelers or guests inspected a town's Catholic church, they could usually count on their local friends or acquaintances for accompaniment. Through all of these channels, Protestant visitors developed a passionate familiarity with Catholic churches.

The tone was set early on by John Adams. When this Puritan son of Massachusetts attended the Continental Congress in Philadelphia in 1774, he, George Washington, and other companions took advantage of spare time one Sunday afternoon to observe services at St. Mary's Catholic Church. In a letter to his wife Abigail describing the visit, Adams declared that "this Afternoons Entertainment was to me, most awfull and affecting." He pitied "the poor wretches" he saw there "fingering their beads, chanting Latin, not a word of which they understood." He was struck by "their holy Water—their Crossing themselves perpetually—their Bowing to the Name of Jesus." And he struggled to express his dread upon seeing "the Picture of our Saviour in a Frame of Marble over the Altar at full Length upon the

Cross, in the Agonies, and the Blood dropping and streaming from his Wounds." Yet Adams was also deeply moved by the chapel's beauties. He observed that "the Dress of the Priest was rich with Lace—his Pulpit was Velvet and Gold. The Altar Piece was very rich—little Images and Crucifixes about—Wax Candles lighted up." He also described the music as soft and sweet. To Abigail and to his diary, he made the startling confession that "the Scenery and the Musick" were so calculated "to take in Mankind that I wonder, the Reformation ever succeeded."[15]

Decades later, in 1847, a Methodist clergyman presented another portrait of this curiosity. Writing for the *Ladies' Repository*, Benjamin F. Tefft recounted a day spent "with the Catholics" in Cincinnati, Ohio. Explaining that he wanted to determine the "true character" of Catholic influence, he and a friend attended the Cathedral of St. Peter in Chains for services. The bulk of his account detailed their admiration for the building's show. Upon reaching the interior, Tefft directed his companion to observe several "beautiful" features, including the decorative panels of the roof and the "dim religious light" cast by the "colored windows." The focal point stood at the far end of the "vast room," a "magnificent recess . . . guarded by a brazen fence or wall, and filled with the sacred furniture." In this chancel sat the bishop's cathedra—"a costly sedan of crimson velvet"—and the marble altar—"figured all over with emblematic sculpture, and covered, though not concealed, by a flowing screen of the lightest and most open texture." Two of the altar's niches held "the sacred books, bound, lettered, and mounted with sumptuous elegance," in addition to "the ordinary utensils of the service." Above stood "ten golden candlesticks, six of them very high and massive . . . all of which are furnished with long and superb waxen candles," whose flames appeared as "radiant spots of fire." And "three splendid paintings" hung behind the altar, respectively depicting the Virgin Mary with the infant Jesus, the crucified Christ being carried to the tomb, and the angel's visit to St. Peter in prison. Completing the sweep, he exclaimed, "Look, now, upon all that brilliant scene—the brazen fence, the velvet-cushioned cathedra, the marble altar and its burnished and blazing furniture, and all that array of masterly and affecting pictures—and then ruminate a moment on the design of all this splendor."[16]

An equally powerful human "drama" soon filled the scene. Again revealing a familiarity with his subject, the clergyman noted "the peals of the mighty organ, rolling and thundering through its thousand pipes," which opened morning services. In the first act, "Two robed priests and a mitred bishop, preceded, in a regular line, by eight small boys in scarlet gowns" entered and performed a series of devotions. Their precise movements struck Tefft as "devout, solemn, and profound." The "second act" began as the bishop found his seat and the officiating priest performed a series of chants and postures with the assistance of the "band of little boys." The "adoring" congregation watched quietly from the pews. The "third act" included a reading from scripture and a sermon, which struck the author as simultaneously obscure, self-serving, and "brilliant." The "fourth act" featured the "awful pageant" of the Eucharist. Here, the priest handled the ceremonial elements with "becoming gravity," his assistants rang bells to signal the transformation of the bread and wine into Christ's body and blood, and "every good Catholic" in the pews bowed and prayed. Then came the formal exit of the bishop, the priests, and the boys, as the drama closed "amidst a perfect volley of learned and laborious thunder from the organ." Thus ended the spirited celebration of morning services. And though most of the ceremony had employed the "dead language" of Latin, the two visitors felt moved.[17]

But their day was not over. Tefft stated that "the spectator, impelled by his fancy, or curious to see the drama concluded, is in his seat again in the afternoon." So the two companions attended the cathedral's afternoon services, which they found to be much more informal. Here, the "rich and the gay" came "to be entertained" by the mostly choral performances. Still, the occasion was devout, with the reverent attention of the bishop, priests, and people on the "inspiring music of the choir." In a beautifully telling comment, Tefft admitted, "All the strangers present, and there are many of them here, sit in mute wonder at the flood of mingled melody and harmony, which comes pouring down upon them from above." The musical performances, the religious ceremonies, and the architectural designs played before an awed public.[18]

The clergyman had immersed himself and his audience in the Catholic scene. His conclusions were not comforting. Reasserting anti-Catholic suspicions, he warned of the enduring, subversive abilities of "Romanism." His companion agreed that the "real skill" with which Cincinnati's Catholics had "united architecture, painting, sculpture, and music" served an ulterior purpose. For "in the structure and furnishing of their house," and "in all the services, they strive to make a bold impression on the imagination, and to captivate the sense." In short, "Every thing, from first to last, is nicely adapted to the prevailing prejudices of the people on whom they desire to act," the "American public." In his own wondrous reactions and in those of the banks of "strangers" in the pews, Tefft found proof of the Catholic ability to pander to "the popular taste" in order to proselytize. Though his experience was influenced by preconceived notions involving submissive Catholic worshippers and manipulative priests, this Methodist had discovered a beautiful, unique, and threatening world in his visit to the local cathedral.[19]

Simpler motives may have brought a crowd of local citizens to attend the consecration of a Catholic church in Lexington, Kentucky. Ironically, their participation was noted by a Presbyterian clergyman publishing a volume of anti-Catholic essays in 1841. Describing the Lexington ceremonies, the pastor recounted a "most uproarous affair" that occurred when the solemnly assembled crowd mistakenly perceived their church to have been set on fire and ran from the building. He began his essay by stating that Lexington had been "a Protestant place," where the few Catholic laborers had met "in shy privacy" at a distant chapel. But in the 1830s, "the Papists seem to have made a simultaneous movement all over the country," and Lexington saw an increase in Catholic activity. Through a variety of means, there soon appeared "a big chapel, erected in the city and holding itself forth with much pretension." Like the later Louisville and Cincinnati cathedrals, this "engine for proselyting [*sic*]" featured much "music and machinery to praise God." When the hour came for the bishop's visit and the building's dedication, the house was full, and "*Protestant spectators*" composed "at least nineteen twentieths of the audience." Though this estimate was perhaps an exaggeration, the pastor made no other explanation of their attendance. It is likely that, given the previously diminutive presence of Catholicism in Lexington and the elaborate preparations for the new building's ceremony, most of these visitors attended out of civic curiosity.[20]

Some may have been donors. The names of Protestant benefactors occasionally appeared on the subscription rolls of new Catholic churches. At times this generosity reflected a proud local boosterism or an endorsement for the programs of refined church leaders. For example, in the early 1800s, a prominent Protestant matron from Boston commissioned painter Gilbert Stuart to execute a portrait of the city's charming Catholic bishop, Jean de Cheverus. At that same time, Boston's Protestant aristocracy donated 20 percent of the total $20,000 needed to build the city's first Catholic church, the Church of the Holy Cross. And with the construction of Louisville, Kentucky's first Catholic church in 1811, Protestants composed ninety percent of the project's contributors. Other instances of Protestant contributions were more economically motivated. One Catholic historian explained that at Albany, Utica, Cold Spring, and indeed "nearly every parish" in upstate New York, Protestant donations "mostly sprung from the desire to keep the working population anchored to a town and an industry," though this did not preclude "kindly feeling." The industrialists behind these gifts to communities of Catholic laborers may have followed their money for a look inside the new buildings. Such donations could stir "a loud denunciation" from "critical brethren," but the pattern remained in place.[21]

Diaries and letters also reinforce the notion of a more casual Catholic attendance. In 1841, an ex-Quaker working as a lawyer in Camden, New Jersey, noted that when a Catholic priest from Philadelphia lectured one night, "Many pious Protestants were led to attend out of curiosity. They had an idea that a Roman Catholic was something like the devil. The house was crammed." Later that year, the diarist attended services at the cathedral in Philadelphia: "Although I got to the Cathedral a half an hour before the time, I could get no seat outside of the orchestra; but I was invited to sit among the singers, and accepted the polite offer." Afterward, he visited an Episcopal service and a Baptist meeting. Maintaining a broad religious appetite throughout the 1840s, he continued to sample nearby Methodist, Baptist, Episcopal, and Catholic churches. Likewise, a young Protestant woman living in Charleston, South Carolina, recorded visiting Unitarian, Episcopal, Baptist, Presbyterian, Methodist, and Roman Catholic churches, plus a Jewish synagogue, all between 1850 and 1851. And an Episcopalian in Wilmington, Delaware, illustrated the role personal relations played in Catholic familiarity. When her Roman Catholic friend died in 1838, she attended the funeral out of respect. On the day of the ceremonies, this diarist recorded: "Early we repaired to the R. Catholic Church. The coffin faced the Altar. The Father and Doct. Climer to whom [the deceased] was betrothed sat near it. The mummeries of the R. C. Church were performed." The diarist did not approve of these "mummeries," but she could discern in them a certain beauty, stating, "The priest in his white robe, the long white scarfs of the bearers, the deep and solemn tone of old Trinity's Bell, were well calculated to inspire thoughts of the departed and to dispose the mind to mournful reflections." A similar appreciation greeted other Protestants whose personal relations or inquisitive tastes led them into Catholic chapels.[22]

Beyond this local exposure, Protestants regularly toured Catholic structures while traveling. The rich explored Catholic monuments in Italy and other European destinations, where the mixed expression of adoration and outrage had become an art in itself. And while memoirs detailing these experiences were plentiful, an equally impressive number of Protestants, like John Adams, visited Catholic sights while traveling through America and Canada.

In the late 1850s, a young man from Cooperstown, New York, entered school at Albany. He explained in a letter home, "On Sunday I usually attend meeting from one to two or three times each Sabbath." One Sunday, he attended the new Cathedral of the Immaculate Conception, "which," he reported, "is built of Stone and is the largest best furnished and most Costly Church in the city." He found that "its interior [is] the greatest and most beautiful piece of Architecture of any Church that [he had] seen in this or any other City."[23]

Two other examples involved tourists from England. One traveler, staying in Philadelphia for a season around 1820, surveyed several of the city's churches, including a Roman Catholic chapel. A few features of the Protestant services had raised his ire, but the trip to the Catholic chapel invoked his full passion. He acknowledged that the church's altar was "very handsome," but he damned its garish decorations as "more calculated for a temple dedicated to Venus" than for a Christian church. He was particularly struck by the crucifix, hanging "as large as life" before the altar: "the first view" of this "sight of horror," he wrote, "must make a sickening impression; but its constant presence deadens the feelings, and renders devotion grounded upon it a mere ceremony." He endured the foreign services until their conclusion, whereupon the organ played *Adeste fideles* "very well but not very àpropos." Though he had a companion, he made no mention of whether this companion was likewise pleasantly revolted. Thirty-five years later, an English Methodist touring America also made a stop in Albany, New York, with similar results. This minister approved of the town's "fervent" Methodist services, held "in a good, commodious church," and he felt lukewarm toward the Episcopal services. Then, when he "looked in at" the crowded Catholic church, he found much to admire: the "decorated" altar, the formal priests, the burning candles, the "powerful" choir, and the earnest congregation. But he added the familiar epithet, denouncing "the show and glare of Popery" before him in this "semi-heathenish sight." Despite the shock in both Englishmen's reactions, their activities fit into a well-defined pattern of Catholic visitation.[24]

Three of the most celebrated destinations included the Cathedral of Notre Dame in Montreal, the Cathedral of the Assumption in Baltimore, and St. Patrick's Cathedral in New York City. These monumental structures overwhelmed their crowds of Protestant visitors. When an American Methodist stopped at Montreal's cathedral in 1852, he told his American readers, "As you stand in front, and look up to the immense central window, nearly seventy feet in height, and then, upward still, to the massive square towers, two hundred and fifty feet above you, an idea of vastness rushes down upon the soul, such as is produced by no other building on the continent." The building's rich interior also impressed the tourist, with "majestic columns"; a "double tier of spacious galleries"; numerous incarnations of "the Madonna and the crucifix, of every material" and "of every size"; "old paintings, delineating scenes from the life of Christ and the saints"; and "long aisles rapidly converging, in distant perspective, toward the altar," again suggesting "an idea of vastness such as is seldom felt." Still, his Protestant heart pitied the souls who came morning and night "to perform the humiliating rites of their refined and civilized idolatry!"[25]

The Catholic beauties of Baltimore rivaled those of Montreal. In 1841, a local Presbyterian pastor granted that "most strangers who visit Baltimore, are conducted to the Cathedral as one of our principal shows." Designed at the beginning of the century by noted architect Benjamin Henry Latrobe, the domed, cruciform Cathedral of the Assumption was widely acknowledged as one of the nation's most impressive churches. For those who could not make the trip, the pastor narrated a detailed description of the building, after his "fifth or sixth visit to this spectacle." Despite the presence of such Catholic "fooleries" as holy water fonts, grotesque paintings, great altars, and confessionals, he ultimately judged the cathedral "a very fine edifice; spacious and imposing; durable and noble."[26]

This Catholic landmark would be partially eclipsed on the American scene in the 1850s with the beginnings of St. Patrick's Cathedral in New York. Planned by Archbishop John Hughes as a mighty tribute to God and the Catholic faith, the twin-towered structure echoed the Gothic designs of France and Germany, and it covered nearly an entire city block. Crowds of Protestants attended the lay-

"The largest ecclesiastical edifice in America," St. Patrick's Cathedral, New York City, New York, as envisioned in *Harper's Weekly* during construction. The building was completed, with some modifications, between 1879 and 1888. From the article "St. Patrick's Cathedral in New York," 808, 812.

ing of its cornerstone in 1858, and when the church was substantially completed in 1878, citizens of all stripes thronged its aisles. The *New York Times* declared that, except for a few details, "there is nothing to detract from the pleasure which the view of the entire grand building inspires." It, too, became one of the area's "principal shows." The exaggerated Protestant reactions surrounding these three cathedrals recalled the quieter encounters taking place in smaller Catholic churches throughout the country.[27]

Actual worship in these churches did not possess the uniformity implied by Protestant observers. But the various churches did illustrate a general willingness to engage the senses with recognizable symbols. Altars, candles, flowers, robes, sculpture, postures, emblems, and images—particularly those involving Jesus on the cross or the Virgin Mary—struck outsiders by their very presence as much as by their comparative uses. These objects represented points of genuine difference between Protestant and Catholic theology, and their tangible peculiarity helped Protestants make sense of the widespread anti-Catholic hype. Further, this "music and machinery" for praising God suggested a key to Catholic growth, since material lures provided easier explanations than the idea of willing Catholic adherents exercising calculated, rational choices.

The accounts of sightseers also highlight the visitors' own ambivalence toward Catholicism. Few longed for the authority of the pope, but the solemnly focused sights and sounds of Catholic worship consistently inspired profound spiritual experiences. Similar tensions led Protestants to explore these appeals through other mediums, including fiction and fine art. Historians of such encounters have often stressed their fleeting or reflective qualities. These scholars describe the fascination with Catholic worship as a vehicle by which Protestants challenged their own constraints or as a temporary "release" followed by an expected "retreat back to the familiar world of Protestant boundaries." But the visitors' immersions were not always fleeting. As Catholic churches became a local commonplace, Protestant exposure to these worlds would be repeated and prolonged. And lurking beneath this exposure and ambivalence lay the specter of conversions.[28]

The physical charms of Catholic churches prompted the conversion of thousands of nineteenth-century Americans. Or so the mythology surrounding conversions would suggest. For while there may have been as many different motives as there were converts, Protestant and Catholic observers consistently trumpeted the ability of Catholic art to sway religious affiliations. A classic example appeared in 1893, when the editors of the *Catholic World* presented the story of one woman who converted after her first visit to a Catholic chapel. Paraphrasing her testimony, the editors explained that decades ago, this daughter of a Protestant clergyman had been living with her family in a small New England village. On one hot day, the woman happened upon a tired, Irish friend walking to Mass. She then helped him to the distant chapel, where the sight of the "little wooden church, with its cross-crowned steeple" beckoned her inside. After she slid into an empty pew, the scene overwhelmed her—the worshippers who "were all kneeling and deeply absorbed in their devotions," the "lighted candles on the altar," the "white-robed priest" and his solemn activities. Feeling an inexplicable thrill, she dropped to her knees, covered her face with her hands, and prayed until the end of the ceremony. She claimed that she was "a Catholic from that moment," and she formalized her conversion soon afterward. The woman recalled that she had "never felt the slightest doubt or uncertainty" about her spiritual path after that breathless morning in the little wooden church.[29]

Other examples were no less spectacular. One American priest recalled that in the late 1840s, an English acquaintance had converted in response to "the incense." The priest quoted the man as saying, "When I went to your chapel . . . and saw the incense rising in front of the altar and curling up, up, up towards heaven, my heart went up with it." Noting the biblical use of incense, the man "wondered that the Baptists didn't have it, nor any church that I knew of; but I saw it in your church . . . and my whole heart felt at home at once. . . . I want to be a Catholic." And a 1905 history related an earlier tale in which a young Boston woman visited her first Catholic church, drawn by "wonderful stories of the Christmas celebration, of the strange vestments, the sweet music and the Infant in the crib." The captivating beauty of those sights ultimately encouraged the woman to adopt the church as a new spiritual home. Narratives surrounding the famous convert Elizabeth Ann Seton struck a similar tone. Seton's conversion in 1806 came after a period of personal distress, but her journal and her early biographers highlighted a moment that occurred when she stepped into a Catholic church in New York City, tired from a long walk. By kneeling "in silence before that little tabernacle and the great crucifixion above it," Seton found "rest." She then rose, declared her newfound faith to the resident priest, and left the building "light of heart."[30]

Protestant testimony could rival these claims. The most glowing appraisals typically contained warnings against the general ability of Catholic art to "seduce." One Princeton professor outlined such "dangers" in a sermon preached before a Presbyterian synod in Baltimore, Maryland, in 1837. Specifically concerned with the practice of sending Protestant children to Roman Catholic schools, he warned that "there is nothing more adapted to captivate the youthful mind than the Popish ritual. Its dazzling splendour; its addresses to the imagination and the senses, can scarcely fail of fascinating every young person, who has not a remarkably enlightened and well balanced mind." And the speaker affirmed that, with the allure of "the Popish ritual . . . thousands have been entangled and enchained by its power before they were aware." In 1845, an ex-priest reiterated the theme of material seduction when he told his Protestant readers about a recent letter from the bishop of Boston, "in which he informs the *authorities* of Rome that he is making converts from some of the *first families* in his diocese." The ex-priest explained that the primary reason for this success lay in the superficial view of the Catholic Church as "fair, brilliant, dazzling, and seductive." "Nothing is seen in their external forms of worship," he continued, "but showy vestments, dazzling lights, and the appearance of great devotion. Nothing is heard but the softest and most melting strains of music. No wonder these should captivate minds." And an 1855 contributor to the *Presbyterian Critic and Monthly Review* stated, "We are not at all surprised, that men of the very first order of mind, and of the highest attainments in all the walks of merely human thought, should throw themselves into the arms of Rome." This was mostly due to the church's artistic appeals, the writer charged, for "that which invests Popery with this tremendous power to entrap and destroy, to blind and kill men, to buy and sell and make merchandize of their souls" was its elaborate "chamber of imagery." Encountering "crosses, surplices, gowns, altars and what not," citizens overlooked modest religion and turned all too easily to the Church of Rome's "beautified" and "complicated machine."[31]

Critics were not surprised by claims of the pageantry's successes because such claims meshed with the basic tenets of Protestant theology. Evangelical denominations largely held that human nature was essentially sinful due to the original fall of Adam. This depraved nature placed every person in constant risk of falling to temptations, and, for many, the glittering promise of material sanctity in Catholic worship seemed a likely enticement. One Presbyterian minister, lecturing before a Philadelphia audience in 1840, spelled out the risk. Evaluating Catholic prospects in America as favorable, the minister explained, "Popery is a system very grateful to the natural principles and sympathies of the human heart." And a decade later, the Methodist *National Magazine* concluded that the ongoing popularity of "idolatry" was due to the "aptitude of man for every kind of sin, and the temptations of the devil." A thorough review of the matter appeared in an issue of the *American Protestant*, where one writer attributed the recent "Success of Romanism" to the predictable effects of its calculated art. Reflecting upon the theme of human depravity, the writer was not surprised to find a certain beauty "throughout the whole structure and furniture of [Catholic] churches." "The pale light entering softly through the painted windows," he wrote, "the ancient Gothic style of the building, the paintings on the walls . . . together with the impression that *the building itself is holy*, are all eminently fitted, as they were designed, to take strong hold of the imagination of all classes in society." The writer admitted, "Such excitement is pleasant; it is grateful to the feelings of men who are naturally super-stitious."[32]

This led some polemicists to try and "unmask" a sinister system behind Catholic splendor. But public appreciation for Catholic art and worship only grew, and Protestant observers personally affirmed its pull. The Methodist visitor to Montreal, while sitting in one of the city's "gorgeous" chapels, found that "here is gained an influence over the young and susceptible heart that is absolutely boundless and ineffaceable." Such statements complemented individual conversion narratives like those published in the *Catholic World*.[33]

Despite the romance of such perspectives, they did not necessarily emphasize exotic or grandiose settings. Narrating scenes in "little wooden" village churches, city parish churches, and seminary chapels, these observers described a unique blend of spirituality and art capable of producing deep religious changes, a blend comparable with that found in large cathedrals. This subject held sensational implications for Protestant denominations, both in terms of their membership rolls and in terms of mission and pride. Thus popular accounts of Catholic art built upon their subject's mystique. "Against this phalanx of ceremonies," concluded one Baptist, "it is vain to hurl arguments."[34]

Beneath the mythology, a fair number of conversions to Catholicism did occur. The actual number remained in dispute, but a reasonable estimate counted 103,400 total American converts from 1820 to 1870.[35] Aside from sanctified worship and art, the channels for conversion included intermarriage, attendance at Catholic schools, the efforts of priests, and personal study. Converts came from every region and background, but a number of typical characteristics did emerge. Most conversions occurred in the free states of the North and West, where there were generally more congregations, chapels, and priests. White converts received by far the most attention, and since free states held a lower proportion of African Americans, it is likely most converts were white. The predominant gender of the converts was not clear. The names of men, especially clergymen, filled published rosters of converts, and the related literature frequently followed conversions of whole "families." Yet anecdotes of female conversions, such as those found in the *Catholic World*, were just as common, and Protestant observers often emphasized the risk to "susceptible" hearts, a veiled reference to supposed "feminine" qualities. References were also made to "young" hearts, and many conversions indeed took place among adolescents and young adults. Two final characteristics remained linked: original denomination and social class. The wealthy—the "first families"—proved to be more open to conversion than the poor, and the two denominations most associated with wealth—the Episcopalians and the Congregational-based Unitarians—delivered higher percentages of their members into the Roman Catholic Church. Wealth may have influenced conversions in the tendency of the upper classes to send their children to Catholic schools, as well as in their broader exposure to Catholic arts.[36]

The most famous converts illustrated these trends. Those who traded the Episcopal Church for the Catholic Church included Elizabeth Ann Seton, the saintly mother of five, and Levi Silliman Ives, who renounced his post as Episcopal bishop of North Carolina upon conversion. In addition, at least thirty-seven other Episcopal clergymen joined the Catholic Church, all prior to 1858. Among Congregationalists and Universalists, Orestes Brownson captured public attention in 1844 when he converted and began a remarkable editorial career. From the evangelical denominations, novelist Anna Dorsey became a Catholic in 1840, and Isaac Hecker, originally a politically active Methodist, converted that same year. Through the mid-nineteenth century, the Archdiocese of Boston alone welcomed prominent doctors Henry B. C. Greene, Horatio Robinson Storer, and Elizabeth C. Keller; industrialists George W. Lloyd and Thomas Moriarty; Brook Farm commune founders Sophia Willard Dana and Sarah F. Stearns; army generals Charles P. Stone and John Gray Foster; and artists Sarah Josephine Tryon and Elizabeth Washburn Brainerd, to name but a few. In addition, prominent British conversions also carried symbolic weight. Examples include architect Augustus Welby Pugin, who converted in 1835, and Oxford theologian John

Henry Newman, who converted in 1845. To be sure, the bulk of the two countries' Protestants were not at risk of rushing en masse into the arms of Rome. But the sum of these notable conversions, taking place within a sea of anti-Catholicism, challenged Protestant assurance and added to the claims for Catholic potency.[37]

So Protestant congregations and building committees of the mid-nineteenth century found themselves in the midst of an artistic swell. They knew of Catholicism's spread, they understood its material distinctions, they observed those distinctions at home and abroad, and they heard of related conversions. Their combination of apprehension and appreciation inspired changes in Protestant church architecture that would acknowledge the new Catholic presence. Using the tools that worked so powerfully in Catholic settings—universal and traditional symbolism, sanctified church structures, and ceremonial worship—they gradually took advantage of the associated surge and began integrating revered elements of Catholicism into Protestant churches. It was not a wholesale appropriation, but it marked a crucial compromise between self-defeating, anti-Catholic vitriol and open conversion to the ancient church. And if the elements brought new complications into Protestant churches, such as the implied, particular presence of Christ in worship and social divisions over the objects' propriety, they also helped Protestants reassert their own vitality before a broader national audience.

In this light, the pointed remarks made by one visitor to the churches of Albany, New York, seem especially prophetic. After arriving in 1850, the Englishman surveyed the town's steeples and declared the local churches to be "large, comfortable, well filled, and usually ministered to by clergymen of very considerable talent." But beneath the prosperity churned, he noted, "a manifest rivalry . . . in the building and ornamenting of their churches. The Presbyterians, Methodists, and Congregationalists . . . equal the Episcopalians in their attention to . . . organs, choirs, and the engagement of professed singers—to towers, steeples, and sonorous bells," and other new artistic attractions. "But," continued the Englishman, "the Romanists are outdoing them all, and probably inciting all the other sects, by the magnificent cathedral they are erecting on the highest part of the city." Additionally, locals complained of the Catholic "art of squeezing out of . . . their humblest followers a liberal quota towards the good work." The visitor's comments illustrate that Protestant innovations were not the result of abstract outpourings of wealth. Instead, the local "Romanists" were challenging the other churches with a specific architectural program. And for some Protestants, the changes would begin with a single, bare symbol.[38]

The Cross

In 1834, the rector of St. Mary's Episcopal Church in Burlington, New Jersey, desired to place a cross atop his newly refurbished sanctuary. No ordinary rector, George Washington Doane also served as the Episcopal bishop of New Jersey. The young bishop had accepted his post in 1832 after a productive career working as a professor, editor, poet, and rector throughout New England. Shortly after taking charge of St. Mary's, he and his vestry had decided to renovate their old church, and their ambitious new design featured a cruciform plan with Greek details, including a pediment adorned with lotus leaves and a tower "derived from that built at Athens . . . commonly called the Tower of the Winds." But when Doane carried out the plans for "an enriched Greek Cross" to be mounted on the roof, the community stood aghast. A local Presbyterian minister chronicled the confrontation, and he began by asserting that most of St. Mary's vestrymen had originally approved the designs without "*noticing the Cross* at the time." The project was thus completed, and to the vestry's "great surprise, as well as that of many in the community, of all 'denominations'—lo! a Cross made quite a Catholic appearance on the apex of the pediment!" Controversy arose, "both in the Vestry and out of it," and "after a very warm meeting, one of the Vestry shortly after declared that unless the Cross was taken down very soon, it should be pulled down." This alarmed several cautious members, "who thereupon employed a carpenter to take down Cross . . . in the night—without the knowledge of the Vestry." But Doane and his congregation must have then settled the matter peacefully, for the cross, "which was sawed down in the night," was "re-placed at the apex of the pediment . . . in the DAY-TIME." At the consecration of the new building, Doane remained uncharacteristically silent on the uproar, and the cross would stay.[1]

Doane was among the few American Protestants of the 1830s and 1840s who risked making "a Catholic appearance" by employing the cross as a church symbol. For the symbol's associations with Roman Catholicism ran deep—Doane's cross had provoked an anti-Catholic fury despite the Greek associations of the piece's design and despite the variety of classical features surrounding it on St. Mary's Church. Like the crucifix, with its bodily representation of Christ's suffering, the cross had served as a sacred Catholic instrument for centuries. One Boston Episcopalian explained in 1847 that "when a stranger enters a city, and passes a church with a cross upon it, his impression is that it is Roman Catholic; and when one visits the cemetery . . . and sees a stone embellished with the same symbol, he takes it for granted that a Roman Catholic sleeps underneath." A similar report came from California, where one correspondent noted that a local "Episcopal chapel . . . has been surmounted by a cross, and in consequence, is frequently mistaken for a genuine Roman Catholic place of worship." Indeed, canon law prescribed set architectural locations for Catholic crosses and crucifixes, thereby bolstering their prominence. These qualities made the cross a regular target for anti-Catholic mobs, like those that cheered the rising flames at St. Michael's and St. Augustine's churches during Philadelphia's 1844 riots, or the mob that attacked a chapel near Boston in 1854, dispersing only after the group had wrenched the cross from the top of the steeple and publicly burned it. Thus, in the eyes of many American Protestants, and in the words of one Presbyterian magazine, the cross was "not a symbol of redemption through the blessed Saviour, but a perverted, abused symbol of a great system of superstition and imposture." The use of this symbol on Protestant churches not only tempted "idolatry," but it also confused religious loyalties.[2]

The rare appearance of this "outward emblem of Popery" on Protestant churches inspired similar fights throughout the country. During the construction of New York's Trinity Episcopal Church in the early 1840s, architect and churchman Richard Upjohn sought to place a cross at the tip of the building's enormous tower and spire. While the vestry debated its propriety, Upjohn privately ordered workmen to prepare a cross, place it on the spire, and immediately remove the scaffolding. When the hostile vestrymen noticed their new ornament, Upjohn slyly insisted that removal of the lofty cross would require an unreasonable amount of time and expense. Elsewhere, anti-Catholic suspicions could condemn decorative touches that merely resembled crosses. For example, in the 1850s, the architect of a new seminary chapel in Alexandria, Virginia, placed "a modest trefoil or poppy-head" at the top of each of the pews. When Virginia's conservative Episcopal bishop, William Meade, arrived to consecrate the chapel, he interpreted these trefoils as foliated crosses. Refusing to consecrate them, Meade summoned a carpenter, and, in the words of one of the seminary students, "every poppy-head was laid low before the opening service." These initial conflicts frequently occurred in Episcopal circles because that denomination was among the earliest of the major Protestant denominations to employ crosses and Catholic-inspired symbolism. Such episodes illustrate the extensive baggage associated with simple crosses.[3]

The Protestant attack on the symbol extended onto the pages of anti-Catholic literature. Even as Doane, Upjohn, and others began to experiment with the cross, the distribution of profane images of the cross reinforced Protestant animosities. One "ex-clergyman," sick of the "abundance of form, ceremony, pomp, and circumstance" that was sweeping "all the churches and church establishments now in existence," opened his controversial 1855 pamphlet with an ominous engraving showing a waste pile of crosses and other elements of "Romanism." Another example appeared in several publications of the 1830s and 1840s, including *Illustrations of Popery* and the *American Protestant Magazine*. This image pictured four notable Protestants standing on "the immoveable rock of TRUTH," academically attired in black robes and holding books. Beneath these four, floundering in "the stormy ocean of theological disputation," appeared four angry Catholic authorities bedecked with crosses, beads, a crosier, and a crucifix. The Protestant figures showed no concern for the sinking papal devices. But the supreme insult was delivered to the cross as symbol in an 1855 pamphlet published in Boston, titled *The Satanic Plot; or, Awful Crimes of Popery in High and Low Places*. In this pamphlet championing free schools and Protestant churches, the cover art centered on a seated discussion between the pope and Satan over a map of the United States. Not only did the cross appear prominently on the back of the Pope's chair, but it adorned the back of Satan's chair as well. In contrast, a Protestant church with a plain spire appeared near the top margin. Such a scene left little doubt that Protestant loyalties to the symbol were thin. In these and other images, the cross served as a Catholic trademark, a piece of visual shorthand representing the sensual tools of Catholicism and the oppressive authority of the church.[4]

Modern churches testify to a dramatic change. Crosses can now be found on nearly every Protestant church in America, from the tops of spires down to decorative cornerstones. Plain and decorated crosses hang above Communion tables, glow in stained-glass windows, trim ministers' vestments, adorn Communion vessels, and mark gravesites in surrounding yards. Several design variations have been available to modern Protestants—including the Greek cross, the design selected by Bishop Doane, which features four arms of equal length, and the cross of St. Andrew, which resembles an X—each with its own unique significance and origins. But specifically the Latin cross, which features a vertical line with a shorter horizontal line cutting across its upper portion, has become the design of choice. This was the form on which Jesus was understood to have been crucified and yet also the one most closely identified with Roman Catholicism. Few members would now ransack their churches to remove the symbols, for

REVIEW OF BISHOP IVES'
"TRIALS of a MIND"
BY AN EX-CLERGYMAN.

PHILADELPHIA.
PUB! BY THOMAS CURTIS, ARCH STREET.

Title page from an 1855 anti-Catholic pamphlet displaying the cross and other shadowy implements. From Ex-Clergyman, *A Review of Bishop Ives' "Trials of a Mind."* Courtesy of the University of Delaware Library, Newark, Delaware.

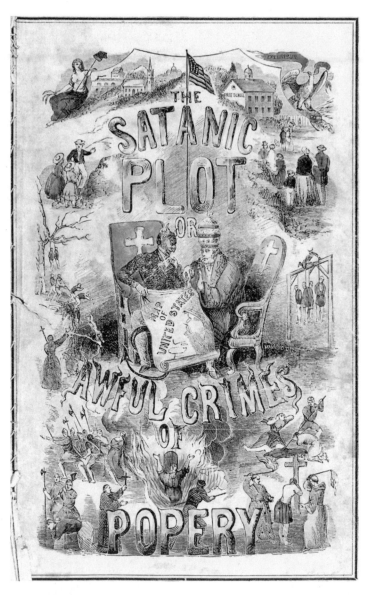

Cover page of an anti-Catholic pamphlet showing the cross on the chairs of the pope and Satan. From *Satanic Plot*. Courtesy of the University of Delaware Library, Newark, Delaware.

A Latin cross featured on the sign outside Westhampton Baptist Church, Richmond, Virginia. Photograph by Ryan K. Smith, 2005.

the Latin cross has become the universal emblem of American Christianity, defining the self-image of almost every variety of Protestant. The largest denominations—including the Southern Baptist Convention, the United Methodist Church, the Presbyterian Church in the U.S.A., the African Methodist Episcopal Church, and the United Churches of Christ—have incorporated the Latin cross into their shields and trademarks. Having lost nearly all of its exclusive associations with Roman Catholicism, the cross has gained an ability to communicate Protestant aspirations for a sacred, common faith.[5]

Scattered fights in the 1830s and 1840s over the use of the cross highlight the beginnings of the symbol's Protestant career in America. And while a variety of theological, commercial, and aesthetic factors encouraged the new use of the cross, it was the rise of Roman

Catholicism itself that provided the major impetus. Bishop Doane admitted as much early in 1827 when he published a bracing article titled "Crosses and Weathercocks on Churches." Here, Doane spoke out for the "restoration of the rood to our steeples" by unfavorably contrasting Protestant timidity toward the symbol with the bolder, more effective practices of "the Papists." Over the next thirty years, Doane's warnings against "the dangerous attraction of the Church of Rome" would gain significance as the Catholic Church increased in numbers and prominence. Doane's own son converted to Roman Catholicism in 1855, causing his father great distress and illustrating how quickly the battle could become personal. Protestant churches, by appropriating the cross, as well as other related implements of Catholic art and worship, harnessed a part of the Catholic surge while refining their own ability to attract and satisfy members.[6]

Reformation Roots

In the religious struggles following the Reformation, England drifted in and out of Rome's orbit. The English Church split from Rome in 1533, but succeeding monarchs held differing views as to how the country's religion should be practiced. By the time that church policies began to settle in the late seventeenth century, the Anglican Church had essentially abandoned the Latin cross and the crucifix as church fixtures. The nation's more extreme reformers, such as the Presbyterians and the Puritans, had dropped the symbols long before then. As a result, the early denominations in America that grew out of the English experience—Episcopalians, Methodists, Presbyterians, Congregationalists, and Baptists—treated the Latin cross as a foreign symbol. Lutherans and a smaller German-based sect, the Moravians, employed the cross as early as the eighteenth century without difficulties. But the symbol did not capture public attention until the early nineteenth century.[7]

Yet the churches of English-speaking Protestants had never been symbolically bare. From the earliest colonial settlements, congregations had supplied their meetinghouses with creative, meaningful

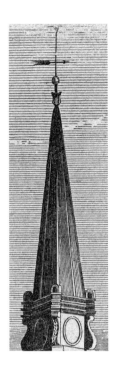

A typical "ball and vane" design, atop the spire of the Second Presbyterian Church, St. Louis, Missouri (1840). From *Presbyterian Magazine* 2 (February 1852): 48. Courtesy of the William Smith Morton Library, Union Theological Seminary and Presbyterian School of Christian Education, Richmond, Virginia.

furnishings intended to illustrate beliefs, facilitate ceremonies, and honor the Lord. By the early 1800s, Protestant churches could draw from a rich store of common symbols. Perhaps the most recognizable was the church spire. Across the nation, these heaven-directed needles topped the church towers of almost every denomination, providing spiritual punctuation to their landscapes. In 1855, a Methodist editor endorsed the opinion that "the *spire*" was singularly useful in granting a "religious character" to a building. And a "ball and vane" was, in the words of one Episcopal bishop, "the usual and appropriate finish" for the tip of a Protestant spire. Below the spire, heavy bells often rang out God's call to worship. Elaborate entrances divided the human and divine realms. Ornate pulpits commanded the center of sanctuaries, demonstrating the importance of hearing God's word. Silver Communion vessels exemplified the durability and value of Christ's sacrifice. And following the Protestant penchant for texts, the words of the Lord's Prayer and the Ten Commandments often hung on church walls, while large Bibles rested on lecterns or reading desks.[8]

Beyond these functional elements of the immediate church environment, a Protestant iconography flourished. Prominent in graveyards and on the pages of religious literature, natural and classical figures addressed the mystery of human experience while respecting the bounds of Reformation traditions. Popular motifs employed by Protestants before midcentury included hourglasses, cherubs, birds, urns, and trees. Accompanying texts or comments frequently helped clarify the religious meanings of these improvised images. For example, in the 1850s, one observer drew strength from a unique pair of headstones erected in Philadelphia's Laurel Hill Cemetery, "upon one of which is a sheaf of wheat, beautifully sculptured, with the sentence 'fully ripe' inscribed beneath; on the other is the effigy of a lamp, with the inscription 'trimmed and burning.'" Anticipating his Protestant audience, the writer exclaimed, "What appropriate and beautiful emblems do these present of the Christian character of those whose graves they mark." But images of the Bible provided the most consciously "Protestant" icons. Sculpted and engraved images of the book, whether pictured open or closed, transformed the Word into a badge needing little explanation. For example, at the headquarters of the Presbyterian Board of Publication in Philadelphia, "an effigy of an open Bible" ornamented the facade. And on the pages of anti-Catholic pamphlets, images of the Bible provided a visual "vindication of Protestantism from Papal assailants."[9]

None of these symbols drew from a recognizably Catholic tradition, nor did they wield any sacramental power. Spires, bells, Communion silver, and the like had centuries of pre-Reformation use, and they commonly graced contemporary Catholic chapels, but their presence had long since ceased to distinguish between Christian traditions. The same held true for the few iconic overlaps, as no "stranger" viewing a gravestone embellished with a cherub or dove could accurately guess the denomination of the deceased. Further, most Protestants remained wary over the role of these symbols. Their rhetoric consistently maintained that Communion and its accompanying silver utensils merely commemorated, rather than reenacted, Christ's sacrifice; that high pulpits and their preachers could only prepare the unsaved for the action of God's hand; and that, in the words of the *Christian Recorder*, "We do not worship that harmless picture [of the Bible], but we feel happy whenever we see it, for it reminds us anew of God's precious gift." If such explanations distorted the role of "Catholic" art in comparison, relatively few Americans had the exposure or experience to argue otherwise.[10]

The Rise of Roman Catholicism

This distance started to narrow in the 1830s. With the sudden expansion of the Catholic Church in England and America, Catholic symbols gained a unique prominence and potency. New Catholic chapels and their flocks brought the cross, the crucifix, and other common Roman symbols into the rhythms of daily life, where they crystallized the mystique surrounding the surging church.

A number of observers noted the symbols' new visibility. In the 1830s, one pastor in Baltimore recounted a visit to "a man under sentence of death to talk to him about Christ." The pastor told his readers that upon his arrival, the man was "gazing intently on a little metallic image of Christ crucified, which a priest had left him." The pastor's own offer of assistance meant little, for, as the pastor put it, "He seemed indifferent to all I said. The priest had *prepared* him!" In 1852, the *Presbyterian Magazine* described the striking, almost admirable, prominence of the cross in Italy, where "in approaching a city, town, or hamlet . . . , the first object seen in the sky is the cross; it gleams upon the banners of her armies, and glistens upon the breasts of her soldiers; it rises upon the pinnacles of her towers, and looms upon the moonsail-masts of her navies." Newspapers and directories that charted the spread of Catholic churches throughout America described similar symbolic details. Also, popular paintings of Catholic subjects, like George Whiting Flagg's *A Nun*, displayed in 1836 at the National Academy of Design, brought images of Catholic crosses into public view. And even when the increasing numbers of anti-Catholic pamphlets visually desecrated the cross and its symbolic companions, as on the cover of *The Satanic Plot*, the objects still demonstrated key associations with power and destiny.[11]

Here, the cross "loomed" forward for appropriation in ways that the crucifix, the visages of saints, and other emblems did not. Its subject—the sacrifice of Jesus and his subsequent victory over sin and death—already corresponded with basic Protestant ideals. In the words of one Presbyterian in 1846, the concept of the cross "is undoubtedly the centre of the Christian system. It is like the sun in our planetary system; the source of light and life." Further, the material cross was rooted in the Bible, and evidence suggested that its form had been employed by Christians before the "corrupt" Middle Ages.[12]

The symbol's stark lines were also appealing, since Protestants remained notoriously squeamish at the sight of Jesus's suffering on Catholic crucifixes and canvases. One convent visitor explained, "One revolts at the endless pantomime of pain, and wearies of the pine or marble Christs in versatile and studied agonies. . . . Gladly, thankfully, gratefully does the Protestant looker-on turn from this low physical plane to that sublime *life* which is the Light of men." Such discomfort arose from an understanding of worship as commemorating rather than reenacting Jesus's passion, as well as from traditional taboos involving raw bodily displays. Another example of such discomfort appeared in a Methodist monthly, where one author declared that the popular transition from cross to crucifix in the Middle Ages marked "the decline of both artistic and religious purity." The author contrasted the crucifix, a symbol "that leaves Jesus in his agony of suffering, and his worshipers in tears and doubt as to the issue of the awful struggle," with the "empty cross" that "looked forward to the moment when it was said, 'He is not here; he is risen;' and that thus became the emblem of a mighty conquering Lord." The continuing preference among Protestants for the view of the "empty cross" as consciously signifying the resurrection's triumph would become a defining theme for their use of the symbol.[13]

While Protestants distinguished between crucifix and empty cross,

Roman Catholics continued to hold both symbols as appropriate reminders of Jesus's sacrifice. And their use of both remained central to the church's broader approach to art and symbolism, which had long drawn charges of idolatry from Protestants. In 1844, one Philadelphia Catholic exclaimed that "surely it is not possible, that . . . men should be found capable of believing, that the majority of the Christian world . . . should be so ignorant, so debased, so stupid, so wicked, as to give divine honours to a lifeless and senseless image," but this perception indeed persisted. James Gibbons, archbishop (and later cardinal) of Baltimore from 1877 to 1921, attempted a definitive answer regarding the church's use of images, crosses, and crucifixes within his widely read *The Faith of Our Fathers*. Gibbons lauded the sympathetic effects "produced by the silent spectacle of our Saviour hanging on the cross." He also explained that "the Cross is held in the highest reverence by Catholics, because it was the instrument of our Saviour's crucifixion. . . . We do not, of course, attach any intrinsic virtue to the Cross; this would be sinful and idolatrous. Our veneration is referred to Him who died upon it." Regarding sacred images generally, Gibbons reiterated the doctrines expressed by the sixteenth-century Council of Trent, which held that images "are to be had and retained, especially in churches; and a due honor and veneration is to be given to them: not that any divinity or virtue is believed to be in them . . . but because the honor which is given them is referred to the originals which they represent, so that by the images which we kiss, and before which we uncover our heads or kneel, we adore Christ, and venerate His saints, whose likeness they represent." Thus in the eyes of the church, crosses and crucifixes each had their own valuable qualities. And images of saints and other holy figures served as valuable tools in worship, provided that they were not venerated as objects in their own right.[14]

For Protestants, images of saints presented their own complications. They implied a need for a high church authority to certify and canonize the elect, and they could appear as improper rivals for the attention and supplications due God alone. "Saints" and human figures would eventually find a place in many Protestant worship spaces, but they would not match the power and reach of the cross. In contrast to the use of human figures and the thornier issues surrounding them, the symbol of the cross was arrestingly simple, even while it conveyed deep yearnings for universality and transcendence. In the hands of America's upstart Catholics, it performed spiritual and denominational work beautifully, thereby encouraging combatants like George Doane and Richard Upjohn to break customs and employ crosses in Protestant settings.

As seen in Burlington and New York City, these experiments provoked heated opposition, despite the symbol's advantages. Beyond Reformation-based theologies and simple inertia, conservative resistance drew strength from several sources. One arose from Catholicism's close associations with unpopular ethnic groups. In a climate where nativist passions blurred the religion and the ancestry of their targets, many congregations were hesitant to identify themselves with the "foreign" traditions of Irish and German immigrants. Also, Protestants had long disparaged the sensual tools of "popery" as being intellectually weak and unscrupulous. Placing a cross atop a tower risked implying that the congregation beneath was taking the low road to "captivate the senses" of their audience rather than striving to uphold the Gospel's evangelical "truth." But these reasons hardly account for the panic expressed by some Protestants who encountered a new cross on their church. Some feared a slippery slope, where the introduction of one new aspect of "popery" meant that countless others would soon follow, including matters of doctrine and polity. One letter published in an 1867 issue of the *New York Observer* argued, "Every such innovation has a plausible beginning, which, like the letting out of water, may be very small, but which, in the end, is likely to sweep away all that is good and holy in the worship of God." And occasionally, Protestants could vent irrational anxieties over "popery." An article in the *Episcopalian* explained the spread of ritualistic devices through its denomination in terms of literal infiltration, where the Catholic Church "has sent among us secret emissaries . . . whose mission it is to introduce one Romish novelty after another, until the congregations in which they are introduced are gradu-

ally but surely drawn into the communion of the Romish Church."
Thus objections to "Romish" innovations ran from the tightly rea-
soned to the emotionally charged.[15]

But such objections gradually eroded as the process continued.
The actual appropriation of the symbol defied categorization in many
ways—Protestant crosses appeared in rural settings near the time that
they first appeared in urban settings, and demand for the symbols
arose among the clergy and laity alike. Still, most of the early crosses
were raised at churches in the North and West, rather than in the
South, and their advocates were typically young and white. Support
also came more particularly from middle- and upper-class congregations, whose members may have been more culturally cosmopolitan
and uncomfortable with the coarse outbursts of nativist mobs.

Redeeming the Symbol

Protestant advocates of the symbol employed several mechanisms to
dislodge it from Roman Catholic settings. Two early strategies were
verbal. The first involved popular meditations on the figurative significance of the cross. Precedents for these meditations had long been
established in hymns, prayers, and sermons, but their popularity in
the midst of explicit anti-Catholic controversies served to "prime the
pump." Their language illustrated the relevance of Christ's suffering
to Protestant worship but treated the material presence of the cross
with ambiguity. For example, while an 1835 Presbyterian article titled
"The Moral Influence of the Cross" proclaimed that "the influence
of the cross is powerful," it outlined the historical and theological
ramifications of its subject rather than the physical or artistic significance of contemporary crosses. Likewise, a reader might have taken
an article titled "On the Use of Crosses" in an 1842 issue of the *New
York Observer* to be a discussion on church symbolism. But the author restricted the topic to an abstract consideration of holy suffering
and the human condition. Perhaps most effusive was an 1848 Methodist article titled "Power of the Cross," as it almost sang: "The cross!
the cross! around it and in it are clustering and centring [*sic*] all our

hopes and all our joys. And if any of the readers of this article, have not, as yet, bowed to the cross of Christ, let me urge you to yield your hearts to its powerful attractions." Such language blurred the boundaries between metaphorical and literal crosses. By their sheer repetition, these meditations made the next step of actually employing "our crosses" an easier leap.[16]

A second verbal strategy surveyed the use of the cross by non-Christian cultures and religions. This endowed the symbol with a spirit broader than Roman Catholicism and simultaneously affirmed a sense of Protestant destiny. Various authors described crosslike icons among ancient Trojans, Greeks, Scandinavians, Aztecs, Mongolians, Egyptians, and Buddhists, as well as assorted pagans. A particularly broad analysis published in *Harper's Weekly* concluded that the cross was used "as an object of worship" by "the aborigines of North and South America, as well as by the most ancient nations of the Old World." One Methodist author went even further, explaining that "the universality of the cross as a religious symbol in all ages and among all peoples is a surprising fact." These mystical appearances of the symbol foreshadowed the ultimate Christian event and illustrated the propriety of the symbol's use, despite the contemporary specter of Catholicism. For Protestants inclined to adopt the symbol, this could provide justification enough. An author in the *New York Observer* held that the cross "was as well a religious symbol of the ancient Egyptians as of the Christians" and that it had, "notwithstanding all the prejudices against it—prejudices arising from the Popish perversion of its uses—often proved an eloquent preacher amid the solemn congregations of the WAITING." Though inconsistent—no author suggested that "ancient Egyptians" or the like had used the cross in a "proper," Christian manner—such passages suggested that the cross could be rightfully redeemed from a Catholic context.[17]

Other strategies operated on a material level. The use of alternative symbolic patterns offered one route. The Latin cross and the crucifix were immediately recognizable as Roman Catholic, but other cruciform designs were less distinct. One example appeared at St. Mary's Church in Burlington, New Jersey, where George Doane's early attempts to sanctify the chapel included an equilateral Greek cross. By using this design, Doane could attempt to circumvent the fear of "popery," though he was not entirely successful in this case. As late as 1871, *Harper's Weekly* declared that "any person of good taste . . . would avoid wearing, for display merely, ornaments in the form of a Latin cross," in part because that was the form "on which our Lord suffered." But this admonishment did not exclude all crosses from personal use, for, the writer continued, "there are the Maltese cross and others used in heraldry, which are more suitable for such a purpose." Another alternate cruciform design found in Protestant contexts was the cross of St. Andrew, with its two arms crossing like an X.[18]

A related method cloaked the cross in natural imagery. By placing flowers or vines on Latin crosses or by framing crosses in sublime outdoor settings, Protestants generated several new symbolic associations. On a spiritual level, foliage surrounding the barren wood of the cross suggested the promise of resurrection and eternal life. On a denominational level, foliage on the cross domesticated the foreign symbol by combining it with an accepted vocabulary of naturalistic icons. Examples of these adorned crosses began to appear frequently in Protestant homes and graveyards at midcentury. One Methodist detailed hers in 1867: "this little memorial gem is a mound emerging from the mouth of a crystal fern-shell, . . . and from the mound goes up a cross formed of tiny, rose-tinted shells." Such mixtures of biblical and natural symbolism hinted at broader spiritual truths than those claimed exclusively by Roman Catholicism. And sublime feelings could be further heightened by natural settings. For example, at Philadelphia's Laurel Hill Cemetery in the 1850s, an individual erected a nondenominational stone monument known as "The Cross" that stimulated much spiritual contemplation. An observer described the piece as "situated on a craggy point," where "masses of rock rise in picturesque grandeur." The monument bore a melancholy inscription celebrating the soothing surroundings. A similar effect was achieved in landscape paintings of the time that featured crosslike forms set within majestic clouds or terrain. Whether seen in person "on a craggy point" or on a popular canvas, these crosses and pictur-esque views mutually enhanced the spiritual qualities of each other. Like the appearance of the cross in non-Christian cultures, naturalis-tic settings sanctified the use of the symbol through a sense of provi-dential destiny. But these portrayals were not exclusively Protestant, for Catholics also employed flowered crosses, indicating the popu-larity of broad decorative motifs.[19]

The interest in medieval architecture opened another door to sym-bolic appropriation. Under the guise of historical accuracy, Protes-tants could demand the use of crosses on their Gothic and Roman-esque church designs. As the nineteenth century progressed, more and more architects and critics advocated rigorously researched de-signs rather than impressionistic fancies. This approach culminated in the work of Anglican "ecclesiologists"—reformers who promoted actual medieval models for the construction of modern churches, as at St. James-the-Less in Philadelphia, complete with symbolic orna-mentation. But other congregations less committed to strict archaeo-logical accuracy also used the romantic atmospheres cast by Gothic and Romanesque designs to introduce new symbols. For example, the Gothic-inspired designs of Grace Church in New York City, built in 1848, moved observers to compare the structure loosely with Euro-pean cathedrals. After audiences accepted these as inoffensive paral-lels, then the crosses adorning Grace's many stained-glass windows seemed less out of place. Though these windows did not draw from specific medieval models, they contributed to the building's overall effect and brought Protestant worship into contact with traditional Catholic symbols.[20]

Finally, denominational approaches to the cross could be starkly straightforward. Rather than experiment with indirect alternatives, some Protestants conceded the power of the symbol and simply advo-cated its use. The Congregationalists' General Convention officially sanctioned the symbol's use in 1853, when it published *A Book of Plans for Churches and Parsonages*. This book illustrated the designs of several eminent architects in the hopes of promoting "convenience, economy and good taste" among Congregational "Houses of Wor-

Design for a Congregational church with a prominent cross
on the bell tower. From Congregational Churches in the United States,
Book of Plans, plate 7. Courtesy of the Winterthur Library,
Printed Book and Periodical Collection.

ship." Many selections featured elaborate examples of the Gothic Revival, but it was a simple chapel design that opened the floodgates to
Catholic appropriation. In the description of "Design VII," the authors stated, "We have shown how an ordinary square tower may receive a church look by the addition of a simple cross, the everywhere
recognized symbol of the Christian faith." Anticipating controversy,
the authors justified their purposeful inclusion of this "peculiarly appropriate feature of a church edifice" by arguing that "the fear or the
dislike of Popery which forbids the use of this hallowed and most significant symbol in such a position, is a fear or a dislike, in our judg-
ment, both unenlightened and harmful." Rather, the cross, "which is
endeared to all Christians as the symbol of the atonement . . . might
safely crown our Christian temples. . . . There is no good reason why
every little chapel of the Mother of Harlots should be allowed to use
what appeals so forcibly and so favorably to the simplest understand-

ing, and we be forbidden the manifest advantage which its use would often give us." In this example, the Congregational Church maintained its attack on "the Mother of Harlots," recognized that Catholic symbolism was an effective proselytizing tool, and adopted this symbolism as its own. The General Convention dispensed money to build missionary churches, and it required prospective applicants to submit their designs for review, thus encouraging "conformity" with its recommendations.[21]

This manifesto confirmed and encouraged a process already under way among Congregationalists. Flirtations with Catholic symbolism had appeared on earlier Congregational churches, as at the First Parish Congregational Church in Brunswick, Maine. This parish had contracted with architect Richard Upjohn for a new structure in 1845, and the resulting Gothic Revival building featured a cruciform plan. Though the minister insisted that "we shall have no steeple, and therefore . . . shall not have 'the sign of the Cross on the steeple,'" the church's plan and its quatrefoil decorations on the tower and transept walls drew charges of "popery" from more conservative Congregationalists. Four years later in the same state, a book reviewer found "the once hated symbol frequently introduced among the rich decorations of the newly finished chapel of an orthodox college," though the symbol was still regarded by some "with as much horror as the fetish of the African savage." But after the publication of the Convention's plan book in 1853, Congregational churches donning quatrefoils or crosses required less justification. "Cruciform" finials topped the Congregational churches in Charlestown and Cambridgeport, Massachusetts, by 1859, when an image of the Charlestown church appeared in the *Congregational Quarterly* without comment.[22]

Methodists could also confront the Latin cross directly. One frank article on the subject appeared in Philadelphia's African American published *Christian Recorder* in 1861. The author prefaced his or her support for the symbol by explaining that the human mind has "always manifested a pleasure in emblems, allegorical representations, and images, beautiful thoughts or holy sentiments." It then followed that if these "fancies" remained within certain limits, they claimed "the highest authority for their existence and popularity, even in religious circles." The cross ably provided such an emblem, though the author acknowledged "the folly and wickedness of the Papists, in their superstitious and idolatrous use of the cross." But the "truth" behind the symbol demanded expression, despite the danger of abuse. So "if we should see it in a Protestant church, on the wall behind the pulpit, or high above, surmounting wall and roof and steeple," the author asserted, "we should be gratified, for it would remind us anew of the precious redeeming blood once shed on such a cross." The author regretted "that we have surrendered so completely to the Papists this appropriate emblem of our holy faith," and he or she hoped that "a more healthy and vigorous Protestant feeling may possibly yet enable us to . . . restore to our churches and altars the expressive sign of the Saviour's atoning work." Other Methodist discussions similarly struck at Catholicism while appropriating its tools. In one 1867 article, a Methodist narrator questioned her friend about a painted "Cross of Flowers" found in her studio, since it recalled uncomfortable Catholic associations. "My dear friend," the other woman replied, "why should we permit the mother of abominations to monopolize every symbol and beautiful token of our holy Christianity?" After some discussion on the symbol's history, the friend concluded, "Let us take [the cross] from sacrilegious hands, who profane the most holy faith by their prayers to saints and their worship of graven images, and let it be our emblem of victory." These arguments bore similarities to those presented in the Congregational plan book, which the Methodist press had quickly endorsed.[23]

And as they did with the Congregationalists, crosses gradually crept into actual Methodist use in the 1850s. In October 1855, the Methodist *National Magazine* published a radiant image of a crown and Latin cross, among other inspirational images and lyrics. A year later, a Newark, New Jersey, congregation dedicated their lavish Gothic-style church, which featured two decorative crosses set halfway up its twin stone towers. Still, the towers were topped with weathervanes, illustrating that the cross had not yet achieved decorative centrality for the congregation. *Harper's New Monthly Maga-*

zine in New York reported another sighting in 1866, when an editor claimed that "the Methodist Church of Jeffersonville is the only church of that denomination in the State which has *a cross* on its steeple." This landmark arose far from the metropolis, and it allegedly drew jeering observations from one of the area's "old citizens," who wished "to defend the 'old style' of church-building." By 1867, articles such as "The Cross of Flowers" in the *Ladies' Repository* testified to the widespread use of decorative crosses in Methodist homes. And by 1876, crosses appeared as interior decorations flanking the chancel of Mystic Methodist Church, Mystic, Connecticut. That same decade, grand Methodist churches in Baltimore and Cincinnati sported flutters of crosses, resting on gable ends and above porch entrances. At the latter, one Methodist enthusiast could exclaim: "Looking at the exterior of the church from any point, it seems to be a perfect building."[24]

Episcopalians addressed the issue under enormous controversy. Though churchmen like George Doane and Richard Upjohn had been among the earliest American Protestants to employ the cross, their denomination experienced the most prolonged, acrimonious debates over the symbol's use. This intensity grew out of church party politics and the denomination's conflicted heritage, both of which came into sharp focus in the 1830s with a unique reform movement sometimes known as "Oxfordism" or "Tractarianism." In 1833, Anglican theologians at Oxford University began reasserting the "catholic" qualities of their church through a series of widely distributed tracts. Their work emphasized the power of sacraments and outlined the divine sanction of church officials. By the mid-1840s, the Oxford Movement had advanced far beyond the earlier positions of its leaders to uphold some of the most controversial aspects of Roman Catholicism. Religious symbolism quickly became relevant, as related groups organized to promote a conscious revival of sacramental art within Anglican and Episcopal churches. Such reformers thereby created their own formal language for informal pressures then affecting Protestant denominations generally. As Anglicans closely considered the historical continuities between their church and its pre-Reformation

Broad-Street Methodist Episcopal Church, Newark, New Jersey (1856),
featuring decorative crosses midway up each tower. The towers
are topped by characteristic weathervanes. From "Methodist Church
Architecture," March 1856, 223. Courtesy of the University of
Delaware Library, Newark, Delaware.

precedents, arguments over the propriety of symbols, "ritualism," and "Anglo-Catholicism" continued to rock the denomination throughout the nineteenth century.[25]

Amidst the decades of Episcopal debates in America, a midcentury crossover moment could be discerned. This moment occurred in the early 1840s, slightly ahead of the symbol's acceptance by other Protestant denominations and right on target with the Catholic swell. One Episcopal editor in Boston commented on this moment in 1847. Uneasy over the change, the editor noted, "The demand for a symbolical use of the cross has been wonderfully increased of late." Beginning with examples from Episcopal publications, he warned readers to "see how rapidly, during the last six or seven . . . years, the picture of the cross has been multiplied upon the covers, the title-pages, and indeed upon all the pages. Ten years ago, it was a comparatively rare thing to stamp a cross upon a new book." Driven by the public's "*demand* for such pictures," he continued, the proliferation of crosses encouraged "a system which exalts trifles into great importance, and constructs a sacramental and sensuous religion out of forms." Material crosses had simultaneously spread across the landscape; surveying Boston, the author claimed that "in three of the older Episcopal churches in this city, the cross is not seen, while it is not only found in four of those more recently established, but, beginning with Grace, the elder of the four, in which it occupies an unassuming place upon the shaft of the baptismal font, it rises rapidly in prominence, according to the age of the parish." Thus the cross was making regular advances into the Episcopal worship environment, despite the controversy surrounding it and despite the warnings of Episcopal editors. The author also noted a similar progression of the symbol elsewhere in America and England.[26]

Other examples affirm the editor's diagnosis. In New York City, a cross topped Richard Upjohn's Trinity Church in the early 1840s and the Church of the Holy Communion in 1845. In 1846, stained-glass windows with cruciform details were installed in James Renwick's Grace Church, as were spire and gable-end crosses. Upstate, a cross topped the Church of the Holy Innocents in Albany by 1850. In New

Jersey, Doane's defiant cross in Burlington had appeared in 1834, another appeared on a new church in Salem by 1838, and a seven-foot-high cross appeared on a church in North Bergen in 1853. In Baltimore, the vestry of the Church of the Ascension acquired a painting with a prominent cross in 1840. In eastern Tennessee, a highly decorated church showcased the symbol from gateposts to altar during the late 1850s, though the bishop of the diocese refused to consecrate the building and it soon fell out of use. In 1877, Catholic archbishop James Gibbons marveled that an acquaintance in Richmond, Virginia, had "adorned with twelve crosses an Episcopal church where, eleven years before, the sight of a single cross was viewed with horror by the minister." By this time, the symbol had also spread to Episcopal churches in the West, like the gable crosses on an 1854 missionary chapel for Indians at Gull Lake, Minnesota, and the "gilt cross" that ornamented the spire on the church in Astoria, Oregon, in 1869.[27]

The growing use of the symbol among Baptists and Presbyterians occurred with much less public discussion. Presbyterians had been quick to criticize other denominations, as in Burlington, New Jersey, but slow to reflect upon similar developments that would gradually change their own houses of worship. Burlington's critic insisted that "Protestant Christians, whilst they 'glory in the cross,' do not, and cannot adopt the badges of Romanism and superstition." Yet evidence to the contrary emerged after a Presbyterian convert to the Episcopal Church, sensitive to the charges of "popery" raised by his previous peers, turned to investigate his accusers in 1853. He claimed that Presbyterians and other "Sectarians" were rapidly clothing themselves in the "rags of popery," and he quoted the proverb "Physician, heal thyself!" These new "rags" included the growing use of the cross. Pointing out that "the symbol of redemption, on brow or church" was once certified as "*the mark of the Beast*," the writer could "see it now on Baptist and Unitarian temples, and glittering upon the bosoms of your children, and even speaking peace upon the sepulchral stone over your dead." And though the writer had defiantly worn a cross on his own breast for nine years as a Presbyterian minister, he could scarcely believe his eyes when he saw a book published by the Presbyterian General Assembly "with a magnificent frontis-piece emblazoned with a gorgeous cross!" Despite his ironic tone, the writer ultimately encouraged such developments, for, he wrote, "our only plan at last must be, to take the good and true in Popery, to conquer the evil and the false." Still, he could not understand how Presbyterians would reconcile these developments with their theology. Indeed, most did not until the Protestant use of the cross had become an established custom.[28]

One curious episode occurred at Princeton, New Jersey, in 1847. That year, the old Presbyterian college's trustees assembled a building committee to oversee the construction of a new chapel, and the group quickly hired John Notman, a respected Philadelphia architect. Notman produced a somewhat plain, Italianate design with an understated cruciform plan. After construction had begun, a conflict erupted over the plan. Due to some trustees' distress over the "semi-popistical" layout, the original building committee was dissolved and a new one appointed with power to alter the rising structure's design, potentially at great cost. The original committee protested, and the college's trustees finally resolved to complete the cruciform plan. But the second committee made it known "that in their judgement, the form of *a Cross*, is not *the* form for a Presbyterian Chapel. Cruciform Architecture, is so identified with popery that it becomes us to beware of adopting its insignia." They explained, "We know that the Cross is a form dear to Christians from all its original associations. Far be it from us to assume a position of irreverence [*sic*] towards this sacred object. But the history of the Church proves, that when the Cross has been imitated externally in buildings and crucifixes it has tended to degrade religion, and introduce superstition." The committee especially resented its use on a college campus, "where the minds of the young can be easily familiarized with a form of architecture condemned by our church in general." Yet after Princeton's controversial chapel was finished, Notman continued to receive major commissions from Presbyterians, illustrating the direction of the tide.[29]

Baptists remained the denomination least engaged with Catholic symbolism. Outside the largest American cities, Baptist congregations were generally poorer than those of other denominations and less interested in the fineries of religious architecture. But in the 1850s and 1860s, the same congregations that had held worship in plain houses, barns, and groves began to emphasize the importance of church buildings and to display more enthusiasm for symbolism. In 1857, one Baptist author bemoaned this architectural penchant for "following" the examples of other denominations, which undermined his denomination's "established principles" of simplicity and Gospel-based worship. As an example, the author described his reaction to one Baptist meetinghouse's windows, "which were emblazoned with a strange variety of mystical symbols that must have amused the children by their grotesqueness, and sorely puzzled any plain man like myself." His puzzlement over these details grew as he wondered why his denomination was "imitating the gorgeous structures of the Catholic church, with which are associated bigotry, persecution unto death, and the most soul-destroying perversion of the doctrines of the cross." It would remain for his coreligionists to redeem the cross and its associated doctrines. Four years earlier, a Baptist congregation in Roxbury, Massachusetts, had built an enormous church and steeple "surmounted with a gothic cross," and in 1869, a Baptist congregation in Philadelphia decorated their new church with almost every sort of Christian symbol, including several rooftop crosses. Farther afield, an image of a simple country church with a cross above the bell tower appeared without comment in an 1883 publication from the American Baptist Home Missionary Society.[30]

By this time, the cross's takeover was essentially complete. In the 1870s, it had advanced to such a degree that one architectural pattern book termed it "the usual symbol of the Christian religion," which "is appropriately placed on the apex of any gable." With technical coolness, the nondenominational book recommended useful sizes, materials, and fastening techniques for cruciform roof ornaments. And in 1877, one Presbyterian could proclaim, "The use of the cross, on spires, in churches, and worn as a jewel, . . . is not now denominational." Such ornaments could be purchased across the country, as markets began to address the new demand for crosses. Iron- and

A serene Baptist chapel scene from 1883 showing a cross atop the bell tower. From *Baptist Home Missions in North America*, 168. Courtesy of the William Smith Morton Library, Union Theological Seminary and Presbyterian School of Christian Education, Richmond, Virginia.

stoneworking shops supplied freestanding crosses, furniture makers engraved crosses on pews and altar furniture, and cloth manufacturers embroidered the design on church linens. The "usual symbol of the Christian religion" could command reliable sales.[31]

A Newfound Beacon

The new crosses acquired by Protestant building committees would have mixed effects. Most immediately, they sanctified their church environments. As a symbol, the Latin cross held distinctly religious connotations, and its presence immediately marked a space as being religious in nature. This characteristic drew upon the Catholic concept of formally consecrated ground, in which agents of the church specifically blessed a site and dedicated its use for religious purposes. American Protestants had long been moving toward such a concept of church property, but the new use of the cross dramatically aided their efforts to distinguish between sacred and secular spaces. New crosses helped satisfy another Protestant need in the symbols' associations with Catholic unity. Though internal conflicts racked the Catholic Church in America and abroad, the church consistently promoted its claim as the uniform faith intended for the entire world. Simple crosses visually linked Catholic congregations from around the globe and expressed the belief in universal salvation made possible through Christ's redemption. In contrast, American Protestants had been notorious for organizational splintering and sectarian rivalries, leading one critic in New York City to deride their churches as "schism-shops." Crosses could not mend these schisms nor override lingering beliefs in predestination, but their commonality did nurture an image of greater religious union and help individual denominations identify their particular faith with a broader "Christian religion." Also, in terms of Protestant devotions, the new crosses fulfilled their intended role by raising Jesus's crucifixion and redemption into view. Capable of inspiring humility and gratitude, the symbol confronted the individual's gaze and recalled the burdens of sacrifice.

These widespread effects, occurring so shortly after Protestant hostilities publicly denigrated the symbol, revealed the remarkable flexibility inherent in Protestant/Catholic relations. The migration of the cross and its associations into Protestant communions demonstrated that surprising points of genuine exchange could take place between established religious oppositions.[32]

Yet the new crosses ultimately upheld these original religious boundaries. The crosses' conservative effects emerged in several ways. First, Protestants employed crosses differently from Catholics. On church exteriors and gravestones, Protestant crosses operated similarly, but in church interiors and within the context of worship services, Protestants attempted to distinguish between "proper" uses for the symbol and "improper," Catholic uses. Protestant critics emphatically asserted the need to avoid treating the symbol as an object of reverence, lest they fall victim to "the Popish idolatry of the cross." In terms of behavior, this meant that one should not prostrate or bow before a cross, nor expect any magical powers to flow from it. One pastor in Baltimore, writing in the 1830s, explained his rhetorical distance from Catholicism in a dialogue: "But, say the Catholics, have not Protestants their pictures and statues? Certainly we have. We do not make war against the fine arts. We can approve of *painting* and *statuary* without practicing *idolatry*. Yes, we have representations of deceased Christians, but we do not kneel before them, nor do we on that account drop the second commandment, as some do." The pastor's reference to the second commandment and its strictures against idolatry illustrated a key concept by which Protestants identified their symbolic tradition. As demonstrated by Archbishop James Gibbons and others, explanations given by Catholic authorities for their own use of the cross did not entirely differ from the Protestant standard. But in the eyes of many Protestants, the behavioral differences were plain, and they sustained distinctions between the traditions despite certain similarities in artistic equipage.[33]

That body of equipage itself pointed to another division facilitated by the cross, for the symbol had been one among many Catholic icons, the vast majority of which did not similarly migrate into Protestantism. Not only did the cross fail to signal a merger of Protestant and Catholic symbolic programs, but the symbol's successful appropriation highlighted the stubborn incompatibilities inherent in the remaining Catholic symbols. The crucifix and its realistic portrayal of Christ's suffering did not make the leap, except in rare, later instances. Protestant households demonstrated an increasing appetite for images of the Virgin Mary, but most evangelical church environments steered clear of any possible associations with "Mariolatry." Sculptures and images of other saints and Protestant luminaries could occasionally be invoked. For example, a new Methodist church built in 1855 in Pittsburgh, Pennsylvania, featured the stone heads of John and Charles Wesley over the front entrance. But these could still be problematic, as the heads drew the disapproval of the Methodist press when the *National Magazine* wondered whether it was "expedient to adorn our churches with sculptured heads of the Wesleys, or any other great and good men[.] Does it not savor a little of canonization, and seem to countenance what, as a people, we heartily abominate[?]" Full-bodied representations of "saints" were even more rare, except for their occasional appearances in stained-glass windows. And finally, the Protestant aversion to papal emblems remained plain enough.[34]

Above all, the new use of the cross lay on a foundation of traditional religious competition. For many ambitious Protestants, the cross provided a tool by which to appropriate the growing Catholic momentum and to enhance the comparative identities of Protestant churches. The aim "to take the good and true in Popery, to conquer the evil and the false" that lay at the heart of the actions of such varied actors as Bishop George Doane and the General Congregational Convention was incompatible with a larger sense of Protestant/Catholic communion. Even as these actors helped to erase the denominational associations of the cross and to identify a new vision of the "Christian religion," they simultaneously affirmed the larger forces that set the Christian traditions against each other. For all the shared effects of the cross atop church spires and abreast denominational shields, the cross in America could not fully transmit the universality implied in its Gospel origins.

Thus the cross was a mixed symbol. In its capacity to accommodate the promises of division and unity, of suffering and hope, it spoke to an impressive range of concerns. These qualities help explain its remarkable durability and its lofty stature as a newfound beacon for an imperfect world.

The Gothic

"Every church of every denomination is now-a-days Gothicized." So observed an anonymous correspondent in the *United States Democratic Review* in 1847. Though an exaggeration, the comment came during the very height of the Gothic Revival, when pointed arches, vertical lines, stained glass, and other medieval design features appeared on countless new structures throughout the Atlantic world. And amidst the puzzle of pointed houses, prisons, and town halls, the style's revival in America indeed found particular focus in church architecture. This trend fascinated the correspondent, who wondered "why every place of worship, Episcopal, Presbyterian, Congregational, and what not, put up, in this democratic land, in this nineteenth century, must be Gothic, and *moyen âge*."[1]

Other observers attested to the prevalence of "miniature cathedrals." In 1836, a contributor to the *North American Review* claimed that architectural Gothic "has come greatly into use, not only in cities, but throughout the country" and that "the Gothic order, where it has appeared . . . has been almost exclusively appropriated to churches." Eight years later, a *Princeton Review* article on churches spotlighted the "increased interest which has been felt, within a few years, in the Architecture of the Middle Ages." That same year, the *North American Review* again reported "a growing taste" for the Gothic and cited several new ecclesiastical examples. In 1853, a critic in New York City commented on "the mediaevalisms in church edifices which have been introduced among us during the past twenty years" and "the rapidity with which" Gothic-style churches "have sprung up in every street." And another contemporary announced, "The mania for Gothic architecture seems to be prevailing throughout the country; and in no part of the Union is it to be seen in more varied forms than in the city of New York, where almost every denomination is represented in one or more churches of this style." A Baptist writer emphasized its rural spread: "From the cities to the towns and the country . . . our brethren are everywhere beginning to rejoice in naves, and transepts, and chancels, and altars, and oriel windows, and stained glass." In a later flourish, one Congregational author reflected that earlier in the century, "a great Gothic invasion came over us, and for the last few years parishes have been hard at work" building variations on ancient cathedrals.[2]

American builders had always looked to history for inspiration. Yet this "Gothic invasion," this "mania" that swept through every denomination in twenty years, was a peculiar occurrence. For not only did it help break long-established classical tastes, it also actively linked Protestant congregations with a controversial era in the history of Roman Catholicism. The bewildered correspondent in the *United States Democratic Review* made this link plain: "The history, the associations and the details of the Gothic style," as demonstrated in medieval cathedrals, "make it the exclusive property of certain forms of religious belief." Namely, "it was *Catholic* faith and *Catholic* art that reared those giant piles. . . . They were built for *Catholic* worship." Thus the new Protestant enthusiasm for the style presented a profound inconsistency—"Protestant Gothic, Puritan Gothic, iconoclast Gothic, what an absurdity!" the writer exclaimed. Scolding Protestant readers directly, he held forth: "Denounce their religion as much as you please—I have not a word to say for it; but at any rate Gothic architecture is their property, and theirs only, and you cannot share it with them." Still, "Presbyterians, Congregationalists, &c." were attempting to share the Gothic. In doing so, they risked the impression of building "churches in a style which necessarily carries us back in thought to the days of Romish darkness, and pontifical supremacy."[3]

Those highly charged associations generated much of the style's appeal. For the "Gothic invasion" occurred at precisely the same time as the related "invasion" of Latin crosses, candles, and robed choirs into Protestant churches. Widely understood as an original product of the Roman Catholic faith, Gothic architecture provided another tool by which evangelical congregations engaged Catholic worship and responded to the rising power of the Roman Church. By adopting the style in colorful bits and pieces, and by carefully filtering the style through English history, Protestants tailored that architecture to their own needs. Yet even so modified, the Gothic maintained a sensational medieval flavor, enabling congregations to lay claim to religious tradition and answer the allure of sanctified Catholic church space.

In no way did this usage exhaust the possibilities of pointed arches. As a loosely defined style, the Gothic involved other, nonreligious themes. It represented a point of international exchange, as builders entered a dialogue with European advocates of the revival. It accompanied the growing sophistication of the architectural profession, whereby designers and critics expanded their roles and experimented with different building styles. On a deeper level, preference for the medieval Gothic signaled uneasiness over modern industrial changes. At the same time, the Gothic offered a vehicle by which patrons could bring the refinement of their churches on par with comfortable new homes, shops, and civic buildings. And at times, the selection of the Gothic illustrated lighter feelings for romance and whimsy.

These considerations help explain the broad resonance of neo-Gothic architecture, which, after all, appeared on railroad cars, state capitols, doghouses, and other disparate structures. But the revival maintained a particular ecclesiastical thrust, and even when employed elsewhere, the style retained links with the medieval church. Its wide appeal, developing during the Catholic Church's rise in America, only deepened the need for a "Protestant Gothic." Most of the revival's historians have overlooked or denied its particular denominational associations. But in "this democratic land, in this nineteenth century," in this atmosphere of religious tension, as outlined by the *United States Democratic Review*, the Gothic could not have appeared as mere fashion or refinement. On churches, it represented a deliberate identification with medieval Catholicism and that subject's attendant legacies.[4]

Making a Gothic "Style"

From its earliest identification as an architectural "style," the Gothic was linked with Catholic architecture. The soaring cathedrals erected at Amiens, Paris, Strasburg, Salisbury, Milan, and elsewhere throughout Europe from about 1150 to 1500 presented fantastic achievements, calculated to inspire a sense of awe and reverence. Their dramatic heights, their masterful use of interior light, and their open expression of materials and structure might have appeared on other medieval building types and during other eras, but their combination in the service of the Catholic faith established an identifiable tradition. A host of related abbeys and parish churches dotted European landscapes and added to the church's mystique.[5]

It was against this tradition that later, Renaissance thinkers rebelled when they first labeled such aspiring medieval monuments as "Gothic," a term not used by the medieval builders. Seventeenth- and eighteenth-century intellectuals, in their renewed appreciation for secular inquiry and classical proportions, found the art of the crusading era embarrassingly devoid of reason. Likening it to the crudity and lawlessness of visigoth invaders of the fifth century, skeptics like French playwright Molière denounced "The besotted taste of gothic monuments / These odious monsters of the ignorant centuries / Which the torrents of barbarism spewed forth." In Renaissance eyes, medieval buildings stood as a heap of asymmetry, distorted glass, melodramatic pointed arches, and unflattering heights. With such critics' explicit historical comparisons, mostly based on common visual characteristics, the modern concept of architectural style began to emerge. And fashionable "styles" increasingly centered on the interpretation of ancient Greek and Roman examples, in contrast to the medieval Gothic.[6]

Yet the surviving "Gothic" buildings remained in use. In England, neither Renaissance criticism nor the Protestant Reformation prevented church and state from appropriating and employing Catholic properties. Apart from some iconoclastic violence, the transition occurred relatively smoothly for the Anglican congregations that adapted cathedrals and chapels for public services. This set an important precedent for later Protestant interpretations of the style and its revival. But the Anglican assumption of Catholic churches took place in part by necessity; excepting a few notable projects around London, the state did not dedicate any significant funds toward church construction until the early nineteenth century. Further, Anglicans employed the old churches' interiors differently. In smaller churches, congregations often blocked off chancels and replaced these ceremonial centers with pulpits and Communion tables set before the pews. And medieval worshippers would have hardly recognized the Anglican services held in large cathedrals, where monuments to kings and lords soon crowded beneath the cavernous vaults, behind the scanty congregations who typically worshipped within the smaller chancels. For dissenters, even these alterations did not go far enough in disassociating public worship from Catholic excesses.[7]

By the mid-eighteenth century, elements of the antiquated Gothic began to occasionally reappear on English estates. Restlessness and romanticism led some members of the gentry, such as Horace Walpole, to revive the Gothic as an exotic ornamental scheme capable of picturesque effects. "One has a satisfaction in imprinting the gloomth of abbeys and cathedrals on one's house," explained Walpole, who reinforced the style's religious associations even as he applied it domestically. At Strawberry Hill, an estate near London, Walpole imprinted this monkish gloom through decorative pointed arches, stained glass, wooden carvings, and various medieval curiosities. He further explored the subject by writing his own Gothic novel, revealing the interplay between literary imagination and the developing taste for medieval art. Such literature grew in popularity, as did antiquarian interest in England's Gothic relics, but modern Gothic architecture remained a superficial ornament comparable to the Chinese style until the early nineteenth century.[8]

American romanticism fostered a similar approach to medieval subjects. The country had few original Gothic examples of its own, but this did not keep late-eighteenth-century Yankees from basking in the Gothic atmospheres found in novels, architectural plan-books, and occasional tours overseas. Behind these medieval retreats lay the desire to explore melancholic and sublime emotions, a desire satisfied by time-worn cathedrals, abbeys, and castles. Following the architectural examples of English revivalists, Americans occasionally employed the gloomy mysteries of pointed arches, spires, crockets, and tracery to enliven boxy Georgian structures. Early, notable projects displaying such tastes included the second construction of Trinity Episcopal Church in New York City, finished in 1794; the Sedgeley estate outside Philadelphia, finished in 1799; the chapel at St. Mary's Roman Catholic seminary in Baltimore, raised in 1807; the Georgia state capitol in Milledgeville, begun in 1807; Philadelphia's Masonic Hall, finished in 1811; and Daniel Wadsworth's Gothic cottage outside Hartford, Connecticut, finished by 1819. Budding architects like Philadelphia's William Strickland frequently had a hand in the design of these local curiosities, which made few claims for historical accuracy.[9]

During the same years, a related change was taking place among Protestant houses of worship. Throughout the country, evangelical congregations were abandoning their multipurpose meetinghouses in favor of more self-consciously "churchly" buildings with towers, spires, bells, elaborate entrances, and longitudinal plans. Anglicans and Lutherans had always employed dedicated church buildings, but most other Protestants had downplayed the need for worship-specific spaces. Emphasizing bodies of believers rather than physical structures, Congregationalists, Presbyterians, Methodists, and Baptists met anywhere that a preacher could be heard—in meetinghouses, homes, courthouses, and taverns, as well as outdoors. Well-established congregations did build fine meetinghouses, though little distinguished them from other buildings except for an occasional tower or steeple. But with the construction of elaborate rival Anglican churches in the mid-eighteenth century, and with a growing demand among members for sentimental and expressive worship, evangelical congregations began to build structures recognizable as "churches" after the American Revolution. This change renewed the importance of church style and opened Protestants to new design possibilities.[10]

In turn, the Gothic received its first true push in America, at the hands of Episcopalians and Roman Catholics. Both groups were struggling for denominational footing in the first years of the nineteenth century; both maintained a formal liturgy and ritual, unlike the larger faiths; and both had direct historical precedent for the style's use. In Gothic designs, these two groups saw opportunities to nurture honored European traditions, pursue beauty in worship, and distinguish their buildings from those of increasingly "churchly" evangelicals. As in other early Gothic projects, their use of the style began with basic details. Pointed windows, slim exterior buttresses, and stone facades were enough to earn churches the "Gothic" label, no matter the plan or underlying structure. But over the next few decades, such revivals became more archaeologically correct, and designers began discerning among different periods of Gothic architecture and different national expressions. In the process, Episcopalians and Catholics gained information and momentum from similar projects among their peers in Europe. Each denomination continued to build churches in other styles, but by 1830, more neo-Gothic buildings had been built for Episcopalians and Catholics than for any other American patron.[11]

Here, the Gothic might have remained an exotic decorative choice and a high church exception. Medieval themes indeed satisfied America's growing romanticism, but so, too, did ancient Greek themes, Italian themes, Chinese themes, and Egyptian themes, all of which offered eclectic architectural alternatives that appeared on the scene before 1830. For example, in 1794, one Annapolis, Maryland, architect advertised his expertise in "Tuscan, Doric, Ionic, Corinthian, Composite, Chinese, Attic, Cargatic, Arabesque, Moresque, Grotesque, Saracenic, Rustic, Antique, Antiquo-Modern [and] Gothic" design. And though influential critics like Andrew Jackson Downing and John Ruskin eventually popularized the virtues of picturesque Gothic designs, neither advocated strict adherence to the style. Even when the Gothic was most fashionable, from 1840 to 1860, evangelical churches might have chosen to simply follow the examples of other classes of patrons, employing the style as an occasionally interesting design scheme.[12]

Yet the country's churches would develop a unique "mania" for the Gothic. Other styles, especially the Greek and, later, the Romanesque, continued to provide important models, but the Gothic worked its way into the heart of Protestant denominations. In 1953, a Presbyterian committee in Chicago discussed this disposition among American Protestants, calling it "the cult of the Gothic Revival." The committee declared that over the past hundred years, "this cult has established the opinion very widely that Gothic is the normal and correct pattern for a church, even a Presbyterian church." In one sense, this widespread adoption complemented earlier evangelical strides toward "churchly" designs and dedicated worship spaces. For those seeking to make their sanctuary "look like a church," the Gothic offered useful associations. But with the respectable growth of the Episcopal denomination, and with the explosive rise of Catholicism, those associations became an active ingredient in Protestants' rush to the style.[13]

The "offspring of Catholicity"

Throughout the nineteenth century, prominent Catholic voices claimed the Gothic as an original product of their church. Architects, critics, and priests consistently upheld the historic connections between the medieval church and its architectural legacy. Further, they explained that the arrangements of Gothic churches were particularly suited to their rituals and that various aspects of the architecture symbolized key points of Catholic faith and doctrine. These efforts challenged Protestant enthusiasm for the style and ensured that Protestant/Catholic relations would become a factor in stylistic decisions.

Still, the Catholic Church did not speak with one voice on matters of art. At least three centuries had elapsed since the original days of Gothic construction, and the church had changed greatly. In Great Britain and America, Catholic churches assumed a number of different styles and plans, reflecting a broad diversity even within single towns. And among the revival's proponents, few claimed that the style should be exclusively applied to all Catholic churches. Indeed, the most widely known and loved Catholic church in the world was the Vatican's Basilica of St. Peter. Completed in the early seventeenth century, this structure served as the literal and symbolic seat of the pope, and it presented an image of extraordinary beauty. Its noble dome, its high round arches, and its marble-smooth interior held little relation with the angular, medieval churches to the north. Thus the Gothic could hardly sustain all the proprietary demands placed on it by its most impassioned Catholic advocates. But their basic observation remained: some of the style's most notable monuments indeed arose under the direct sponsorship of medieval Catholics and in the service of their particular brand of worship.

Such observations motivated Benjamin Henry Latrobe to promote Gothic designs for the first cathedral in the United States. In 1804, this English-born, professionally trained architect offered his design services to Archbishop John Carroll in Baltimore, who was beginning to plan the highly symbolic project. Latrobe submitted two alternate design schemes—one Gothic and one Roman. The former design was not an accurate reflection of Gothic structure, but it contained so many features from the old cathedrals that its appearance on the American scene at that time would have been revolutionary. Latrobe, a master of the neoclassical, claimed "an equal desire to see the first or the second [design] erected." On one hand, his talents and experience lent themselves to the Roman scheme. On the other, his intellect demanded the Gothic for the archbishop's project because of "the veneration which the Gothic cathedrals generally excite by their peculiar style, by the associations belonging particularly to that style, and by the real grandeur and beauty which it possesses." Denominational "associations" prompted Latrobe to submit this radical Gothic design to his unique client. In the end, the archbishop selected the Roman design—choosing a marvelous plan and linking his embattled faith with metropolitan, progressive, and republican tastes. Carroll's decision again demonstrates that the relationship between Catholicism and the Gothic was never one-to-one. Nonetheless, Latrobe's reasoning illustrated the lingering cathedral associations of the Gothic, as well as the style's larger denominational identity.[14]

Other Catholic builders in America did find the Gothic appropriate. Their early use of the style stimulated public interest in the revival and refreshed the links between architecture and tradition. During the early years of construction at Baltimore's cathedral, a Catholic chapel in Gothic dress appeared across town. Designed by the newly arrived French architect Maximilian Godefroy in 1806, St. Mary's Chapel served the Sulpician seminary of which it was a part. With pointed windows, flying buttresses, and a vaulted roof, it stood as one of the first "Gothicized" churches in the country at the time of its completion. Another ecclesiastical Gothic landmark was the first St. Patrick's Cathedral, New York City. When raised in 1815, this structure may have been the largest neo-Gothic building in the United States. Two more monumental projects solidified the Gothic's relationship with Catholicism in North America. One came early, in 1829, when the Basilica of Notre Dame opened its enormous doors in Montreal as one of Canada's first neo-Gothic churches, initiating a passion for the style among Quebec's Catholics for the next seventy-five years. The other came later, in 1858, with the vision of New York City's archbishop, John Hughes. The militant Hughes conceived of a new cathedral whose size and splendor would outstrip those of any other church in the nation. The church purchased an entire city block for the project, and New York architect James Renwick drew mostly from continental Gothic precedents. Workers laid the cornerstone in 1858, and the structure was finally completed in 1888, at a cost near

St. Mary's Seminary Chapel, Baltimore, Maryland (1808), as it appeared
around 1850. The chapel (right) was one of the earliest examples of the
Gothic Revival in America. Its design emphasized the building's particular
religious function on the seminary campus. From *Memorial Volume of the
Centenary of St. Mary's Seminary of St. Sulpice*. Courtesy of the U.S. Province
of the Society of St. Sulpice Archives, Baltimore, Maryland.

one million dollars. The massive, elaborate cathedral boasted a cruciform plan, twin towers, rows of stained glass windows, heavy buttresses, and rich sculpture. Easily the largest church in America, St.
Patrick's became one of the country's architectural wonders.[15]

Elsewhere, the church continued to make Gothic strides, before
the style took serious root among evangelicals. In 1828, a Rochester,
New York, directory described the town's Catholic chapel as having
"large Gothick windows." In the early 1840s, German and Austrian
congregations in Baltimore and Pittsburgh erected continental
Gothic-inspired churches, the design features of which included hall
plans and telescoping towers. The Midwest saw similar activity, including the parish churches of architects Franz Georg Himpler and
Adolphus Druiding. In Ohio, an 1851 guidebook surveyed Washington, a "thriving village" south of Cleveland, and found "1 Lutheran,
1 Presbyterian, 1 Methodist, 1 Union and 1 Catholic church—the last

of which is an elegant and costly gothic edifice." The South held at least three notable examples of Roman Catholic Gothic, aside from Louisville's cathedral: St. Patrick's Church, New Orleans, Louisiana (1837); St. Peter's Church, Memphis, Tennessee (1852–58); and the Cathedral of Saint John and Saint Finibar, Charleston, South Carolina (1854). As in the Ohio guidebook, a magazine from 1859 described the townscape of Edgefield Court-House, South Carolina, as having "four churches: one Methodist, one Baptist, one Episcopalian, and one Roman Catholic. The last is a magnificent stone structure, in a Gothic style, not yet quite finished. When completed, it will be undoubtedly the finest ecclesiastical edifice in any village of the State." And throughout Texas, almost all of the new Roman Catholic churches built during the 1840s and 1850s employed the Gothic style, due to the exertions of its newly arrived priests. Overall, Episcopalians made similar identifications with the Gothic. But Catholic projects appeared early enough and with such force that they helped define the very course of the revival in America. Their presence stood as a constant historical reminder.[16]

As did other denominations, Roman Catholics modified the medieval style to suit their current needs. Beyond practical accommodations for lower costs and available materials, most of these modifications were directed at the space around the altar in the chancel. Original Gothic designs featured deep chancels to seat liturgical choirs and the assisting clergy. Medieval congregations did not necessarily need to see or hear the high ceremony taking place in the chancel; indeed some churches' size and interior arrangements prevented an easy view for many worshippers, and other ceremonies may have been taking place simultaneously at other altars. But in America, the church faced a general shortage of priests. Also, post-Tridentine theology emphasized the need for the laity in the nave to participate more closely in the Mass by witnessing the miraculous transformation of the host into the body of Christ. Thus, Roman Catholic Gothic Revival churches tended to include shallow chancels, eschewing excess clergy seating for dramatic, decorated altars nearer the congregation. Further, Catholic church music had changed to include both men and women performers, and since women were generally prohibited from the chancel area, choirs were often moved into the galleries. And different ethnic parishes, such as those of the Germans and the French, demonstrated particular loyalties to the Gothic signatures from their homelands. But the nineteenth-century Catholics who employed stained glass, pointed arches, pinnacles, battlements, crockets, spires, and buttresses still conjured the history and spiritual atmosphere spun by the style. They just were not tied to outdated worship patterns.[17]

This point was often lost, as Protestant and Catholic commentators alike consistently stressed the church's historical continuity. Perhaps the most outspoken and the best known of these was A. W. Pugin, primary theorist of the revival. Born in England in 1812, Pugin was the son of a successful draftsman who specialized in medieval designs. In his teen years, Pugin himself became a skilled illustrator and cabinetmaker, producing Gothic playthings for such varied settings as Windsor Castle and London stages. Around the age of twenty-three, Pugin experienced a profound spiritual conversion and embraced Roman Catholicism with a rare fire. Thereafter, he dedicated his architectural talents to reviving the beauty and truth he saw in the medieval church. In over one hundred sanctuaries built in England and Ireland, and in eight widely read publications, he explicitly promoted "pointed architecture" as the organic product of Catholic faith. He held that "everything glorious about the [medieval] English churches is Catholic" and argued that the style offered the "only correct expression of the faith, wants, and climate of our country." Linking aesthetic design with the morality of its patrons, Pugin sharply denounced the "pagan" origins of classical architecture, and he dismissed modern art since the Renaissance and the Reformation as confused or godless. He contrasted both periods with the piety and honor he saw in the art of the Middle Ages. This was fanatical stuff; but in his personal example of conversion and in his brilliant, passionate grasp of historical designs, he exploded any conceptions of the Gothic as a neutral design choice. His direct influence could be seen in the work of English and American builders of all religious persuasions, including such notable American architects as Richard Upjohn, James Renwick, Minard Lafever, and Robert Cary Long.[18]

The Catholic press in America elaborated on Pugin's claims. Several examples appeared during the 1840s in the *United States Catholic Magazine*, where architect Theodore E. Giraud held up the Gothic as a mirror of Catholic heritage and excellence. Giraud opened his first article titled "Christian Architecture" in 1843 with a quote from Pugin, "the celebrated advocate" of pointed architecture. Paraphrasing Pugin's message and borrowing his terminology, Giraud asked his readers to look back and consider the origins of "Gothic or pointed architecture." This "Christian style," which had "attained its highest degree of purity and perfection in the twelfth and thirteenth centuries" and which "the whole Christian world had adapted to the dwellings of the Son of God," was thus "formed in the bosom of the Church" and "modeled to suit our sacred rites." Giraud then tossed in a jab at Protestants to make his point for the "Christian style" more clearly: "I understand 'Christian,' in the sense it had before the dawn of that age of light, the sixteenth century, gave it its many different, nay, even opposite meanings." He then explained why the city of Rome offered few Gothic specimens, rationalized "prejudices existing against the style," and concluded by reaffirming its denominational associations. One year later, Giraud again quoted from Pugin extensively, this time in an effort to rail against the misguided "Modern Catholics" who preferred classical, "revived pagan" architecture. He then offered a neat summary that would ring in Protestant ears: "The pointed style is the offspring of Catholicity; we should thence naturally conclude that it is better suited for its churches than any other." Finally, in an 1845 article, Giraud reiterated many of these claims and advocated a revival of the Gothic for "the faith which created it." But when he warned that "Catholic art . . . does not acknowledge" the "monstrous" examples recently built in America, Giraud's editor attached a telling note. "We think that Trinity [Episcopal] church in New York, with the exception of the chancel," the editor wrote, "and St. Alphonso's [Catholic] in Baltimore, may be ranked among those buildings of which Catholic art could justly boast." Thus the editor, while retaining the option of denying Catholic associations with shoddy examples, capped off Giraud's series with a direct claim for such non-Catholic examples as Trinity Church.[19]

The *Catholic World* provided another outlet for such claims. In 1877, an unsigned article traced the story of the Gothic Revival for its readers. Superficially a review of one of the first major studies of the revival, the article championed the "many Catholic associations" of the style and the later role of Catholic priests and architects in its revival. Like previous writers, the author reserved a special significance for the Gothic. Even though the Catholic Church had "sanctified" other historical styles, the Gothic "seems somehow more especially her own child; the others are but children of adoption—wayward children that she has rescued from pagan parents." Looking back on the century's renewed appreciation for this notable style, the writer felt that Catholics "should feel justly proud of the large part that some of their co-religionists have had in that revival, and should refer with feelings of pleasure to the influence brought to bear upon it by the adoption of many Catholic doctrines and practices by their Protestant brethren." With such Protestant comparisons, the writer ventured even further into rival denominational territory than had the *United States Catholic Magazine*. Aided by a later perspective, the writer could connect the simultaneous Protestant "adoption of many Catholic doctrines and practices" with the use of the Gothic, a combination that underscored the Catholic identity and influence of each component.[20]

America's Catholic bishops, for their part, also laid official claim to the Gothic. After John Carroll's early reserve, Archbishops Martin Spalding and John Hughes vigorously defended the medieval heritage it represented. In a lecture delivered in Kentucky and Maryland in the 1850s and published while he served as archbishop of Baltimore, Spalding sought to remove some of the Reformation's stigma against the "literature and the arts in the Middle Ages." Toward this end, Spalding listed twenty-five "great improvements and inventions, which we owe to those much abused ages." Among them was "a new style of Architecture," of which the church had produced "splendid specimens." Spalding lauded their complexity and unified effect, their play between mass and lightness, their pointed arches, and their tracery. Citing the cathedral at Pisa as an example, he exclaimed: "Let men of the present day build an edifice like this; let it stand six hundred years, and then, if it be still firm and uninjured, they may sneer at the darkness of the Middle Ages!" Spalding could expect that few in his mixed audience would object to either these associations or these compliments. Also during the 1850s, the archbishop of New York, John Hughes, undertook to rebuild his city's cathedral. In the powerful Gothic design procured for the project, Hughes defined its mission: "for the glory of God; the exaltation of Our Holy Mother, the Church; the honor of the Catholic name in this country; and as a monument of which the city of New York . . . need never be ashamed." The enormous structure filled these various roles, two of which involved public perception of Catholic achievements.[21]

Archbishop Hughes's exaggerated approach did not characterize standard Catholic uses of the style. By the mid-nineteenth century, the Gothic could be employed by beleaguered Catholics to conform to accepted American tastes as much as to distinguish denominational achievements. But even if "fitting in" was their motive, various American Catholics made sure that the public recognized the original inspiration and continuing participation of their church.

A "Popish Church of the fourteenth century"

Some of these claims might have sounded a bit thin had not numerous Protestants seconded them. Amidst many interpretations of the Gothic, a broad selection of Protestants upheld the style's Catholic associations. Whether sympathetic or critical, their observations projected the perceived power of Catholicism onto the concrete image of Gothic architecture. And in their acknowledgment of specific religious tensions, these observers revealed a simmering contest at the very center of the rapid Gothic invasion.

The most dramatic examples came from the revival's critics. Often seeking to halt the broader Protestant "adoption of many Catholic doctrines and practices," anti-Gothic conservatives ridiculed the use of such blatantly problematic designs. An Episcopal pamphlet published in 1850 struck this tone. Written by an anonymous "layman," perhaps from New York, the pamphlet was directed against the New York Ecclesiological Society, an organization of Episcopalians promoting medieval architecture and symbolism within the denomination. The author made his main point on the title page by "dedicating" the pamphlet to Levi S. Ives—a notorious convert to Catholicism who had previously served as an Episcopal bishop and a patron of the Ecclesiological Society. In twenty pages, the author trounced the ecclesiologists and their enthusiasm for crosses, liturgical colors, and correct church orientation, arguing that such features flew in the face of Protestant theology and promoted conversions to Rome. The ecclesiologists' favor for Gothic architecture made the list of offenses, and the layman dissected the society's published opinions on the subject: "Thus, we are told, 'For transparency of Christian truth and temper, the Gothic or pointed Church of the fourteenth century is unparalleled.' . . . Again, we are taught that the Gothic Church is 'the embodiment, in *wood* and *stone*, of Christian doctrine and spirit.' We have heard of persons who could see into a mill-stone, but our Protestant Ecclesiologists can do more—they can see into the *wood* and *stone* of a Popish Church of the fourteenth century, and there discover Christian *truth*, and *temper*, and *doctrine*, and *spirit*." Here, the author employed the Gothic enthusiasts' own language to illustrate inconsistencies. In his view, their attempts to revive Gothic church architecture plainly recalled "a Popish Church of the fourteenth century." The author's satire conveyed two bitter suggestions: Protestants could not rightfully employ "Popish" architecture, just as "Popish" architecture could not possess Christian truth and spirit.[22]

Several outspoken Methodists offered similar strikes at the Gothic and its Protestant use. In 1852, layman and historian J. H. McCulloh published a religious study in which he decried American trends toward expensive church architecture. Demonstrating Methodist skepticism toward artistic appeals, McCulloh worried that rich churches promoted "superstitious feelings" among worshippers. He found that "this is especially the case with Gothic churches, the invention of the darkest and most superstitious time the Christian world has ever seen, when . . . the mere imagination was excited by the fanciful proprieties of an ecclesiastical opera-house, that substantially only represented religious melodramas." These words directly linked the image of the Catholic past with modern attempts at the style's revival. In 1853, the *Methodist Quarterly Review* endorsed McCulloh's observations in a book review. Directly following the republished attack, the editor heartily thanked the author "for this plain and fearless declaration of unfashionable and unwelcome truth." "Like him," the editor continued, "we think we see the three stages of declension manifested in choirs, organs, and Gothic churches. . . . Even Methodism is infected with this evil spirit of sensualism." Thus both McCulloh and the editor specifically identified the Gothic as a popular style and a particularly popish threat to Protestant identity.[23]

In 1855, the Presbyterian *Princeton Review* tackled the problem. In an article on church architecture, one author spoke for "our own church, that is, of the Protestant church," indicating a comparative sense of unity in the face of secular and Catholic pressures. After noting "the return to the perpendicular art of the middle ages which is now going on in our church architecture," the author concluded that the style clashed with Protestant worship and ideals. The author was "certain" that "whatever the style of our Protestant art may be, it cannot be Gothic." For "we cannot imagine ourselves entering *con amore* these mediaeval temples to worship without having retreated from our present position. The Christian church of the Reformation has no service to which the visible glory and symbolism of Gothic art are other than a waste or a degradation." The author could respect the style's landmarks but could only "tremble at the idea of the Protestant world generally making experiment of genuine cathedral art," due to that art's Catholic pull. Later in the century, another Presbyterian continued the attack on imitations of "the old cathedrals, designed in sin, founded in iniquity, cemented with the tears and blood of the living temples of Christ, the monuments of idolatry and tyranny." He likewise found the Gothic a synonym for "cathedral art," which

The public square of Elyria, Ohio, where the town's Presbyterians built a
costly new Gothic church (left) next to the county courthouse in 1847.
From Howe, *Historical Collections of Ohio*, 314. Courtesy of the Manuscripts
and Rare Books Department, Swem Library, College of William and Mary,
Williamsburg, Virginia.

exerted an undeniable Catholic pull; "a Gothic nave is a fearful place,
and cathedral art has a power that would . . . compel cathedral worshippers to a cathedral service." Presbyterian experiments with turrets
and stained glass may have been a far cry materially from Catholicism's great cathedrals, but their imagined distance was slight.[24]

Congregationalists critiqued the style's identity as early as 1843.
During that year, a conservative member in Boston entered into a
newspaper war with advocates of the revival. Debating the merits of
a local Gothic church under construction, the critic opposed the design choice on the grounds that the style had originated in the Middle
Ages, "when a false philosophy, aided by a corrupted Christianity,
and despotism in Church and State, had fettered and stifled the soul."
The design's defenders were hardly more charitable. After reject-
ing Greek architecture as pagan—"indelibly associated with a most
sensual and voluptuous mythology"—they accepted the Gothic as
having certain Catholic faults. One sheepishly pronounced that "the
Gothic, however dark and barbarous may have been [the period of its

beginnings], sprang into light and flourished and had its chief glory under christian auspices." Though these Protestants argued about the style's propriety, they did not dispute the style's Catholic origins or its "chief glory" in Catholic examples.[25]

The differences between these denominational critiques of the Gothic and outright anti-Catholicism were small. As hinted by Bishop Spalding in his defense of the "dark ages," anti-Catholic activists throughout the nineteenth century poured condemnations on the pre-Reformation age, indirectly condemning the modern Gothic Revival. An extreme example of the tendency appeared in the provocatively titled *Illustrations of Popery: The "Mystery of Iniquity" Unveiled: in its "Damnable Heresies, Lying Wonders, and Strong Delusion," With the Sanguinary Persecutions of the "Woman Drunken With the Blood of the Saints,"* published in New York in 1838. This was something of an anti-Catholic encyclopedia, and it contained an extended section on the "magnificent frippery" developed for the church during the Middle Ages. According to the author, this was a time when "the indulgence of an unbridled imagination, and the captivation of the bewildered senses, constituted the sole object of all religious observances," thus obscuring true Christianity. As "popery" mimicked the "paganism" it replaced, "the followers of the Italian Pontiff constructed buildings to emulate the Pagan edifices." Here, the author cited the example of Gothic architecture, "for the Gothic Cathedrals are similar to the ancient Heathen temples; each containing the vestibule, the portico, the hall, and the choirs; to which the Papists superadded diverging wings in the shape of the cross." As in other, similarly inflammatory publications, Gothic architecture sank below a misguided, superstitious vision of Christian worship into a debased, "pagan" holdover that contradicted basic Christian principles.[26]

These critics would have been just as happy to leave the Gothic to Roman Catholics. But others more sensitively acknowledged the style's Catholic associations while accepting, or even endorsing, its modern revival. Such observers understood the appeal of the Gothic and held a more fluid view of Protestant identity. For example, in 1859, a Congregational minister from New England published an extended essay on his denomination's "Meeting-Houses" in which he welcomed the Gothic Revival and its associations. He admitted that "the simple truth is that the cathedral churches—and all others . . . which have been copied, in little, from them . . . are not the outgrowth of the unadulterated Christianity of the primitive ages, but rather of the corrupted forms of a later period." He even went so far as to label "basilican and cathedral architecture," which included the Gothic style, as the "congenial outgrowth of false and Pagan ideas engrafted on the Christian system." And yet, he continued, "It would be foolish not to take advantage of whatever associations exist in the popular mind, with the consecrated edifices of the past, which rightfully belong as much to us as to any branch of the Church." The minister proposed to use those powerful associations to his denomination's advantage by modifying publicly recognized styles for Congregational worship. And though he found that "almost all styles of the church architecture of the past may be so adapted to Congregational use as not to be incongruous with it," the author held that "this is particularly true of the [G]othic."[27]

Likewise, Episcopal minister Charles Comfort Tiffany desired a modification of Catholic architecture for his denomination. In an 1875 address to a New York church conference, he outlined his views on Christian symbolism. Much of his attention centered on the Gothic, because "what we call Gothic architecture was a growth out of Christian thought and life." He praised the style's features and effects: "Turret, pinnacle, flying buttress and roof, all contribute to assist the aspiration of the beholder." Yet Tiffany felt that "in the great cathedrals," the style had embodied too many of Catholicism's errors. This was not surprising, for this architecture "arose in the period of mediaeval Christianity; a period when the conventual life was in its greatest glory, and when the church was rather an hierarchical than a social power; when it emphasized far more the relation of men to the priest, than their relations to each other." Though these early models had been saturated with Catholic identity and theology, the style could yet be redeemed. Tiffany proclaimed that "Protestant Christianity with its modification of mediaeval Christianity, demands a modification of mediaeval architecture to adapt it to its wants, and to make it the adequate expression of its nature." So, even as late as 1875, Episcopalians struggled with the style's essential associations.[28]

Outside the denominational machinery, professional architects and designers meditated on the style's Catholic foundation. A critic in the *New York Mirror* observed simply that "the [G]othic order seems to be the fittest for religious edifices; and it was invented and perfected when the Catholic church was in the zenith of its power and magnificence, by ecclesiastical personages, expressly for religious purposes." And notably, Andrew Jackson Downing, New York's internationally known landscape designer and arbiter of taste, recommended Gothic church designs in 1848. This was not terribly surprising, since Downing had previously promoted the style for country houses because of its picturesque irregularity and its compatibility with rural materials and settings. Yet Downing's basis for recommending the style to churches involved a different emphasis. In his monthly periodical, the *Horticulturist*, he declared that churches should adopt the Gothic because "all its associations, all its history, belong so much more truly to the Christian faith," and he cited several successful revival examples on the Hudson River and in Massachusetts. Three years later, he published an even more explicit reading of the style's unique religious associations. Again advocating ecclesiastical Gothic, he charged that America's existing Protestant churches were "the ugliest . . . in christendom"; their "bareness and baldness" revealed only the "hatred which originally existed in the minds of Puritan ancestors, against everything that belonged to the Romish Church, including in one general sweep all beauty and all taste." While his proposed Gothic solution matched his well-established rural aesthetics, Downing's understanding of the style retained Catholic connotations.[29]

Practicing architects like Baltimore's Robert Cary Long also reflected this view. Forty years after Benjamin Henry Latrobe drew up a Gothic design for Bishop Carroll, Long won the commission for the Church of the Immaculate Conception, soon renamed St.

Alphonso's Catholic Church, in Baltimore. During the construction of his Gothic design, Long outlined his views on the style in an article published by the *United States Catholic Magazine*. Here he claimed that early revival architects had experimented with Gothic features because of "the unvarying monotony of the Greek style." But he then looked back to the more profound origins of the Gothic: "When this great style was conceived 'the whole earth was of one speech and one language,' one faith was universal in the church." Long did not become mired in medieval controversy; sounding ecumenical notes, he praised "the efforts of Mr. Pugin" and celebrated that "all sects are beginning to see beauty and fitness in a style of building generated by the genius of Christianity." Long did not ignore religious tensions, but he believed that "even those whose religious creed has prejudiced them against any impression to be derived from art, connected with the services of the Catholic religion have borne witness of the feeling of veneration which has come over them" upon entering Gothic cathedrals. By implication, Protestants could architecturally reunite with Catholics through a specifically medieval heritage.[30]

Thus it was not only the opponents of the Gothic who saw Roman Catholicism in the shadows of pointed towers, buttresses, and window tracery. Long's experience illustrated how such a conception of the style did not require religious conflict. Throughout the United States, Catholic architects such as Philadelphia's Napoleon Le Brun occasionally contracted with Protestant congregations to build romantic designs, and Protestant architects such as Long and Latrobe served on Roman church projects. Further, wealthy Protestant congregations occasionally selected renowned Catholic glassmakers and other artisans for church ornaments and construction, with a minimum of conceptual conflict. And during the course of the entire revival, observers casually compared America's Gothic strivings to their European originals. These associations, whether seen as hostile or benign, provided Protestant attempts at the Gothic with much of its power. But such associations did require some adjustments in order to satisfy denominational pride and worship needs.

Protestants never wholly disassociated Gothic architecture from its Catholic roots. Unlike the arguments over the use of the Latin cross, debates over the propriety of the Gothic extended well into the twentieth century. Those Episcopalians, Presbyterians, Methodists, Baptists, Congregationalists, and others who adopted the style, amidst the contemporary swell of anti-Catholic hostilities, did so with great care. To better embrace "Catholic" architecture and its associated momentum, Protestants employed common strategies. Verbally, Protestants complicated the underlying meaning and identity of the Gothic. Architecturally, Protestants wove the exotic features into more traditional worship environments. Between the two informal strategies, an ideal image of a parish church emerged, and it would become something of an American icon.

Verbally, Protestants spent a great deal of time theorizing the origins of Gothic architecture. By offering alternative explanations for the source of Gothic inspiration, Protestants deflected some of the attacks on medieval superstition and "Romish" authority, and they created a broader sense of Protestant heritage. In this regard, perhaps most insistent were Anglican "ecclesiologists" in England and America who lauded cathedrals and parish churches as products of English artistry rather than the leadership of the church. Ecclesiologists did not dispute the buildings' Catholic roles, but they did seek a deeper essence of the style in English nationalism. A classic example came from the pen of American architect Joseph Coleman Hart. In an 1857 book of designs for parish churches, Hart explained that in the Gothic, "the peculiar habits and religious faith of the old English people" had produced "a characteristic mode of buildings, a national Ecclesiastical Architecture for their religious requirements." Hart further concluded that "the church architecture of England can have no true existence under a system foreign to her own," a statement that circumscribed the historic leadership of the Roman Church. Likewise, American ecclesiologist Frank Wills championed the "old English art," as he outlined its implications for modern Episcopalians.

After describing the sublime aspiration of Gothic churches, he declared, "Such is the teaching of a genuine pointed church when freed from the frivolities and heresies with which Rome has encumbered it." Thus an essentially Anglican past emerged: "There is a catholicity in Architecture as well as in the Church, and may be separated from Popery as well in one as the other; the dross being removed, the rest is all our own, and let us use it as our inheritance." Here was a tricky yet authoritative license for Episcopalians to build new Gothic-style churches. Such celebrations of the Gothic's peculiarly English qualities were occasionally cited by members of other denominations as well.[31]

Protestants also muddied the origins with an assortment of other theories. One outstanding example appeared in Episcopal bishop John Henry Hopkins's *Essay on Gothic Architecture*, published in 1836. In this early work, Hopkins granted that Europe's Catholic "ecclesiastics were the architects, and often the very workmen, by whom those splendid edifices were erected." Yet when he probed deeper, he found evidence that the style had originated in Palestine and then traveled back to Europe with crusading priests. But this only begged another question: "What produced it in Palestine?" Here, Hopkins floated an argument for the Gothic's biblical precedent. He matched the divinely inspired plan for the temple of Solomon with the basic features and proportions of Gothic cathedrals, arriving at a fantastic and de-Romanizing conclusion—that "the style in question is the most ancient in the world which has been applied to sacred purposes; and that it deserves to be esteemed, not only for its solemn beauty . . . but for its special application to those very objects by the chosen people of God." In this conception of Gothic art, medieval Roman Catholics became the late vessels for ongoing scriptural traditions.[32]

But nothing muddied the Catholic waters more than outright denials. A few bold observers confronted the Catholic legacy of Gothic architecture and denied its relevance or truth. In 1844, one Presbyterian made the case that "the forms that enter into a Gothic cathedral" spoke "a universal language." Since their forms had struck such a common, transcendent chord among visitors, the writer exclaimed,

"How preposterous . . . , to mix up with this natural symbolism, deriving its efficacy from that which is true as the human mind and permanent as the race, the purely technical symbolism of any particular creed or age!" Thus the reader should understand, the writer concluded, "We dissent utterly from the sentiment often expressed, that the Gothic architecture is a development of Papal Christianity." Such protests were not entirely persuasive, since they confirmed the "sentiment often expressed" toward "Papal Christianity" and Gothic architecture as much as they legitimately refuted it. More often, defensive Protestants did not deny Roman Catholic connections so much as they attempted to reclassify the style under a more generic identity as "Christian."[33]

The relationship between Gothic architecture and the natural world offered another opening in defense of the Gothic style. As noted in regard to the cross, by the 1840s, Americans had developed a particular reverence for the concept of "nature," nurtured by poets, artists, and philosophers. In wilderness, Americans envisioned the promise of rugged nationalism and the sublime power of the universe. Protestants responded forcefully to suggestions that Gothic architecture grew from natural models. Various observers saw groves of slender, curving trees behind rows of high, pointed arches; they saw branches of colorful leaves in glittering stained-glass windows; they saw frost and ice crags behind spires and pinnacles; and they saw a yawning cavern with a complex of stalactites beneath the high, fretted roof. These observations did not receive the support of professional architects, but they did plant medieval architecture on more universal ground. And when such comparisons began to seem trite, Protestant theorists backed away from literal comparisons and endorsed the view of Gothic architecture as mimicking organic processes generally. One artist explained that the construction of a cathedral like that at "Chartres or Ely is a tree, growing freely and boldly, encountering obstacles and surmounting or working them in with an energy that makes deviation a new and higher illustration of principle." John Ruskin, England's popular architectural adventurer, vigorously promoted this organic view of Gothic architecture, at the expense of

Roman Catholicism. America's Protestants, when told that Gothic church designs derived from nature's forests and caves, or perhaps from England's native genius, or from Palestinian traditions, or from biblical command, or even from some vague "universal language," could rest assured that there was something else going on in "Catholic" architecture, and that they had a stake in it.[34]

Finally, Protestants maintained a naming tradition that distinguished their sanctuaries from the Catholic chapels down the street. Neither Catholic nor Protestant church names referenced architectural style, but their established differences helped uphold religious distinctions even as congregations tapped the same medieval sources. Many Catholic churches in America were named after patron saints, often reflecting their devotees' ethnic background. Among Gothic-style structures, the name of St. Patrick's Cathedral, New York City, recalled its Irish sons and daughters; the Church of St. Louis, Louisville, Kentucky, raised in 1811, reflected a French influence; and St. Philomena's of Pittsburgh, erected in the mid-1840s, recalled firmly continental connections. Catholics also named their churches after sacred objects or concepts, as at the Church of the Holy Redeemer in New York City and the Church of the Assumption, Philadelphia. In contrast, Protestants typically named churches after their location or their successive relation to other congregations. The name of First Presbyterian Church, Baltimore, implied its early organization, as compared to that city's Second Presbyterian Church, both of which were Gothic by the 1850s. The names of Green Street Baptist Church in Newburyport, Rhode Island, and Freemason Street Baptist Church, Norfolk, Virginia, both Gothic by the 1850s, cited their local addresses. These types of names denied formal recognition to saints and to their role as divine mediators, while they stamped a modern Protestant identity onto their structures' antiquated forms. And if such church names raised a stylistic tension with their exterior massing, they also reasserted the loyalties of their congregations. Episcopal churches and, occasionally, Methodist churches, offered important exceptions. Episcopalians commonly adopted saints' names and pious concepts for their churches, like those of Trinity

Church in New Haven, Connecticut, and St. Mark's Church in Palatka, Florida. Methodists proved the most unpredictable, with names varying from such Protestant standards as Broad-Street Methodist Episcopal Church in Newark, New Jersey, and Arch Street Methodist Church in Philadelphia, to more high-church names like Grace Church in Buffalo, New York, and Christ's Church in Pittsburgh, Pennsylvania. As the century wore on, Protestant names in general became more eclectic, but these general characteristics remained.

In addition to such nonmaterial strategies, Protestants maintained architectural distinctions in their use of the Gothic. One avenue for distinction involved the selection of English models of the Gothic rather than continental models. In the early 1840s, Anglican ecclesiologists had selected England's early parish church format as the ideal revival type, to the exclusion of later and foreign variations on the Gothic. American Episcopalians followed this direction—the construction of St. James-the-Less in Philadelphia, on the basis of exact plans from a thirteenth-century parish church in Cambridgeshire, representing the logical extreme. Most American sanctuaries inspired by the English parish church model did not similarly draw from historical plans, but they did employ characteristic features of the early English Gothic: modest proportions, asymmetrical massing, pronounced chancels and naves, heavy materials, and narrow lancet windows. Evangelical denominations did not take this model as seriously as did Episcopalians, but their selections of Gothic models could still carry Protestant significance. For example, there is evidence that architect Robert Cary Long selected a Tudor Gothic style for Baltimore's Franklin Street Presbyterian Church because it held a relevance to the Reformation. The design's flat roof, broad hall, and octagonal towers suggested a later era in English architecture, near the birth of Presbyterianism. Other congregations were satisfied by merely avoiding the most showy elements of French, German, and Italian cathedrals until later in the century when the style had become more established.[35]

Protestants also distinguished their Gothic Revival churches through artistic details. Aside from a more restricted use of symbols and statues, Protestants handled stained glass differently. For example, mid-nineteenth century Catholic churches in the Boston area employed continental glass traditions in which the human figures pictured in the windows took on a realistic, three-dimensional appearance. At the same time, the area's Protestant churches favored English glass traditions, in which flat-looking human images were compressed into two-dimensions with abrupt shifts in color. Not only did this bring the comforts of English associations, but it also suited Protestant modesty over portrayals of the human body in worship settings. And shortly after midcentury, evangelical churches throughout the country created a new stained-glass tradition by installing windows picturing sublime landscape scenes. These images of hills and trees avoided the need for human representations entirely and, in their largely Protestant popularity, marked subtle differences between Gothic-looking sanctuaries.[36]

An incident at Philadelphia's Second Presbyterian Church illustrated these concerns. When this Gothic-inspired building was dedicated in 1872, one member donated a new stained-glass window portraying the scene at Jesus's empty tomb. At the top, an angelic trumpeter proclaimed the Resurrection, and below, Mary of Magdala, Mary the mother of James, and Joanna greeted two angel figures pointing to the empty tomb, with graveclothes in the foreground. This was the church's first window in which human figures appeared. The member who had donated the adjoining stained-glass window, which featured a written inscription and floral design, protested the addition as contrary to Presbyterian principles. Other members formally backed his protest, but the church decided to allow the new window's placement. Additional images of angels and saints eventually followed it into the building, but they were barred from the chancel, where the stained glass contained only geometrical and emblematic designs.[37]

The most persuasive distinctions were "modifications" to Gothic plans. Every revival-inclined congregation adapted the style freely to suit their individual needs (the literal replication of St. James-the-Less in Philadelphia notwithstanding). Typically, this involved an emphasis on utility, with special attention paid to two areas: the chancel and the audience's line of sight. Whereas Catholic congregations had resized historically deep chancels in order to focus worshippers' attention on the high altar, Protestants could gain a sense of Gothic differentiation by restricting the size of their new chancel's Communion furniture and by clearing the nave of any columns or obstructions within earshot of the all-important pulpit. Toward these ends, some congregations filled chancels with organs and experimented with timber roofing systems that did not require bulky piers. These alterations offered a nod to Protestant theology, which emphasized hearing the scriptures and their interpretation from the pulpit and which denied any special divine presence in church sacraments. The fact that recessed chancels and cavernous church spaces were appropriated at all indicates how deeply some congregations wanted to make a Gothic impression. In 1859, one Congregational minister from New England championed an example of such modifications in a "beautiful" new dissenters' church near Liverpool, England. He explained, "Here the chancel of 12 feet depth, is retained for its outside effect, but used in its lower floor for a rear entrance and two retiring rooms, and in its second story for an organ and choir gallery open to the house; so that externally we have the old look, while all internal incongruity is removed." The minister reemphasized his point with another instructive example in "the cruciform style," where congregations had used "one transept as a chapel for evening service; the other for a Sabbath school room; and the chancel for the minister's retiring room and church library: the structure thus having an external Gothicity which, in its internal arrangements, is entirely shorn of all that is irrelevant to simple Congregational use." Likewise, an Episcopal minister addressed the importance of modifications to scale, insisting that medieval-style churches should "not be of such size that the voice of the minister, either when he preaches or prays, may not be distinctly heard and intelligently responded to." And Protestants should avoid "rows of columns which uphold the clerestory, and serve to divide the body of the building into nave and aisles. These not only obstruct

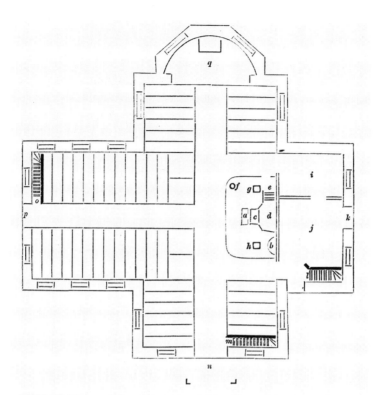

a. Holy Table.
b. Credence.
c. Reading Desk.
d. Pulpit.
e. Steps to Pulpit.
f. Font.
g. Bishop's Chair.
h. Assistant's Chair.
i. Robing Room.

j. Vestibule and Parish Library.
k. South Door.
l. Staircase to Organ Gallery.
m. Staircase to West Gallery.
n. West Door and Porch.
o. Staircase to North Gallery.
p. North Door.
q. Benches for Parish School.

St. Mary's Episcopal Church, Burlington, New Jersey (1834). This is a fine example of a traditional medieval floor plan adapted for Protestant use. The most significant changes centered on the pulpit's primary location, the transformation of the rear chancel area into a "Robing Room" and "Parish Library," and the inclusion of a parish school in one of the transepts. From Hills, *History of the Church in Burlington, New Jersey*, 435. Courtesy of the University of Delaware Library, Newark, Delaware.

the eye and the ear, intent upon the chancel and the pulpit, but they divide the congregation, and break up its unity of effect." Most Protestant pattern books of the time illustrate this concern over chancels and access to the pulpit. Also, individual denominations further domesticated the Gothic by adding specific features from their own worship traditions. Baptists occasionally constructed large baptistries near the front of their Gothic churches for immersions, just as Methodists arranged meeting rooms around the sanctuary for classes and small group activities.[38]

West Spruce Street Baptist Church, Philadelphia, built in 1869, offered a prime example of such denominational modifications to Gothic plans. Though it was an enormous and costly church raised by a fashionable congregation, the building still made important denominational links in its design. Its standard Gothic features included a high, open-timbered roof, stone walls and buttresses, a cruciform plan, a prominent tower, pointed arches, stained glass, a rose window, and rich symbolism. But Protestant peculiarities peeked out. First, a smaller lecture room and a "Sunday-school" formed the entrance to the larger nave, with a movable screen separating the areas. Thus, according to the construction announcement, "the church, lecture-room, and school can be thrown into one grand auditorium, or be used separately," while still keeping the external Gothic plan intact. Additionally, a rich marble baptistry for full immersions, enclosed in a lofty wooden tabernacle, sat behind the pulpit in place of a medieval altar. And above the baptistery, the primary chancel window would feature an image of "the baptism of our Saviour in the river Jordan." The congregation's flexible approach to the historic style accommodated particularly Baptist worship needs.[39]

And Philadelphia's Second Presbyterian Church, in addition to struggling with its first figural window, also wrestled with the placement of its pulpit. The trustees were committed to building a cruciform plan, but they wondered whether to follow Gothic tradition in placing the pulpit to one side of the divided chancel, or even forward somewhere in the nave. Their pastor remarked that he had never seen a Presbyterian pulpit placed off-center, nor anywhere but up front.

He wondered if it were thus moved, "we might be taunted with copying." Presbyterian tradition won out, and the pulpit was placed in the center of the Gothic-styled chancel.[40]

In such ways, Protestants created their own brand of Gothic. Given the earlier strides toward "churchly" designs and the piecemeal nature of Gothic "style," this change did not require dramatic shifts in theology or program. Yet it still captured part of the history, authority, vigor, and romance attributed to Catholicism. In 1853, six years after the anonymous correspondent in the *United States Democratic Review* had warned Protestants that they could not share the Gothic, another observer celebrated the revival's religious success. His subject was New York City's Trinity Church, the cathedralesque Episcopal sanctuary that architect Richard Upjohn had topped with a cross in 1844. Praising its cost and form, the observer admitted, "It is pleasant to see the emigrants when they swarm up Broadway from the ships, stop in front of the Church, which they take to be a Roman Catholic Cathedral on a small scale, and kneel before it on the pavement, thanking their God for bringing them safely to land." If this pleasing sight could be ascribed to the immigrants' fatigue and naïveté, the same could not be said for the staid ladies and gentlemen who thronged its aisles every Sunday. For here was a Catholic church without the stigma of foreign ethnicity; a "popish church" without the authority of the pope; a medieval church without the distance or "superstition." And here was an answer to Catholicism's surge. Most Gothic churches erected by midcentury Protestants did not approximate Trinity's richness or scale, but they did express its inspired, ambiguous relationship with Roman Catholicism.[41]

Debates over the meaning and role of the Gothic would follow the style and its use well into the twentieth century. Builders, patrons, and critics continued to make steady comparisons between new cathedrals or parish churches and their medieval models. These debates lost some of their sting as American church architecture became more eclectic overall and Byzantine, Romanesque, Colonial Revival, and modernist styles grew in popularity. But the continuing Protestant "cult of the Gothic" looked to stained-glass windows, pointed

Lyman Beecher's Hanover Street Congregational Church, Boston,
Massachusetts (1826). From Beecher, *Autobiography*, 2:49. Courtesy of the
William Smith Morton Library, Union Theological Seminary and
Presbyterian School of Christian Education, Richmond, Virginia.

arches, recessed chancels, and soaring heights as essential features of
church architecture. The ability of these features to retain a specifically
"Christian" effect, especially when combined with related symbolism
and ceremony, mirror the style's earliest definitions in America. So
the style never entirely lost its historic associations, as did the Latin
cross, but it did propel the spirituality of Protestant sanctuaries with
a similar force.[42]

Such an outcome would not have surprised Lyman Beecher. This
renowned Congregational preacher spent much of his career battling
Catholicism like no other American, yet he felt at home in a Gothic
sanctuary. In a typical speech, this one given in 1827 to the American Board of Missions, he acknowledged the resources of his enemy,

warning that "considering the civilization, and wealth, and science, which the system comprehends, it is from popery, no doubt, that the Gospel is destined to experience the last and most determined resistance." Beecher's true notoriety came in 1834, when he delivered such a fiery string of anti-Catholic sermons in Boston's churches that many held him personally responsible for the ensuing riots that destroyed a nearby convent. But when this warrior had first moved his family to Boston only seven years earlier, he began his work at Hanover Street Congregational Church, notable as an early example of the Gothic Revival. This structure featured a rough stone facade, a large front tower topped with battlements, and rows of pointed windows filled with tracery—an unmistakably medieval experiment. When Hanover Church burned to the ground in 1830, Beecher and the congregation erected a nearly identical building one year later. The group left few documents explaining their choices, and it is sometimes difficult to imagine Beecher's antipapal tirades echoing off his church's Gothic walls, but Beecher offered something of an explanation twenty years later. At a convention of Congregational ministers in 1852, where Beecher attended as president of a Cincinnati seminary, he entered one particularly lively discussion on the need for more church buildings to establish Congregationalism in the West. Here, he announced, "If you want to get martins about your house, you must put up a martin box." And Hanover Church, like countless other "miniature cathedrals" across the country, had welcomed many fluttering crowds of curious, colorful martins.[43]

The Flowers

The decorous worship services at Ginter Park Baptist Church conceal a long-forgotten struggle. Every Sunday morning, visitors park their cars along the wide, tree-lined streets of this Richmond, Virginia, neighborhood and stroll toward the church's great doors. Above them, the building stands much as it did when raised in 1920, with heavy brick walls, two front towers, stepped buttresses, and rows of pointed, stained-glass windows. Once inside, a few hundred people, primarily white, settle into long, wooden pews and await their typical program of songs, prayers, sermons, and sacraments. The bright worship that follows would hardly suggest its embattled roots. For much of the congregation's colorful ceremonial derives from nineteenth-century Roman Catholic introductions and would have scandalized earlier generations of Baptists. Beyond their use of symbolic crosses and medieval-themed architecture, these Protestants have draped their entire worship experience with the flowers, choral music, vestments, candles, and related flourishes that once belonged only to their Catholic neighbors. As in countless other Protestant congregations across the country, the members of Ginter Park Baptist Church now freely employ these particular sights and sounds to

Ginter Park Baptist Church, Richmond, Virginia (1920).
Photo by Ryan K. Smith, 2002.

heighten the air of festivity and holiness surrounding their services, without a wisp of difficulty.[1]

Let us take one recent Sunday for an example. On a sunny April morning, the church doors open early for the weekly service. Ushers greet newcomers and regulars alike and hand out program leaflets that proclaim this day to be the "Second Sunday of Easter." Within the program, visitors find that the day's roster of hymns and scriptural readings—such as the hymn "Christ Is Risen"—are specifically oriented toward the spiritual season. Two hundred years ago, America's Baptists had rejected the annual feasts, fasts, and holidays that marked the Catholic liturgical year, but here at once we find an easy celebration of the formal, extended season of "Eastertide."[2]

Stepping inside the sanctuary, visitors move into a broad center aisle dividing two banks of pews. The eye is drawn up the aisle, which runs toward a recessed chancel with a pipe organ on the far wall. While people mingle, find seats, and prepare for worship, there is time to reflect on the season and its symbols. The cover of the program leaflet pictures a lamb with a radiant halo aside a flagpole and flag bearing Latin crosses, referencing the scriptural lamb of God, as well as the traditional *Agnus Dei* design motif. The Latin cross and other transformed symbols also twinkle throughout the sanctuary's tall stained-glass windows, which reflect geometric rainbows into the spacious nave. In front of the nave, a small Communion table stands before a raised pulpit, flanked by a wooden baptismal well. The pulpit is dressed with a white linen cloth, which may have raised earlier eyebrows even without its embroidered cross and crown. Certainly the heavy brass cross on the Communion table would have offended mid-nineteenth-century Baptists, as would the two lighted candles flanking it, for they would have mimicked the Catholic "superstitions" of lighting unnecessary ritual flames during the daytime and reverencing an altar. And despite the season, the two fresh-flower arrangements blooming in brass vases on either side of the chancel opening would have appeared out of place, given their previously common associations with "popery" and pagan temples.

This whole scene is soon awash with the organist's playing. Such tunes might have soothed the ears of some earlier Baptists, but if those churchgoers had glimpsed the organist's maroon robe and silver stole and the incoming, similarly attired choir, the pleasantries would have passed. Vestments hinted at an authority and ceremonial distinction previously unwelcome among Baptist congregations. And separate choirs—though popular among visitors of all faiths in Roman Catholic and Episcopal chapels and concerts—sounded a distinctly un-Baptist note by signaling that the entire congregation would not be united in singing every song. Nevertheless, the choral introit here featuring the German folk tune "Christ the Lord Is Risen Again" brings only approving expressions to the congregation's faces.

The choir members then take seats in the chancel facing the congregation, as two men in dark suits enter the sanctuary from the side. One is the pastor, and the other is the minister of Christian development, who issues a call to worship, to which the congregation responds in unison. Next comes an Easter hymn, for which the congregation stands to sing. More words of welcome follow, and the congregation sits to listen to a young layman deliver a short sermon to the children present. Then, a laywoman stands to read aloud several seasonal Bible verses and offer prayers on behalf of the seated congregation. After another hymn, the pastor stands to offer a thoughtful sermon on the apostle Thomas's skeptical response to Christ's Easter victory. A hymn, "We Live by Faith and Not by Sight," concludes the sermon. The ushers then retrieve brass collection plates from the front table, while members of the congregation dig in their pockets for the offertory. The final collection is returned to the front table under the strains of the traditional doxology hymn, after which the congregation hears a final prayer and a solo choir performance. As the organist begins a postlude, everyone rises and turns to head for the doors, chatting comfortably on the way. Back in the sunlight, the visitor is returned to the secular world of sidewalks, swaying trees, and passing cars.

The previous hour inside represents only one portion of the spiritual life at Ginter Park Baptist Church. But it is a prominent portion—one that constitutes the congregation's primary worship before God, involves every church member, and introduces nonmembers to the congregation's beliefs. And in this portion, the church displays a decidedly mixed heritage. Its worship remains steadfastly Baptist in its plain-clothed ministers, its focus on scripture and song, its members' preference to sit or stand during prayers rather than to kneel or bow, and its prominent baptistry. Yet the church has set these traditions within the material milieu of a different communion. It observes a cyclical spiritual year filled with ordained events; it seats a separate choir in a recessed chancel where the group performs independently; it adorns the choir and organist with formal ministerial vestments; it displays lighted candles on an ornamented Communion table; and it hangs expressive floral arrangements about the worship center. All of these ceremonial "flowers" lift the faith of the believers and illustrate respect for the house of God. Far from being simple decorations, they define the congregation's activities even as they quietly point to a key religious exchange that took place 150 years ago.

Down the street, across town, and around the country, an array of Baptist churches welcomes Sunday visitors into worship services. Other Protestant churches, descended from the nineteenth-century Methodists, Presbyterians, Congregationalists, and Episcopalians of this study, offer even more jarring variations. While Ginter Park Baptist Church cannot provide a model for the Protestant worship of Anglo-America, it can illustrate the action of accommodation in these churches. After Roman Catholicism burst onto the American religious scene in the 1830s, differing degrees of traditional Catholic ceremonial found their way into Protestant sanctuaries. Some parishes adopted more of the controversial implements—such as incense, ministerial vestments, and high altars—and some adopted less, but nearly all moved in some way to accommodate the sensuous sanctity of Roman Catholic worship with their own venerated theological traditions. As in the example at Ginter Park, most did so by stripping the items of their original associations with the tangible presence of God and yet retaining their softer abilities to bring worshippers closer to him through feelings. In the items' widespread appropriation from the 1840s through the 1890s, they prepared Protestant churches to meet the challenges of a competitive, upstart denomination and an increasingly commercial society. When combined with symbolic crosses and medieval architectural styles, this ceremonial helped Protestants put their new designs in motion, bringing their worship to bloom.

"Baptized paganism"

In 1895, one elderly Episcopal clergyman recalled that "flowers on the altar were like red rags to a bull" forty years earlier. His comment probably drew chuckles at the time as a quaint curiosity, for the threat that could be found in a vase of fresh-clipped buds—the idea that a congregation or its minister might respond with animosity to a stray yet strategically placed flower arrangement—had already become lost to modern Protestants.[3]

The change in attitudes that took place over those forty years is illustrated most vividly in the earlier era's anti-Catholic literature. In scores of books and pamphlets, hostile authors frequently critiqued Roman Catholicism's distinctive worship and dress, unwittingly foreshadowing the later staples of Protestant sanctuaries. Writing from the comforts of a plainer Protestantism, these authors classified sanctuary flowers and the like as shallow stage props for idolatrous melodramas. The instruments' presence in Catholic churches caricatured that denomination's supposed errors as a bastion of "baptized paganism." One example appeared in 1834, when W. C. Brownlee of the Reformed Dutch Church in New York illustrated the "sisterhood" of Catholic cathedrals and "pagan temples" by pointing out their common use of candles, incense, altars, and vestments, among other features. Similarly, in 1851, a Presbyterian pastor attempted to show that "the religion of the modern Romans is derived from their pagan ancestors" by citing their common employment of incense, "tapers and lamps," "pomps and processions," and robed acolytes. A year later, New Jersey Presbyterian Nicholas Murray singled out the use of ritual candles for ridicule. Murray had seen them burning in various Catholic settings, including the Baltimore cathedral, "as thick and countless as trees in a nursery." This practice, a "prominent peculiarity of the Romish service," struck Murray as excessively superstitious, and he bragged, "We have learned how to express our joy without lighting lamps or candles." He finally dismissed the practice by exclaiming, "The whole thing . . . is ridiculous, and is transferred bodily and confessedly from Paganism. There is nothing in the Christian Scriptures to countenance it." The implications of such attacks were clear: "true" Christians, that is, Protestants, had no business lighting decorative candles, or kneeling at altars, or donning ceremonial robes and surplices, or lighting incense, or marching in ceremonial processions. To do so might signal an alignment with Catholicism and its "pagan" holdovers.[4]

These midcentury charges were largely free of hypocrisy. Since colonial times, America's non-Germanic Protestants had gathered for worship with a sober eye toward Reformation strictures. Minimizing church sanctity and authority, they had built their services around the celebration of God's word through sermons, songs, and readings, as well as the commemoration of two sacraments—baptism and the Lord's Supper. Neither called for an elaborate atmosphere, and church furnishings were comparatively sparse in even the most lavish buildings. Indeed, Baptists, Methodists, and, to a lesser extent, Presbyterians had forged their styles in rugged revival meetings along the nation's frontiers. Into the 1830s, Methodist ministers throughout the country preached in drab street clothes; Baptist congregations sang without the assistance of choirs or instruments; Congregationalists passed around Communion utensils from hand to hand, on days with no reference to ecclesiastical holidays; and Presbyterians shunned formal processions in church. Episcopalians were a trickier lot, since they observed a rotating calendar of ecclesiastical events, decorated with evergreens, organized church choirs, received communion from ministers who wore white surplices, and occasionally indulged in processions. Yet, like all four of the other denominations, Episcopalians avoided incense, colored vestments, ritual flames, fixed altars, midweek services, and sanctuary flowers before the 1840s. These commonalities did not mean that Protestant services lacked art or ceremony. Rather, without the assumptions that God was specially present in church or that ministers could impart spiritual grace through church sacraments, Protestant services developed independently from references to the traditional pageantry employed by Rome to convey a sense of reverent awe.[5]

Thus Catholicism's rising public profile in the 1830s and 1840s brought fresh worship alternatives before the eyes of America's Protestants. Onlookers who were less antagonistic than anti-Catholic pamphleteers still linked sacramental instruments like candles, vestments, and flowers to the Roman Church with a similar consistency. A sprinkling of Jewish and Lutheran groups throughout the country had also been employing such ceremonial articles in their worship for years, but their aesthetic results were quite different, and their customs made comparatively little impression on the chief Protestant denominations, with the notable exception of new Christmas celebrations inspired by German immigrants. In contrast, Protestant visitors to Catholic churches were so taken by the unique ceremonial found therein that they invoked a specialized vocabulary to describe the items as a class. Examples include the Episcopal diarist in Wilmington, Delaware, who had noted Catholic "mummeries" at the funeral of a friend in 1838, the Presbyterian pastor who had described the ritualistic "fooleries" found in Baltimore's cathedral in 1841, and the Methodist clergyman in Cincinnati who had spent a day reviewing the local "splendor" and "drama" of "Romanism" in 1847. Whether uttered in outrage or adoration, terms such as "mummeries" or "trumpery" knit together Catholic variations across time and space, establishing a convenient point of contrast to Protestant worship.[6]

Popular images of Catholic worship cemented the effects of visitations and vocabulary. Circulated in books, magazines, and art shows, these pictures displayed various Latin ceremonies before wide audiences, whetting Protestant curiosities while standardizing Catholic mysteries. New York pastor John Dowling presented one such image, titled "Elevation and Worship of the Wafer at Mass," as the frontispiece to his 1846 handbook, *The History of Romanism*. Set in a generic Catholic sanctuary, the pictured ceremony shows a robed priest holding the Host aloft at the altar, while robed attendants and crowds in the pews kneel reverentially. Six tall candles on the altar illuminate various symbols and statues surrounding the scene. Intended to illustrate the idolatry of Catholicism's central ritual, the image outlines a detailed yet nonspecific setting filled with classic Latin "mummeries." Another image published in an 1871 anti-Catholic treatise reveals even more "trumpery" at a generic "High Mass," including a smoking incense censor and fresh-flower arrangements. This publication also included an image of the interior of the Church of the Immaculate Conception in Boston showing a group of candles, statues, and paintings around an altar. A more sympathetic painting, completed by Episco-

Generic Catholic worship scene from a Roman Catholic guidebook for
Protestants. From Barnum, *Romanism As It Is*, 422. Courtesy of the
University of Delaware Library, Newark, Delaware.

palian Robert W. Weir in the early 1860s and displayed before New
York gallery crowds, centered on the ceremonial induction of a young
female novice. *Taking the Veil*, which was set in Italy but emphasized
a universal tone, featured a variety of customary implements: robed
choir, mitred bishop, kneeling maiden, curling incense, scattered rose
petals, rich drapery, Gothic arches, hanging crucifix, and decorated
altar. The flood of other comparable images that greeted midcentury
Protestants helped establish a pattern for Catholic worship as exotic
yet recognizable. Whether considering local chapels or Rome itself,
whether viewing scenes in person or on the page, Protestants identified an alien tradition in the "equipage" of "Romanism."[7]

Thus the few early mainstream Protestant experiments with these articles aroused immediate suspicion, since their origins and implications were clear. This held true even for such simple additions as sanctuary flowers. In 1867, New York Episcopalian Morgan Dix related an example from ten years earlier, when, "in one of the leading churches of this city, for the first time, it was decided to dress the altar on Easter day with flowers." Dix, a minister, did not say whether the clergy or laity initiated the change. The unnamed leadership adopted a strategy based "on the principle of . . . plunging in head foremost as the best way of getting into deep water," so it was "resolved to make the decoration elaborate, striking, and very unmistakably conspicuous." On Easter morning, when the newly fragrant "Lord's table" greeted the entire congregation, "everybody looked and wondered, and to their honor be it spoken, everybody said, 'How beautiful!'" But questions over the change still lingered just below the surface:

> An old lady, who, with another old lady, approached the chancel after service, and gazed upon the flowers with troubled mien. Said the second old lady to the first, after a while, "How did you like the services to-day?" Said the first old lady in reply, "Very much; they were delightful; it is all beautiful; I like it all except one thing." "What is that?" asked the friend. "Why, those flowers!" was the reply. "But why do you dislike the flowers? What can you object to in them?" inquired the second old lady. "I don't like them," was the answer, "because they look so Roman Catholic!"

When one of New York City's most cultured Episcopal congregations tread so carefully around this subject as late as 1857, other Protestant congregations across the country could hardly be expected to view such "red rags" less sternly.[8]

The "prevailing prejudices" of the American People

As with the Latin cross and Gothic architecture, the Catholic associations of certain ritualistic devices did not necessarily discourage their use. Rather, given Protestants' ambivalent passions for Catholic worship, such associations could actually enhance the appeal of church flowers, candles, vestments, and celebrations. Not only did the items suggest the mysteries surrounding Catholic ceremonies, they also recalled the church's ancient tradition and reflected the church's recent vitality.

These qualities might have been enough to recommend the items for Protestant use, but there was another dimension to the items' appeal. In their rich textures, these objects and festivities tapped directly into the nation's growing preoccupation with material prosperity. It was this dimension that moved occasional observers to bemoan Catholicism's suitability to the "prevailing prejudices," or tastes, of American society. By the mid-nineteenth century, the country had been transformed by an expanding industrial base, an advancing market economy, a burgeoning middle class, and a spreading transportation network. All of these changes fed a drive toward greater and greater cultural refinement, as American tastes increasingly demanded beauty and gentility in the fabric of everyday life. Buildings of all types grew more elaborate and their furnishings more plentiful, offering decorative public "stages" for polite society. Protestant churches had moved with this tide, but their patrons remained ambivalent about the relationship between religion and modern fashions. If churches were too sparse, they risked alienating the mainstream and projecting an image of impoverishment. If churches were too rich, they risked appearing too worldly and losing their claims to moral authority. Catholic churches, coming into prominence in the midst of these currents, offered a solution to this tension. In their beautiful equipage, Catholic churches satisfied broad desires for uplift and material sophistication. Yet those Catholic beauties simultaneously stood apart from modern fashions; the specialized vocabulary of robes, candles, and altars carved out a uniquely religious sphere. Thus Catholicism's ritualistic implements held the potential to help situate churches within the modern prosperity while retaining an air of separation and authority.[9]

These issues peppered Protestant journals and sermons as observers established a basis for the implements' appropriation. One article published in the Congregational *New Englander and Yale Review* in

1848 outlined with clarity the dual pressures of denominational competition and general cultural refinement. The author began by affirming the role of "the arts" in Christianity, since a "sense of the beautiful" was "a part of our [human] nature." The religious possibilities of art became most apparent in the link between church "architecture and worship," for "an imposing or attractive edifice creates in the minds of the worshipers associations favorable to the effect contemplated, and may alone often bring the undevout within the reach of the more powerful agencies that are at work within." Here, the Congregational author underscored the sway material attractions held on worshippers while celebrating church ornamentation as a distinct proselytizing tool. If the demands of refinement did not convince church committees to upgrade their worship, he asserted, then "the score of sectarian emulation" should: "Those denominations and those particular societies that are too . . . sluggish or prejudiced to make their houses of worship more agreeable or convenient, and will not keep pace with the public mind in this direction . . . will suffer as they ought to suffer by comparison with others." Surely the author had Roman Catholics and Rome-leaning Episcopalians in mind for the bar of comparison. Societies that disregarded such churches' "aids and embellishments of devotion," he continued, faced a dire prediction: "They will fail to gain adherents, they will lose some they now have, among those whom they would most wish to secure"—the art-loving, "youthful part of the community." Old-timers might be content to worship in tradition and simplicity, but an age of quickening beauty and competition required changes in Congregational sanctuaries.[10]

A similar appeal came from a Presbyterian pastor in his 1854 dedication of a new church building near Pennsylvania's mountain resorts. Calling the structure a "temple" and God's "own holy habitation," he advised his audience, "You must take men as they are." "Christians might come hither from a sense of duty, or from the love of religious exercises themselves," he suggested, "even though the house should be neglected, poorly furnished, poorly warmed, and cheerless, but not so the worldly and impenitent; they will be influenced by the pleasantness of the place and the character of all its appointments and its services." In this admission, the pastor made the refinement of Presbyterian arts and rituals imperative: "You must appeal to those motives by making the place and the ordinances of religion attractive," with the hope of properly edifying worldly visitors once they had actually arrived. Yet such visitors would necessarily find Presbyterian novelties in newly "attractive" services. The pastor's reflections drew from a strikingly Catholic conception of the church as a receptacle for the special presence of·God, "a place wherein you will feel a reverent interest for the sake of its associations with the holiness of Heaven; its inhabitation by the high, most high God." This same understanding bolstered the explanations given by Bishop Martin Spalding and other Catholic contemporaries as to why they employed decorated altars, vestments, incense, and other ceremonial implements. Again, worldly refinement and denominational mingling called for Protestant innovations. The pastor offered his audience and congregation a new license to outfit their church.[11]

Methodists likewise set a path between the lures of Catholicism and the world. An 1856 article on Methodist church architecture in the *National Magazine* reviewed the recent progress of traditionally austere churches toward the fine arts. Observing comparative developments in Britain, the author endorsed one Wesleyan's opinion that "the esthetic element in religion" must extend beyond architecture to employ "music and painting, and even . . . sculpture." Opposition to "Popery" had "debased" the fine arts, sending music to "concert-halls and opera-houses," sculpture to the subjects of "licentious gods and goddesses," and painting to "scenes of revelry and drunkenness, or . . . pampered puppy-dogs and favorite race-horses." The author was ashamed, insisting that art should be redeemed from these degraded tastes and set to the service of the Methodist faith. If a tack toward popery and the fine arts involved "departing from ancient landmarks," he asserted, then it was a necessary change. For "a religion that renounces the beautiful, and true, and tasteful in nature or art is either mere affectation, or will one day drive its votaries to the hermit's cell or the monastery." With these outcomes in mind, some Methodists saw their future in the exercise of "tasteful" religious art.[12]

Just as these observers were giving voice to denominational pressures, a host of critics mocked the improvisations. For example, a pastor from Iowa entered a tirade in the *Congregational Quarterly* in 1859 to refute the propriety of sensory appeals. He held that if his denomination's standard offerings could not "attract, [then] it is not our business, by other appliances, to play upon human nature on the Sabbath and in the Church." Indeed if his coreligionists felt that they needed new churchly refinements for reasons of "self-defense" or "our comparative denominational respectability," the pastor could only wonder "whether Jesus Christ has any more use for the Congregational branch of His house." But despite the thunder of such criticism, and despite the well-worn themes behind it, these critics still acknowledged the unmatched material appetites of their modern audiences. One Baptist author noted that "while the temporal power of the Pope of Rome is waning, it cannot be denied that there is a widespread revival of ritualism, which is felt even within the most evangelical churches." Though the author opposed these sophisticated deviations in church services, he located their roots in popular fiction, which was "glowing with gaudy imagery," and he announced that "the progress of this 'strange revival' will keep pace with the prevalence of novels, theatres, pomps, parades and gewgaws." Considering the bright future for social pomps and shopkeepers' gewgaws in America, plus the renewed fortunes of the country's "Papists," this critic faced a true challenge.[13]

Other influences prepared the way for increased ceremonial in Protestant churches. The religious revivals that had swept the country during the first half of the century placed a new focus on worshippers' emotions and the atmosphere for conversion, thereby directing attention to the form of Protestant worship. Changes in Protestant theology also prepared the way, as the various denominations began placing greater emphasis on the role of sacraments in church life. And after 1861, the violence and mourning arising from the Civil War stimulated a wave of ceremonies and memorials that would involve Protestant faiths. All of these movements would come to a head in the popularity of Roman ritual devices. Catholic flowers engaged a world steeped in memorials, emotion, and material refinement while retaining a religious edge within that world. If Protestants complained that Romanists held an unfair advantage in such a scenario, certain steps could be taken to address that advantage.

"Novelties in the Church Service"

Catholic-inspired celebrations and ceremonial entered Protestant sanctuaries a bit later than symbolic crosses and medieval-themed architecture. The bulk of the appropriations took place between the 1850s and the 1870s, but the full process was long and uneven, with initial experiments beginning in the early years of the century and late disputes lasting into the twentieth century. Ritualistic flowers comprised a looser category of items than Latin crosses or Gothic architecture, and congregations selected from the various implements in stages, according to their own desires. Candles, choirs, vestments, and processions interposed directly upon the act and substance of prayer and so required a unique care in their installation. Protestant denominations moved toward the implements gradually, after symbols and architectural styles had established new directions.

Church furnishings and festivals also brought parishioners' gender roles into greater focus. Unlike the more impersonal results of a pastor and building committee's architectural decisions, church flowers required ongoing member participation. Here, designs and duties often divided along culturally established lines that positioned women in the realm of nurturing, domestic concerns and men at the head of public affairs. "Romanized" church interiors provided arenas for both models, as women took charge of the preparation of vestments, banners, and decorative linens, plus the upkeep of furnishings and altar equipment, while men directed choirs, processions, and services. Responsibilities for musical programs and holiday plans were often shared. And while men's activities remained in plain view, the participation of female parishioners often remained behind the scenes, excepting special notices. In 1861, the *New York Observer* offered one example when it reported the dedication of Morrisville, Pennsylvania's First Presbyterian Church and added that "the interior has been elegantly and tastefully furnished with carpets, cushions, &c., reflecting great credit upon the ladies who superintended that department." The writer Constance Fenimore Woolson toyed with these expectations in an 1874 story in which she described a frontier Episcopal chapel as owing "its existence to the zeal of [an Eastern] director's wife, who herself embroidered its altar-cloth and bookmarks, and sent thither the artificial flowers and candles which she dared not suggest at home; the poor Indians, at least, should not be deprived of them!" Still, the basic roles proved durable, as the evangelical author of *Arranging Church Flowers* in 1951 casually referred to the chairperson of flower guild committees as a "She" and recommended that "the use of lighted candles should be cleared with the church fathers to be sure no one disapproves." From a denominational perspective, differing internal roles did not alter the course of the appropriations, but they did reveal the changes' broadening support, and they showed how exotic Catholic elements became "domesticated" under the traditional assumptions of Protestant culture.[14]

Gender implications and meditative delays aside, the flowering process still held much in common with the earlier appropriations. First, it involved the selection of a few specific Roman elements rather than a wholesale adoption of the Catholic worship catalog. Also, participants remained aware of the selected items' denominational associations, as illustrated by Morgan Dix's Easter anecdote. Only by the end of the nineteenth century would the Catholic origins of popular ceremonial implements cease to be a meaningful issue. Finally, denominational dynamics during the latter appropriation remained much the same as in the previous ones. Episcopalians initiated most of the changes, sparking bitter public debates, while Methodists, Congregationalists, Presbyterians, and Baptists followed thereafter with less fanfare. In each denomination, changes were propelled by the informal experiments of various congregations rather than by the concerted efforts of governing bodies. As with the cross and the Gothic, support came from the younger laity, as well as the clergy, though urban churches would come to lead church fashions more prominently during this phase. Clearly, few churches distinguished their symbolic, stylistic, and ceremonial innovations; all were part of the larger attempt to harness Catholicism's material momentum.

Changes in church music proved the earliest and most far-reaching element. Throughout the country's history, Protestant church music had reflected the extraordinary variety that characterized Americans' religious expressions. From African American spirituals to traditional psalms, from revival shouts to intricate instrumentals, Protestant congregations drew from many musical traditions to suit their evolving worship styles. In general, evangelical congregations favored full congregational singing without instrumentation, while Episcopalians and Lutherans employed separate choirs and organs. But even these characterizations were breaking down by the early years of the nineteenth century as urbanity began playing a greater role in musical tastes than denominational identity.[15]

Catholic congregations showed no less diversity in practice, but the publicity surrounding their spread after the 1820s emphasized certain patterns. The most basic centered on the means of performance —on those choirs and instruments that seemed to ring every Catholic chapel. In 1835, one Congregationalist discussing organs could remark casually that "Catholics and Episcopalians have used them [for] so long," while as late as 1869, the *Princeton Review* identified one of the features of Romanism in "the music of her choirs." Catholic leaders plainly defended the propriety of trained musicians in worship, and some of the church's ceremonies required regular passages to be sung or chanted by a separate choir, thereby lending a special authority to their performances. Another hallmark of Catholic music lay in the church's historic roster of masterful compositions. America's Catholic churches may not have routinely ventured into Mozart's masses and oratorios, but few Protestants questioned the musical brilliance at Rome's fingertips. In 1848, the Unitarian *Chris-*

tian Examiner granted that "among the voluminous compositions of the writers belonging to the Church of Rome, from the time of Palestrina to the present day, they have maintained an undisputed preëminence." Catholic churches frequently showcased this music in special concerts or recitals, popular among people of all faiths, thereby feeding Protestant laments. So Catholic music played into the country's growing appetite for refinement even as it generated a spiritual atmosphere, just as the Methodist visitor to Cincinnati's cathedral sat "in mute wonder at the flood of mingled melody and harmony, which comes pouring down . . . from above" while disparaging the service's willingness to address "the popular taste." The thrust of these impressions helped set a formula for effective church music, a formula built around a diverse catalog of historic musical selections, a willingness to enjoy aesthetically pleasing music in the sanctuary, and a special role for choirs and instrumentalists in congregations' musical offerings.[16]

Evangelicals began to accommodate these pleasures soon after the 1820s, building on the earlier, scattered popularity of organs and choirs. As early as 1843, one historian in Philadelphia perceived that the city's new Catholic congregations were influencing local Protestant music. The historian recalled that within the past few decades, plain songs and congregational singing had given way to fashionable "innovations," which were "first witnessed in Philadelphia in the Papal churches, and came to be but slowly imitated." These new trends featured trained choirs and more complex pieces, and their spread seemed to erase previous denominational peculiarities; the historian marveled that "in the present day, there is no very marked difference in the general appearance of the congregations who worship in the different churches in the city." Curiously, in a city simmering with anti-Catholicism, the "Papal churches" had seemed to spur more uniformity among Protestants than a century of local Episcopal and Lutheran examples. By 1847, Philadelphia's once stolid First Presbyterian Church was even offering weeknight public concerts of choral and instrumental "Sacred Music," as were a growing number of other evangelical congregations around the country. In 1879, a correspondent to *Harper's New Monthly Magazine* confirmed the movement. She observed that "lines once clear, broad, and distinct, separating the musical services of churches, have been blurred, and in many cases obliterated," though creeds remained distinct. This blurring was due to three causes: the "close juxtaposition of so many widely different sects," the "influence of Catholic Church music," and the lack of oversight among the clergy. Yet the author upheld the changes, as she asked, "How was it possible for the severe simplicity of the Puritan form . . . to hold out against the inroads of Catholic pomp and splendor?" She concluded, "It has been but natural that in the attempt to satisfy the modern demand for a religious music which shall be at once pleasing, popular, and effective, the Catholic Church music should be our first resource."[17]

This growing, "Papal"-inspired musical uniformity could be exaggerated, but evidence of its progress came from the movement's own critics. In 1867, one Presbyterian correspondent to the *New York Observer* decried "the apings of the Romish ritual" among evangelical churches desiring "to compete with other churches, by catering to a refined public taste." The correspondent took particular issue with musical changes, explaining, "I have been in Presbyterian churches in the city of New York in which, in the midst of divine service, all worship has been suddenly suspended, and the congregation has been informally invited to listen to a performance by the organist and a quartette of trained singers." The singers' words "may have been sacred," but their performance dripped with sensuous vanity; church music of this style, he complained, "has as little power to awaken devotional feeling in others as the childish frippery and mummery of the professed ritualists." Likewise, a Baptist observer of the same era complained of his denomination's musical "imitation." He noted, "We have organs in all our city churches at the North, and they are now deemed essential in our small towns and villages." And he ridiculed the reasoning that since "other denominations employ professional musicians, . . . we must do it also or we shall be behind the times, and lose our congregations." Such critics were concerned about the spiritual commitment behind professional musicians—it was not so much a question of sophistication as of sincerity and unified congregational praise. Though critics could point to tradition and theology to challenge the growing emphasis on trained religious "performances," they could not neutralize their congregations' desires to stay abreast of denominational challenges.[18]

The use of instruments and choirs would grow to define mainstream Protestant worship by the 1890s. In 1895, a directory for New York and Brooklyn listed choirs in nearly all the area's congregations, including those of the Baptists, Congregationalists, and Presbyterians. In 1903, the General Assembly of the Presbyterian Church in the U.S.A. surveyed the denomination's ministers to discern common worship practices and concluded that "choirs were almost universally present" among its congregations. Protestant church music would continue to evolve and display innumerable variations, many arising from racial, ethnic, geographical, and class differences. But whether or not the musicians in First Presbyterian Church, Huntington, West Virginia, ever performed the various medieval "Ancient Hymns and Canticles" printed in its 1933 hymnal, the very presence of such selections among its pews was proof enough that ripples of denominational exchange had occurred.[19]

In a similar sweep, evangelical denominations moved to recognize the Christian year. While Episcopalians and Lutherans had always observed a cyclical year of regular festivals and sacraments, evangelicals began their experiments in the 1820s and 1830s and brought them to fruition over the following seventy years. Christmas celebrations led the way, followed by Easter and then, less emphatically, by the recognition of such seasons as Lent and Advent and the opening of churches to occasional midweek services. These celebrations developed in close relation to the marketplace and the Victorian home, but their observance within the context of public worship involved a particularly religious shift. Just as Catholic church music had fascinated early Protestant crowds, the rich productions surrounding Catholic festivals like Easter and Ash Wednesday enchanted their Protestant audiences. In 1863, one journal acknowledged, "We are noticing more habitually and affectionately the ancient days and seasons of the Christian Church." Indeed, Christmas's "Saint Nicholas is making his way into universal regard, and is likely to stand as high upon the Puritan as the Catholic Calendar." The author then went on to advocate Protestants' rising appreciation for "the second great festival of the ancient Church, Easter." Two years earlier, the *New York Observer* published an article about Easter Sunday in which the writer felt the need to define, as well as advocate, this newly recognized holy day: "The last Sabbath, known among the Roman Catholic, the Protestant Episcopal and several other denominations of christians [*sic*] as Easter Sunday, was appropriately observed. It is the close of Lent, and commemorates the Resurrection of our Lord and Saviour Jesus Christ." Contrary to the opinions of previous generations, this writer found it appropriate for evangelicals to celebrate the Easter Resurrection annually, praising "those Churches that devote a Sabbath annually to the contemplation of this theme." And in 1884, a popular magazine declared, "The celebration of Easter in the United States is now an established practice." The writer found it "impossible to name the exact time when Easter began to commend itself to many people and many Churches that had looked upon the Christian festival as a Catholic or quasi-Catholic error." Yet, he continued, "it appears that about twenty years ago the Presbyterians began to preach Easter sermons and to adorn their churches with Easter flowers. These churches seem to have followed the example set to them by their sister societies" in other denominations. It was a rather broad example—since neither Baptists, Methodists, Congregationalists, nor Presbyterians followed established liturgies and each congregation's worship celebrations took their own form. Whatever the particular format, church festivals helped stimulate a circular demand for refined, timely music and florid decorations, all of which combined to enhance church sanctity and authority.[20]

While the Rome-inspired changes in Protestant church music and calendars unfolded slowly over the course of the century, a spark came in the mid-1840s that would provide immediate focus for the movement. This spark centered on developments in the Anglican Church, as ministers and congregations sympathetic to the Oxford "high-church" reform movement of the 1830s began elevating the format of their rituals and services. By the mid-1840s, certain Anglicans in England and America had advanced their rituals to such a degree that they drew prominent attacks from within and without the denomination, and these attacks helped identify and systematize the various Roman flowers popping up in Protestant worship as a class. Our Presbyterian pamphleteer in Burlington, New Jersey, satirically named the pattern "Newmania," after John Henry Newman, a leading Oxford theologian who had recently converted to Catholicism. In an 1845 booklet on the subject, this pamphleteer targeted the "rubrical and ritual changes" that had taken place under Episcopal bishop George Doane, in order to denounce their "Romeward heresy." The author identified sixteen new "foot-tracks" of this "extraordinary monster" across New Jersey's parishes, ranging from "daily prayers in the church" to "the affectation of FEAST DATES"; from the use of church "Processions" to "Preaching in the Surplice" rather than in the traditional black gown. Not all of the innovations identified would gain broad popularity, but by linking all of these concurrent changes as part of a larger system, the writer illustrated that new altar decorations, new prayers, and new postures were not simply innocent aberrations in his neighbors' worship. Two years later, an Episcopal editor pleaded the same case with many of the same exhibits. Defending himself against the charge of "magnifying trifles," the editor explained that when the various "new usages" in church worship were "viewed in connection with each other," it could be seen that they possessed a single "voice and aim" as "dangerous whisperers of Roman falsehood in the ears of the people." Examples of these "new usages" entering Episcopal churches included ministers' adoption of the white linen surplice, the treatment of the Communion table as an altar, "Kneeling at the Communion," and the "observance of saints' days." From "their resemblance to Roman practices," the author continued, such outward gestures "beget Romish views, and Romish feelings." Their multiplication "completes the drapery of Romanism itself." These and other critics sounded an anti-

Catholic alarm, outlining a concerted slide toward "popery" in the details of Protestant worship.[21]

By the 1860s, Anglican worship experiments had advanced to extreme heights. Denominational debates now centered on the term and concept of "ritualism," as advocates emphasized the need for impressive forms over precise doctrines. Boston and New York City held the nation's leading "ritualist" congregations, which offered sensational spectacles that began to rival Catholic churches in public attention. In 1868, an "old-fashioned churchman" published a thorough review of a ritualist service for the readers of *Putnam's Magazine*. His subject was St. Alban's Episcopal Church, New York, an unassuming Gothic building on the city's northern end. Drawn by rumors of its advanced "ceremonial observances," the author attended one Sunday morning's services. Arriving early, the author was immediately struck by the interior arrangement and decorations. He particularly marveled at the elevated chancel with its ornate altar pressed against the rear wall. On the altar sat a "large gilded cross" flanked by two towering candles, with several more candlesticks and candelabras surrounding the display, though none of the candles were yet lighted. An organ's tune signaled the beginning of worship, when a remarkable procession emerged from the front vestry room. Several boys wearing white robes and carrying a cross and banners led the way, followed by the adult choir in full song. As they advanced toward their places in the chancel, "three officiating priests or ministers" brought up the rear, wearing "purple-velvet, crown-shaped caps on their heads, and white garments, made like sacks, and ornamented with various colors and symbols." The party made un-Protestant-like bows as they passed the altar, and one boy ceremoniously lit the chancel's candles. A minister then began reading the service, and at one point he announced "a high celebration" to be held in the church during that week. After a fair sermon and the passing of the offering plates, the officiating party prepared the elements for Communion. After some bowing and whispering, the priests invited the congregation forward to kneel at the chancel rails in order to receive the bread and wine. Concluding prayers and songs followed, and the whole congregation stood to watch the line of altar boys, choristers, and priests disappear back into the vestry.[22]

The author was left to wonder about the future of the Episcopal Church. He granted that many regular members of St. Alban's congregation appeared "exceedingly devout" but found that "a large portion" were "visitors, drawn by curiosity, and anxious to see the strange and novel things, as they seemed, in an Episcopal church." From the opening to the closing procession, the service had employed so many controversial details of Roman Catholic worship that visitors burst into discussion outside the church's doors. Among those "with old-fashioned notions and habits," the author felt that "it was no matter of astonishment . . . to hear the charge of 'popery,' folly, extravagance, &c., made freely against St. Alban's." The church's decorated altar, colorful ministers, attentive altar boys, obeisances, processions, and daytime candles seemed "to an ordinary looker-on, very much resembling the public performances in a Roman Catholic church." The author refused to condemn all the innovations outright, but he did end his report by questioning "how far all this is to go." Battle lines had been publicly drawn, and for those Protestants inclined toward appropriation, St. Alban's demonstrated that there were now few limits to a congregation's options.[23]

Unlikely as it may have seemed at the time, many of these controversial elements of worship soon entered evangelical churches. Building on the successes of musical innovations, holidays, and bold Episcopal examples, evangelicals faced their own debates over "ritualism." In 1867, the *New York Observer* published an article titled "Presbyterian Ritualism" that warned, "The evil tendency of this system is not confined to the . . . Episcopal Church in this country. The leaven is spreading itself among the non-prelatical churches of the United States." Two years later, a trade magazine celebrated the fact that "Protestant churches, by recently rapid movements, brought on by curious and remarkable religious reactions, are, with the zest of Romanists, reinstating the gorgeous rituals and reviving the beautiful decorations of the past, now most strikingly represented by the

Roman Catholic churches, and that ritual form of the Protestant Episcopal known as High-Church." In turn, these "reactions" were creating an unprecedented market for "church fixtures or decorative gas-fittings, pew-fittings, pulpits, altars, stalls, lecterns [*sic*], . . . vestments, . . . surplices, chasubles, albs, cassocks, etc.; also altar-cloths, . . . [and] sacred vessels of brass, silver, gold, etc.," among other products. An "ex-clergyman" blamed this revival on America's ministers, who "all and everywhere are tending to Romanism; its mummeries, ceremonies and services, are more or less attractive to every priestly eye." The clergy certainly played a key role in instituting the changes, but they relied upon the volunteer and monetary contributions of the laity as altar guilds, choristers, musicians, holiday decorators, vestrymen, and attendees. When lightning did not strike St. Alban's and other radical Episcopal churches, evangelical congregations from the urban centers outward began adopting aspects of Catholicism's enviable religious "drapery."[24]

The primary locus for evangelical changes was the Communion table. Each congregation approached this sacramental center in its own way, but Congregationalists, Baptists, Methodists, and Presbyterians increasingly treated the table as something of an altar in practice if not in name. An altar was a place of spiritual sacrifice rather than a mere prop, and as such it invited decorative reverence. The popularity of Gothic Revival architecture, with its distinct chancels, facilitated the rise of this ritual center. Such changes consistently drew critics, for, in the words of a Presbyterian pastor from Philadelphia, "What has an altar to do in a Protestant place of worship?" Evangelicals denied the Catholic claim that priests could reenact Christ's spiritual sacrifice at Mass, thereby negating any need for altars, and they turned to the Bible's description of the Last Supper for evidence that Jesus intended his sacrament to be performed at a table. But while the theology made for an imperfect fit, the aesthetic appeal of altars fit well, so evangelicals moved to raise their Communion tables and lavish their chancels with protective, embroidered linens, with flowers representing life and rebirth, and with candles radiating God's presence and truth.[25]

Advertisement for church furnishings, from J. & R. Lamb Co., New York City, New York. From *Methodist Quarterly Review* 59 (January 1877): facing p. 3. Courtesy of the William Smith Morton Library, Union Theological Seminary and Presbyterian School of Christian Education, Richmond, Virginia.

These items first entered evangelical churches during celebrations and newly recognized holidays. In 1863, *Harper's New Monthly Magazine* noted that "Easter flowers are making their way into churches of all persuasions. One of our chief Presbyterian churches near by decked its communion-table and pulpit with flowers for the third time this Easter season." The author endorsed these changes on the familiar grounds of anti-Catholicism and cultural refinement, arguing, "We can make no greater mistake than to take it for granted that religion must be of necessity rude and ugly, and leave to superstition and priestcraft the work of illustrating that there is such a thing as the beauty of holiness." And a year earlier, a comment in an article in the *Continental Monthly* illustrated the new interchangeability of the concepts of altar and Communion table: "Flowers on the altar are most appropriate and significant, but strict attention should be paid to their symbolism. For the communion-table there are lilies of the valley, and in its season, the rosy snow of the blooming fruit-trees." Church photographs taken a few decades later show the results of these changes. A picture from a Methodist church in Orange City, Florida, shows a chancel area decorated for Easter morning. Lilies and other flowers are strewn about the scene in vases, on the Communion table, and interwoven among the Communion railings. And a picture of Union Baptist Church in Mystic, Connecticut, shows a view down the center aisle to a decorated Communion table with flowers in the shape of cross on either side of chancel opening. As these fixtures migrated from special occasions into ordinary worship services, new groups sprang up in congregations to maintain the arrangements—often ladies' "circles" or "societies," the forerunners to formal altar guilds.[26]

In 1877, an "old" Virginia Presbyterian presented a thoughtful meditation on the change. He told how "after nearly a half century of wandering," he returned to "the up-country village" where he was born. There, he visited the Presbyterian church in which he was brought up, "where the faith once committed to the saints was, in those days, kept by noble old Scotch Christians." Entering its "new and stately building" on a "peaceful summer Sunday morning," he

Interior of a Methodist church in Orange City, Florida, 1880s, decorated
with flowers and crosses for Easter. Image PR07914, Florida Photographic
Collection, State Archives of Florida, Tallahassee, Florida.

found that "on the communion table before the pulpit was a vase of
fresh and glorious flowers, filling the great building with delicious
perfume." He paused, remarking, "I know that the stout old elder
on whose lap I remember many a time sitting in childhood, and the
mighty Scotch divine, who was a neighboring pastor, often conduct-
ing services in that church, would have had more than hesitation in
their day in permitting that perfume; for they would have been un-

able to see exactly the difference between the odor of the summer blossoms and the sweet incense from a golden censer." He imagined that the venerable pastor "would have thundered in his broadest Scotch dialect, 'You might as well put a gay cloth on the table and set candles on it and call it an altar.'" The visitor then admitted, "I am not quite clear myself, even in these days of greater enlightenment, that they were not correct, so far as this, that the flowers and the altar-cloths, the incense and the candles, all originate in the same idea." He was cryptic in explaining what he meant exactly by this "idea," but he ultimately recommended the flowers at least, for "we all like the flowers" and "their use is one of the most beautiful acts of reverence for the house of God and the services of the Church."[27]

Decorative caution lingered well into the twentieth century, but the question by then had become one of degree. One 1950 work, *Arranging Church Flowers*, offered a practical guide for "the Evangelical Protestant churches whose sanctuaries have no visible altar." The author related that flowers first appeared in these churches for "funerals and weddings, then for special occasions and, finally, their use each Sunday has become firmly established." Suggesting arrangements for Easter lilies, the author explained that the flowers might be "flanked on either side by tall old brass cathedral candlesticks bearing heavier-than-usual white candles." Three years later, another evangelical guidebook belatedly observed that "candles are becoming common in non-liturgical churches" and recommended that "if candles are used upon the altar or communion table, they should always be burning during the service of worship." Further, the author explained that "the candlelighter usually wears a robe" to light "the candles on the altar or communion table" and that "a single candle on either side of a cross is the usual arrangement in the Protestant church." Evidence to support the author's claim of the candle-cross-candle custom is illustrated in the pre-1961 seal of a Methodist Church altar guild, which pictured a solid altar with a decorative cloth supporting a cross flanked by two lit candles. Whether or not this could fairly be called the "usual arrangement" among all Protestants, it is clear that by the beginning of the twentieth century, a Catholic vocabu-

Methodist Church altar guild seal, showing an altar with linens, a cross, and two flanking candles. From Arnett and Clark, *Methodist Altars*, title page. Courtesy of the William Smith Morton Library, Union Theological Seminary and Presbyterian School of Christian Education, Richmond, Virginia.

lary directed the decoration of Protestant chancels throughout the year.[28]

Evangelical ministers personally reflected this ceremonial turn in their growing use of decorative vestments and church processions. Academic black gowns, suits of "parsons' gray," or street clothes served as the typical minister's dress into the early nineteenth century. But following Episcopal experiments with white surplices and then colored vestments, the pastor's dress became generally more reflective of the priest's. These changes corresponded with the increasing refinement of the chancel area, and they added color to new seasonal celebrations, even if they implied a widening of the divide between minister and congregation. In 1955, a pastor and his coauthor summarized changes in America's "nonconformist" dress and found that "gowns are now almost universal in the pulpits of America with the exception of the Pentecostal sects." They cited the example of one ministerial job applicant opposed to gowns who soon discovered—in an ironic turn of phrase—"that when one was in Rome it was best to don Roman garb." Advocating a variety of colors and symbols for these new robes, the authors acknowledged some remaining resistance to such features but argued that they "gave a dignity to a service which was lacking, at least in part, without it." Methodist ministers generally took to such changes first, ultimately adopting the alb, an ancient Roman robe extending to the feet and often tied with rope at the waist, along with the stole, a long, decorated scarf hung around the neck and extending to the knees. Methodists were followed by Congregationalists and Presbyterians, some of whom eventually began coordinating garments with the color of the season of the Christian year and with matching sets of altar cloths. As seen today at Richmond's Ginter Park Baptist Church, many Baptists remained hesitant to join the movement. Still, like decorated chancels, ministerial vestments had entered general usage by the early twentieth century.[29]

In turn, the evangelical laity contributed to worship changes in both the processions and in the pews, beyond their decorative activities. Although acolytes and choir vestments remained rare in evangelical churches until the turn of the century, choirs gained broad prominence in processionals, seatings, and services. The earliest choirs of men and women in America had not been robed, and they often stood behind congregations in lofts or balconies. By the mid-1800s, several ritualistic Episcopal churches had introduced "boychoirs" wearing white surplices. These were deemed more historically appropriate for chancel seating and for singing choral services than mixed choirs of men and women. The two traditions eventually merged, with white surplices giving way to different types of choir robes and mixed choirs regularly participating in Sunday services, though their seating locations varied from congregation to congregation. In 1892, a Brooklyn newspaper described the local St. Thomas's Episcopal Church as one of the first in the area to adopt "a vested choir of boys, men and women." They all wore "cassock and cotta," and the women marched with the men and boys in the singing of the processional hymns. Their list of names reveals that most of the choir's women were unmarried "misses," possibly highlighting their relative youth or independence. Another Episcopal church in the area hazarded a vested choir of "forty men and boys and six women," in which the women also joined in the processional hymns, "marching to and from the choir room to their seats in the chancel, preceded by the crucifer bearing a processional cross." Such processionals could be as controversial as the sight of women in cassocks. New York's

Robed Baptist choir with male and female members, circa 1910.
"Choir, First Baptist Church, Easter, St. Paul," Photograph Collection,
location no. B1.32p22, Minnesota Historical Society, St. Paul, Minnesota.

famed Trinity Episcopal Church began hosting processional hymns as
early as 1866, though other parishes like St. Paul's Episcopal Church
in Buffalo waited until around 1890 to institute cross-led processionals. Catholics, long accustomed to robed choirs and processionals,
viewed the vesting of women in Protestant choirs with alarm. In 1888,
the *Catholic World* denied the propriety of "surpliced women" but
held that "the [vested] sanctuary choir of men and boys belongs properly to the Catholic Church; she owns it, and when others adopt it
they are but wearing borrowed plumage in this matter as they do in
many others, for whatever is best and most praiseworthy in Protestantism it has stolen from the Catholic Church and tried to make its
own." Nevertheless, mixed, robed Protestant choirs did represent an
important and lasting innovation.[30]

Among the audiences, a newfound interest in devout postures arose, leading many to adopt the habit of kneeling during prayers or sacraments rather than standing or sitting. Episcopalians and many Methodists had always accepted kneeling as appropriate during public worship. Methodist tradition called for kneeling at confession, ministers' ordinations, the baptismal prayer, and the Lord's Supper, though the denomination's *Discipline* acknowledged this as a tender subject: "Let those who have scruples concerning the receiving of [the sacrament] kneeling be permitted to receive it either standing or sitting." For Presbyterians, Congregationalists, and Baptists, this previously suspect posture suddenly emerged as a popular option. In 1846, "A Presbyterian" explored the subject in the *New York Observer*. The author acknowledged dissenters' traditional "opposition to kneeling" but then cited several scriptural sources in favor of the practice during prayer. Dismissing the argument of "inconvenience," the author advocated the posture "above all others" for public prayers, given its humility and reverence. Prejudice against this position was strong; "because the corrupt communion of Rome, and what some consider the imperfectly reformed Church of England, in all its branches, have strenuously maintained the posture of kneeling in prayer," certain evangelicals "feel bound to reject it." But the author held the course and even suggested that it could be appropriate to kneel at Communion. Three years later, the General Assembly of the Presbyterian Church U.S.A. officially advocated "the posture of standing in public prayer, and . . . kneeling in private prayer," as "indicated by examples in Scripture." But calls for public kneeling continued, as exemplified by one Baptist advocate in 1857. He explained, "According to our former custom, we stood in prayer, and sat in singing." Lately, the positions had reversed, he noted, with the result that "our congregations sit, too commonly, gazing about irreverently, while the minister is offering up solemn petitions and adoration." The writer complained that therefore the "solemnity of our service is diminished" and advised, "To kneel in prayer is exceedingly appropriate, and I wish it could be universally adopted." Hymns also referenced a new disposition to kneel. For example, an 1872 Baptist hymnal included one number reading, "Come at the morning hour, / Come, let us kneel and pray." The growing presence of prayer-desks and wooden "kneelers" in the pews attested to the spread of this practice. Thus the churches' new atmospheres swept the behavior of the congregations along with them, inspiring physical devotion even as observers ridiculed the routine kinesthetics of their Catholic and Episcopal counterparts. Though evangelical Protestants continued to maintain that their communions did not host the real body and blood of Jesus Christ, their new, reverent postures indicated that something greater than mere decoration had transferred with the churches' altars, candles, holidays, and processions.[31]

"Popery" and Its Flowers

By 1900, Protestant churches had largely assimilated their new spiritual tools. Plucked from larger Catholic contexts, the innovations excluded many other common Catholic fittings. Holy water and oils were not welcomed into Protestant churches. Incense appealed to certain Episcopalians, but for most Protestants, fragrant censers were not adopted. And the use of the Latin tongue for worship services remained beyond consideration. Refashioned Protestant additions also differed from their original settings in terms of degree. Again, barring a few minor exceptions, Protestants did not erect superaltars or tabernacles on their Communion tables; they did not establish multiple altars within their sanctuaries; nor did their ministers tend to don as much finery as the Catholic hierarchy. And Protestant processions appeared as rather tame affairs in contrast to some of the lavish trains that led into many Catholic churches, especially those found in immigrant communities. The two traditions' worship environments had narrowed considerably, but there still remained essential differences to fire the arguments of denominational critics.

The root of these differences hinged on conceptions of the supernatural. Whereas Catholics routinely celebrated the activities in their sanctuaries as miraculous, mainline Protestants tended to regard God as more removed. In Catholic worship, Protestants sensed the power of certain objects and motions to move their spirits toward God, without accepting the church's underlying claim that such objects and motions also brought God closer to them. Thus their selections and translations from Catholicism shared certain characteristics, limiting direct access to the sacred. First, the selections centered on the senses of sight and hearing rather than the more intimate senses of touch, smell, or taste. While Catholic churchgoers dipped fingers into holy water basins, breathed in frankincense, and swallowed Christ's body and blood each week, mainline Protestants preferred to savor devotional atmospheres with their eyes and ears, except on extraordinary occasions like baptism. At the same time, Protestants also favored arts that allowed for lay involvement, thereby downplaying the role of a sanctified priesthood. Choirs reflected the laity's participation in ceremonies, while altar guilds, sewing clubs, Sunday schools, and individual donors worked behind the scenes to prepare church furnishings and seasonal celebrations. Finally, Protestants tended to square their innovations with biblical teachings and precedents, shunning practices that hinted at mere "superstition." This was not a fine science but an opening for debate, though most congregations could agree on the unscriptural status of multiple altars, tributes to saints' relics, and certain authority-bound sacraments like penance and unction. As a result, the only miracle taking place in mainline Protestant sanctuaries continued to be the effect of God's grace on individual souls—an action that paradoxically depended to a greater and greater degree upon the soft, external atmosphere of worship. In the right light, God touched believers, even if believers could not touch him.

Worship conflicts and differences still lingered around those Protestant innovations that had been selected. As urban models of high ritual and festival rippled out across the countryside, they left a great deal of conservative tension among the denominations in their wake. The Episcopal Church hosted debates over the movement into the 1870s, when a portion of the traditionalist clergy and laity spun off in protest. As late as 1895, a Presbyterian seminary professor from Virginia struggled against church organs and the like, exclaiming, "What madness is it to come down from that lofty elevation on which

God and the blood of our martyred fathers have placed us, to go into the market and bid for men with the gew-gaws and follies of those who, we say, are totally apostate or only half reformed!" Indeed, the churches' new "gew-gaws and follies" might have spurred deeper changes in denominational beliefs. Yet, given the care shown in the selection and installation of new features, the items proved able to sustain Protestant piety while engaging Catholicism, the world of the market, and the hearts of worshippers. Vital differences continued to mark the settings of Protestant worship, but the experiments in the latter half of the nineteenth century had established a general baseline of acceptability for certain Rome-inspired flowers. This baseline would allow for gentle jokes about the threat posed by altar bouquets, and it would offer a common store of devotional arts from which churches like Ginter Park Baptist Church now draw.[32]

Church flowers helped galvanize the earlier symbolic and architectural appropriations. Crosses and Gothic Revival architecture largely addressed the streets, but Roman ceremonial helped integrate all of these features into the weekly devotions of worshippers. This often occurred literally, as when crosses were held aloft at the head of processions or when choral cantatas reverberated beneath high, pointed ceilings. As changes in one element of design activated others, contemporary observers noticed the connections. For example, in 1853, an editor for *Putnam's Monthly* found that "there would be no great difficulty in tracing the tendency to purple chasubles in many of our Protestant clergy, to the mediaevalisms in church edifices which have been introduced among us during the past twenty years." It seemed "a natural result" that "those who rebuild the churches of the fourteenth century, will also desire to revive the worship to which they were consecrated." But these concurrent impulses did not spring from a desire to replicate historic stage sets; rather, their interplay marked efforts to create dynamic sanctuaries. Throughout the nineteenth century, envious anti-Catholic onlookers had attacked the whole drapery of "Romanism"—its symbolic, ritual, and architectural traditions, as well as its theology and church polity. From a sensory standpoint, it became necessary for Protestant churches to adopt a broad spectrum of material in order to meet the rising seductions classified as "popery." If few congregations verbalized such a strategy, the plain harmony among these design changes revealed its own end.[33]

The rise of Roman Catholicism presented only one struggle that America's Baptists, Congregationalists, Presbyterians, Methodists, and Episcopalians faced. As the nineteenth century unfolded, Protestant denominations contended with internal theological splintering, the advancing authority of science, the lures of commercial society, battles over women's rights, and the war over slavery and reconstruction. Each struggle threatened to upset the denominations' unique visions of Christian progress. The uplift of de-Romanized art helped address these other issues. It buoyed Protestantism with a meaningful trademark in the Latin cross, with an expression of tradition and authority in Gothic architecture, and with the potential for refined religiosity in lush worship. In sum, it enhanced Protestantism's position while offsetting the strengths of surrounding stages. For the restless rich, these middle-ground appropriations may not have gone far enough, spurring escapist antiquarian fascinations. For the wary poor, the changes may have gone too far toward worldly means, encouraging a turn toward Fundamentalism. But for the mass of America's Protestants, the changes ultimately brought a satisfying compromise. Without altering the status of the clergy or overturning theological assumptions, the appropriations had outfitted the churches with a durable new identity.

Roman Catholics responded to the appropriations in several ways. On one hand, militants like Archbishop John Hughes of New York City sought to outdistance Protestant developments with grander, more brilliant churches and ceremonies. In contrast, others like pattern-book architect Charles Sholl sought to help beleaguered parishes blend into the architectural fabric of their communities with practical designs matching "the taste and style of our times and country." Behind differing solutions lay a common acknowledgment that surprising artistic developments had overtaken Protestant churches. In 1879, the brash *Catholic World* mulled over the changes, posing the natural question: "Why has this reformation taken place?" Its response—typically jingoistic—held a kernel of truth in the conclusion that "Catholicism has forced Protestantism to wear its 'Sunday best.'" Appropriations had not dampened rivalry on either side; when Catholicism's "monopoly" on sanctified religious art eased, the nation's denominational machinery moved on to other, familiar debates.[34]

Within the machinery, individuals found the possibilities for their faith enriched. Those Protestants so inclined could now approach God through several new channels from the comforts of their own communions. From St. Mary's Episcopal Church in Burlington, to Hanover Street Congregational Church in Boston, to First Presbyterian Church in Philadelphia, and to Ginter Park Baptist Church in Richmond, a fresh store of churchly sights, sounds, and occasions activated personal devotions. The altar of the Methodist Church in Orange City, Florida, pictured in the 1880s photograph as lovingly decorated with Easter adornments, illustrates where its parishioners turned to cultivate the beauty of holiness, thereby offering their prayers another dimension.

So the same ugliness and competition that drove American anti-Catholicism also helped bring forth an apparent elevation of Protestant devotion. That most worshippers would soon forget the source of these changes does not dampen their ultimate promise. Around the sanctuaries, at least, where there had once stood cannons and militias, there now budded flowers. Art had done its share—greater changes would lie beyond the reach of the material world.

Epilogue

A wave of revivalism swept through America's Catholic parishes during the mid-nineteenth century. Led by traveling, charismatic priests, these "missions" featured thunderous preaching and prayers aimed at awakening the souls of the attendees. The revivals drew from established European traditions, but they also mirrored a practice perfected by generations of American Protestants. Indeed, their conspicuous similarities led some Catholics to complain that the popular missions were "an imitation of the old Methodist revivals." Clearly, denominational accommodation could run in more than one direction. Earlier in the century, lay trustees in various Catholic parishes throughout the country had claimed the right to control church finances and to appoint or dismiss their own priests. This democratic initiative, which reflected the customs of neighboring Protestants, soon clashed with the church's hierarchy and produced an extended battle over parish control. Other examples abound: the furnishings in Catholic family parlors began reflecting the pious advice given by such Congregational daughters as Catherine Beecher and Harriet Beecher Stowe; Catholic "summer schools" and Chautauqua-like institutes popped up in response to successful Protestant lecture programs; and by the twentieth century, Southern-style gospel music echoed throughout many Catholic parishes. Such exchanges only hint at the cross-pollination that has taken place among America's denominations.[1]

Though the Protestant appropriation of Catholic art was only one element among these encounters, it proved to be a decisive element. For it articulated a shift in the very nature of the church itself. Among earlier generations of America's Congregationalists, Presbyterians, and Baptists, the definition of a "church" centered on people, not a building or an institution. A "church" consisted solely of a closed body of believers, sometimes described as a fellowship of saints or God's "elect." As seen in colonial churches' recorded minutes, the vision of such groups focused squarely on the activities of their own respective memberships—on their births, deaths, conversions, transfers, and excommunications. Meetinghouses held significance for such congregations, but they rarely interfered with the believers' concept of their bonds.

After the mid-nineteenth century, the "church" had become more of a place. Aspects of the older concept remained, but members could now talk of "going to church," of attending their spiritual home rather than strictly embodying it themselves. Further, these new institutions increasingly engaged the ranks of sinners or unbelievers surrounding them, as membership boundaries eased and audiences widened. Part of this change had to do with the softening of old Calvinistic beliefs in predestination, and part of it resulted from the expansion of denominational resources. But the shift hinged upon the new church buildings themselves. Roman Catholics in Europe and America had long balanced spiritual and material concepts of the "church" by emphasizing a universal body of believers set within an essential context of sacred worship facilities. When Protestants adopted the products of this balance, skimming the recognizably "sacred" qualities from Catholic chapels, they fixed their turn away from an exclusive society, toward public institution. As church spaces grew more and more distinct from houses and other buildings in their crosses, stained glass, ceremonial candles, and the like, they became focal points for congregations, as well as instruments to perpetuate the same. This new art played into traditional rivalries, but it also refashioned the self-definition of the participants.

As these effects settled in the early twentieth century, apprehension over the changes lingered. Nostalgia for an earlier, seemingly more pure faith has been a common religious theme, especially among American Protestants, and several commentators viewed the church design changes through this lens. "Protestantism was built on the preacher and not the performer," lamented one Methodist pastor from Pennsylvania. Writing in 1902, he stated, "Once we had plain people, and the worship agreed with their simple lives and tastes," but "now we have cathedrals." The demand for refinement was partly responsible, as Methodists abandoned "the naturalness and often rudeness of the Spirit-moved man for the ordered and ornate ceremonies more agreeable to the finer few who attend our grander temples." He listed more innovations, making it clear that he was also grappling with his church's relation to Rome: "We had a hymn book; we have a hymnal. We once took a collection; now it is the offering, and the choir gives us the offertory." There were more: set forms, "a liturgical service with no sermon for the communion day," as well as "vested choirs and processionals and recessionals." The pastor asked, "If a little ritual creates a craving for more[,] is it wise to set in our members a taste that will take them where they can get all they want of this diet of forms?" The question was inevitable—where would appropriation lead and where would it stop? Yet by the time of his writing, the trend was already halting. The vast majority of members displayed great satisfaction in their limited, measured Catholic selections. These had helped transform their churches, but it was no less of a transformation than that of the country around them.[2]

As a specific result, we are left with a common catalog of churchly fixtures. The catalog's piecemeal quality has allowed for its adoption by radically different congregations. And it has thrived alongside such later artistic currents as the Colonial Revival and modernist innovations. This catalog has assumed such a sheen that its combination of arches, colored glass, sanctuary flowers, and organs have spread from churches to other structures attempting to strike a spiritual pose, including funeral parlors, amusement-park sets, and Las Vegas wedding chapels. Other consequences have followed: the catalog aided the separation of church and state by helping to carve ideal visual boundaries between the two. It also spurred the network of retailers, advertisers, and consumers through new festivals, new products, and a new religious "brand." Further, it may have made assimilation more difficult for Jews and newcomers from Asia, India, and the Middle East who struggled against hardening notions of what religious worship should look like. "The cult of the Gothic Revival," as described by the Presbytery of Chicago in 1953, as well as its related symbols, "the cross, the cup, and the candlestick," as described by the *Christian Examiner* in 1849, remain a defining presence. In this catalog's long, vibrant legacy, there is as much mystery as in the original artistic exchange.

An important aspect of the story remains elusive—that of the exchange's international context. It is clear that leading artists and critics wielded influence on both sides of the Atlantic and beyond. To what extent did international factors shape the results? In Great Britain, a similar convergence of anti-Catholic hostilities, Gothic Revival art, and Protestant "ritualism" accompanied the resurgence of the Roman Catholic Church. Yet the dynamic was not the same as in America. England had a powerful, state-controlled church, and its Gothic Revival, rooted in the country's own historic traditions, involved issues of national identity that were absent in the United States. France and Germany followed England with their own medieval revivals that were also tied to patriotism and nationalism. In all three countries, romantic literature and industrial prosperity inspired the artistic changes, though architects on the Continent focused on the restoration of old landmarks rather than the construction of new edifices as in Great Britain and America. In Germany, a religiously divided country, a midcentury outburst of anti-Catholicism shared many qualities with its English and American cousins, but it is unclear what effect this might have had on the country's Protestant worship. In North America, Canada presented an even more mixed scenario. Its neo-Gothic churches and Catholic institutions played directly into American developments, and there is evidence that Canada's own Protestant churches also struggled with Catholic art. For example, in 1840, a Presbyterian newspaper in Ontario featured an article bemoaning the spread of crosses into "Protestant places of worship," since the symbol was known as "the *sign of the beast*, the *armorial bearings* of Popish Rome." Yet while Canada's Protestant churches may have felt related pressures, the country's long-standing divided English and French heritage was radically different from the situation in the United States, where the Catholic Church had previously had few footholds. So it is difficult to make direct comparisons. Americans continuously drew important ideas from Europe and Canada, but their country was unique in its Protestant history and its lack of a medieval past. The evidence suggests that American churches adopted the dress of Gothic architecture and ritualistic worship for their own pressing reasons.[3]

A fitting summary of this mixed heritage and inspired localism can be found in the windows of New York City's Riverside Church. This Baptist-based congregation, led by notable philanthropists and a progressive preacher, sought to establish a monumental new home in 1926. By then, choir robes, candles, and crosses were common. The Gothic Revival had received fresh energy at the hands of Boston architect Ralph Adams Cram, who suggested that churchbuilders pick up where the fifteenth century had left off to create their own Gothic wonders. The decade also witnessed renewed anti-Catholicism, stirred by Italian immigration and reflected in immigration restrictions, a revival of the Ku Klux Klan, and the controversial presidential campaign of New York's Roman Catholic governor, Al Smith. These conflicts had largely become divorced from attacks on Catholic churches or "Catholic" church art, and the leaders of Riverside Church turned to the graceful French Gothic for inspiration, adopting the medieval cathedral at Chartres as a model for much of the plan.

When the builders considered window designs, they decided to duplicate those of the revered cathedral precisely. After the high windows were installed—such as one luminous portrait of St. James—critics found that the artists had indeed re-created the originals, including every crazed fracture that had subsequently appeared and then been repaired over the centuries with lead lines. Other American churches were not so precise in their appropriations. Still, this installation—this apparently naive faithfulness to the windows' centuries-old fractures—illustrates the complexities inherent in borrowing. Did Riverside's builders intend to re-create the original designs or the modern surfaces? Did they understand the history embedded in their models? Would it have made a difference in their approach? Or are the designs, with or without repairs, somehow transcendent, or universal? Undoubtedly, the windows' red and blue colors reflect the light beautifully, and their tones and technique represent a modern artistic achievement. The windows gleam with a new light, hiding their secrets well.[4]

Notes

Chapter One

1 Philadelphia *Native American*, quoted in Billington, *Protestant Crusade*, 225 (first quotation); "Local Affairs" (last quotations).

2 Mickle, *Gentleman of Much Promise*, 2:445 (first quotation); *Full Particulars of the Late Riots*; *Address of the Catholic Lay Citizens*, 3 (last quotation). For overviews of the riots, see Billington, *Protestant Crusade*, 220–37, and Feldberg, *Philadelphia Riots of 1844*.

3 Stanton, *Gothic Revival*, 91–115; Pierson, *American Buildings and Their Architects*, 2:184–95; Downs, "America's First 'Medieval' Churches"; R. A. Smith, *Philadelphia As It Is In 1852*.

4 Thomas E. Peck, quoted in Melton, *Presbyterian Worship in America*, 69.

5 Standard accounts of the Gothic Revival include Stanton, *Gothic Revival*; Pierson, *American Buildings and Their Architects*, vol. 2; Andrews, *American Gothic*; and Loth and Sadler, *Only Proper Style*. An exception to this model can be found in Early, *Romanticism and American Architecture*, 112–36.

   The primary reference on American anti-Catholicism is Billington, *Protestant Crusade*. Later studies, such as David Brion Davis, "Some Themes of Counter-Subversion," and Franchot, *Roads to Rome*, de-emphasized the literal Protestant/Catholic clash, treating the antagonism as a mirror for Protestant insecurities.

   Recent histories of Catholicism include Dolan, *American Catholic Experience*; Orsi, *Madonna of 115th Street*; and Kane, *Separatism and Subculture*. Recent histories of evangelicalism include Butler, *Awash in a Sea of Faith*; Hatch, *Democratization of American Christianity*; Schneider, *Way of the Cross Leads Home*; Heyrman, *Southern Cross*; and Frey and Wood, *Come Shouting to Zion*.

   Examples of worship histories include Tucker, *American Methodist Worship*; Melton, *Presbyterian Worship in America*; James F. White, *Protestant Worship*; and Taves, *Household of Faith*. James F. White presented a radical example of this scholarly divide by claiming that after around 1570, "Protestant and Catholic worship existed in virtually airtight isolation until after World War II" (White, *Christian Worship in North America*, 6).

6   For evidence of Protestant/Catholic ambivalence in America, see Billington, *Protestant Crusade*, 18–19; Vance, *America's Rome*; Franchot, *Roads to Rome*; John Davis, "Catholic Envy"; McDannell, *Christian Home in Victorian America*; McDannell, *Material Christianity*; Gerber, "Ambivalent Anti-Catholicism"; and Lears, *No Place of Grace*.

7   For the connections among romanticism, the marketplace, and religion in the early 1800s, see Buggeln, *Temples of Grace*; Kilde, *When Church Became Theatre*; Sweeney, "Meetinghouses, Town Houses, and Churches"; Benes, ed., *New England Meeting House and Church*; Bushman, *Refinement of America*; Schmidt, *Consumer Rites*; and Campbell, *Romantic Ethic*.

8   For the growth of Roman Catholicism in America, see Shaughnessy, *Has the Immigrant Kept the Faith?* 113–36; Finke and Starke, *Churching of America*, 110–15; and Gaustad and Barlow, *New Historical Atlas of Religion in America*, 155–62, 388.

9   "Editor's Drawer," 677 (quotation).

10 "Romanists and the Roman Catholic Controversy," 234 (quotations). For details on the sectional, denominational splits over slavery, see Goen, *Broken Churches, Broken Nation*. John Wolffe ("Anti-Catholicism and Evangelical Identity," 179) suggested that "antagonism to 'popery' served, in a positive as well as a negative sense, to help define evangelical identity" among competing Protestant denominations and organizations on both sides of the Atlantic Ocean.

11 Schmucker, *American Lutheran Church*, 42–43 (quotation). Schmucker also illustrated Lutheran sympathies for anti-Catholicism, proclaiming that his church had been the first to "come out from the Romish Babylon" (p. 43). In contrast, the Episcopal Church, which was comparable to the Lutheran Church in size, received much more denominational attention and inspired many attacks upon its Catholic tendencies.

For Lutheran artistic traditions, see Shelley, *Lewis Miller*, and Milspaw, "Pioneer Churches in Central Pennsylvania." Other Germanic denominations, such as the Moravians, likewise operated under pre-Reformation assumptions regarding art and worship, and their effect upon other denominations' art seems to have been similarly small. See Dillenberger, *Visual Arts and Christianity in America*, 35–36.

12 Gaustad and Barlow, *New Historical Atlas of Religion in America*, 155–62. Overviews of nineteenth-century American Catholic history include

Dolan, *American Catholic Experience*; Debra Campbell, "Catholicism from Independence to World War I"; and Ellis, *American Catholicism*.

13 Tefft, "Day with the Catholics," 281 (quotation).

14 George Washington Doane, quoted in "Bishop Doane and the Oxford Tracts," 454 (quotation). See also Doane, *Life and Writings*, 1:420–21.

15 "C. W. E.," "Our Monthly Gossip," 414.

16 "Editor's Easy Chair," January 1875, 281 (first quotation); E[llis], "Artistic and Romantic View of the Church," 345, 346, 378, 382 (second quotations). This was a Unitarian publication.

Chapter Two

1 My information on church buildings comes from Gaustad, *Historical Atlas of Religion in America*, 43, 103–11, 176, and *Laity's Directory to the Church Service, for the Year of Our Lord MDCCCXXII* (1822), reprinted in "Our Earliest Printed Church History." Population figures are taken from Shaughnessy, *Has the Immigrant Kept the Faith?* 63–73.

2 Gaustad, *Historical Atlas of Religion in America*, 43, 176; *Metropolitan Catholic Almanac*; Shaughnessy, *Has the Immigrant Kept the Faith?* 137–46. The number of buildings listed by state comes from the Seventh Census of the United States, 1850. Although it was issued just three years later, the *Metropolitan Catholic Almanac* offered different figures for some states. For example, this source listed twenty-eight churches in Connecticut and Rhode Island in 1852, while the U.S. Census had only counted nineteen in 1850.

   Membership figures are also under some dispute, as Roger Finke and Rodney Stark have revised Shaughnessy's figures and comparative U.S. proportions slightly downward for the period before 1890. See Finke and Starke, *Churching of America*, 110–5.

3 "Progress of Popery."

4 Morse, *Foreign Conspiracy*; Beecher, *Plea for the West*; "Progress of Popery in the United States" (first and last quotations); Dowling, *History of Romanism*, 642–43; McLeod, *Popery in the United States*; Rufus Clark, *Popery and the United States*, 3, 11 (second quotations); Hogan, *Synopsis of Popery*, 43 (third quotation). See also numerous articles in the *American Protestant Magazine*, including "Roman Catholic Statistics of the U.S." and "Grounds of Hope and Fear." A later example can be found in Barnum, *Romanism As It Is*, 666–72, which drew from figures published in the *Catholic World*.

5 "Progress of the Roman Catholics in the United States," (quotations) (this article was derived from the *Christian Watchman*); Walker, "Reaction in Favor of the Roman Catholics" (this article took its information from the *Laity's Directory for the Year 1837*); "Action and Reaction Between America and Romanism." See also "Roman Catholics," which took its figures from the *Metropolitan Catholic Almanac* for 1848; and "Rapid Increase of Romanism in the United States."

6 "Progress of Popery in Great Britain" (first quotations). "Popery in Britain" (last quotation). This article took its figures from a publication titled *Roman Catholic Directory*. See also Dowling, *History of Romanism*, 644; "Romanism in England"; and "Romanizing Tendency."

7 "*Popery in Wisconsin*" (first quotations); "Summary of Religious News" (second quotation); "Romanism in Cincinnati"; "Letter from Bishop Young," 799–800 (last quotation). See also Dowling's coverage of the Catholic facilities of St. Louis, Missouri, in *History of Romanism*, 643–44, and Barnum's descriptive chapter on Catholic church edifices in *Romanism As It Is*, 543–51.

8 Nevins, *Practical Thoughts*, 212.

9 Spalding, *Lectures on the Evidences of Catholicity*, 194–228.

10 Ibid., 203–7, 226. An example of the Protestant view of these distinctions can be found in Barnes, *Christian Sanctuary*, 16–20.

11 Spalding, *Lectures on the Evidences of Catholicity*, 204, 214–16.

12 Crews, *Presence and Possibility*, 30–40 (quotation); "Roman Catholic Cathedral of the Assumption."

13 Dolan, *American Catholic Experience*; Crews, *Presence and Possibility*, 16–29; *Story of St. Joseph's Proto-Cathedral*; "New Catholic Cathedral, Cincinnati." For the fight over lay trusteeism, see Carey, *People, Priests and Prelates*.

14 Kevin F. Decker, "Grand and Godly Proportions," 23–34, 68; James F. White, *Roman Catholic Worship*; Sholl, *Working Designs for Ten Catholic Churches*. See also "Plan for a Country Church." For the necessary components of a Catholic church from the view of the hierarchy, see O'Connell, *Church Building and Furnishing*.

15 Letter from John Adams to Abigail Adams, October 9, 1774, and diary entry for Sunday, October 9, 1774, Diary 22, John Adams diary, September 4–November 9, 1774, Adams Family Papers electronic archive.

16 Tefft, "Day with the Catholics," 281–83.

17 Ibid.

18 Ibid., 283.

19 Ibid. For another example of a similarly published visitation, see Parton, "Our Roman Catholic Brethren."

20 Breckinridge, *Papism in the XIX. Century*, 175–81. Breckinridge suggested that the Catholics in the crowd thought that the panic was a result of "a premeditated affair—and that a Protestant mob was about to lynch the whole brotherhood." Their fears had foundation. Elsewhere, Catholic property had been targeted for attack, and about twenty years later, Louisville saw a vicious outbreak of anti-Catholic violence. See Crews, *Presence and Possibility*, 41–46.

21 John Davis, "Catholic Envy"; Raguin and Powers, *Sacred Spaces*, 120; Crews, *Presence and Possibility*, 18–20; John Talbot Smith, *Catholic Church in New York*, 1:110–11 (quotations); Kevin F. Decker, "Grand and Godly Proportions," 124.

22 Mickle, *Gentleman of Much Promise*, 2:117, 148–49 (first quotations); Markley, "Memorandum Book 1850–52"; Bradford, "Phoebe George Bradford Diaries," 347–48 (last quotations). See also Steen, "Journal."

23 Lewis Coon, quoted in Kevin F. Decker, "Grand and Godly Proportions," 64.

24 Welby, *Visit to North America*, 168–69 (first quotations). Jobson, *America, and American Methodism*, 380–81 (last quotations).

25 Lattimore, "Recollections of Summer Rambles," 45–48.

26 Breckinridge, *Papism in the XIX. Century*, 56–65.

27 *New York Times* quoted in Pierson, *American Buildings and Their Architects*, 2:262.

28 For interpretations of the fascination for Catholic worship as self-critique or as temporary "release," see Lears, *No Place of Grace*; Franchot, *Roads to Rome*; and John Davis, "Catholic Envy," 108–9 (quotation).

29 "Some Conversions," 816–18.

30 Walworth, "Reminiscences of a Catholic Crisis" (first quotations); John Talbot Smith, *Catholic Church in New York*, 1:111–13 (second quotations); William Harper Bennett, *Catholic Footsteps in Old New York*, 442–44 (last quotations). For Seton's letters, see Seton, *Elizabeth Seton*. For more Catholic conversion narratives, see Hewit, "How I Became a Catholic"; Huntington, *Gropings After Truth*; and Herbert, "Story of a Conversion." Also, for a story showing the ability of Catholic art and worship to recall apostate members, see "At the Church Door."

31 Miller, *Dangers of Education in Roman Catholic Seminaries*, 7 (first quotations); Hogan, *Synopsis of Popery*, 169–70 (second quotations); "Chamber of Imagery in the Church of Rome" (last quotations). See also

E[llis], "Artistic and Romantic View of the Church"; Benjamin M. Smith, *Popery Fulfilling Prophecy*, 36–37; and Walker, "Reaction in Favor of the Roman Catholics," 13.

32 Boardman, "Is There Any Ground?" 11 (first quotation); "Idolatry—Its Origin and Effects," 162 (second quotation); "How Account for the Success of Romanism," 195 (last quotations).

33 Lattimore, "Recollections of Summer Rambles," 47 (quotations). For examples of the polemical "unmasking" of Catholicism's beauties, see [Henderson], *Head and the Heart Enlisted Against Popery*, 86–97, and Cobbin, *Book of Popery*, 5–7.

34 Wightman, "Fundamental Law of Christian Worship," 195.

35 Shaughnessy, *Has the Immigrant Kept the Faith?* 71, 185. In a balanced report, Shaughnessy found that "no reliable statistics are available" for American converts to Catholicism, but his calculations are based on logical formulas that hold true to the few statistics that are available. Due to his interest in European immigration, Shaughnessy explained that "only the white race is to be considered" in his figures, thereby omitting Asians, Native Americans, and African Americans (see ibid., 34–35). He did not compare the number of conversions to Catholicism with the number of conversions from Catholicism. Alternative estimations of conversions to Catholicism could run much higher than those listed by Shaughnessy. Sydney E. Ahlstrom's standard work, *Religious History of the American People* (p. 531), suggested that the number of American converts may have reached 700,000 for the period between 1813 and 1893. See also Barnum, *Romanism As It Is*, 669, and Lord, Sexton, and Harrington, *History of the Archdiocese of Boston*, 2:355.

36 Moore, "Gospel and the Female Sex"; Rameur, "Progress of the Church." Some Episcopal and Unitarian observers defended their proportion of converts by noting that these wanderers had often originally been members of other denominations, including Presbyterianism and Methodism. See Barnum, *Romanism As It Is*, 669–72, and Mines, *Presbyterian Clergyman Looking for the Church*, 512.

37 For lists of notable nineteenth-century American converts to Catholicism, see "Romanizing Tendency," 94; Lord, Sexton, and Harrington, *History of the Archdiocese of Boston*, 3:407–14; John Talbot Smith, *Catholic Church in New York*, 1:114–22; Clarke, "Our Converts"; Young, *Catholic and Protestant Countries Compared*, 592–611; and Curtis, ed., *Some Roads to Rome in America*.

38 Johnston, *Notes on North America*, 259–61.

Chapter Three

1   Hills, *History of the Church in Burlington*, 424–34 (first quotations); A
    Presbyterian, *"One Faith,"* 37, 69 (last quotations). See also Doane, *Life
    and Writings*, 1:104, 402–36. A description of the new plans for St.
    Mary's Church, which included details on the "Greek Cross," appeared
    in the Episcopal *Missionary* prior to the church's completion.

2   Warren, *Causes and the Cure of Puseyism*, 168–69 (first quotation); "Cali-
    fornia," 596 (second quotation); "Cross in Italy" (last quotation). Bur-
    lington's Presbyterian pamphleteer offered an extended discussion of the
    cross's Roman Catholic associations in *"One Faith,"* explaining that "for
    many ages, the Cross has been specially identified with the Church of
    Rome. Some of the ablest commentators have supposed it to be the
    'mark of the beast,' so frequently mentioned in Revelation. It is indeed
    the public and private badge of Anti-christ. . . . It adorns the vestments
    of Popes, Cardinals, Bishops and Priests; it is erected inside and out-
    side of their Churches; it is prominent, both in outward form and by
    manipulation, in all their services of religion, public or private." The au-
    thor warned of "this Papal mark," asserting that "to set up a Cross on a
    Protestant Church is only a declaration that the doctrines of the Refor-
    mation are there growing in less and less repute" (70–72). And a New
    England editor declared that "the idol cross stands as the symbol, not
    of the Gospel that makes free, but of the superstition that debases and
    enslaves" ("Romanists and the Roman Catholic Controversy," 252).
        For the Catholic Church's canon law regarding church symbols, see
    O'Connell, *Church Building and Furnishing*, 5–7, 105–6, and 205–8, and
    England and Rosati, *Ceremonial for the Use of the Catholic Churches*.
        For the Boston cross-burning episode, and for a broader view of
    Protestant violence directed at Roman Catholic churches in America,
    see Billington, *Protestant Crusade*, 305–9.

3   A Presbyterian, *"One Faith,"* 70 (first quotation); Upjohn, *Richard Up-
    john*, 55–56. Bishop Meade's story was recounted by seminary student
    C. A. L. Richards, quoted in Allen, *Phillips Brooks*, 45–46 (last quota-
    tions). For other cross-inspired struggles from the 1840s and 1850s, see
    Clarence E. Walworth, *Oxford Movement in America*, 27–28, and "Diffi-
    culties of the Cross."

4   Ex-Clergyman, *Review of Bishop Ives' "Trials of a Mind,"* 16–17 (first quo-
    tations); *Illustrations of Popery*, facing title page, 4 (second quotations);
    Satanic Plot, cover. The four notable Protestants featured in the image

in *Illustrations of Popery* were listed as "Luther, Zuingle, Cranmer, and Calvin." This image also appeared on the cover of the *American Protestant Magazine* 1 (1845).

5 See Hall, *Dictionary of Subjects and Symbols in Art*, 77–78, and Tyack, *Cross in Ritual, Architecture, and Art*. For the general capacity of religious symbols to cross broad cultural boundaries, see Drummond, *Church Architecture of Protestantism*, 270–312; Goodwin Watson, "Psychologist's View of Religious Symbols"; and Fleming, "Religious Symbols Crossing Cultural Boundaries."

6 "Crosses and Weathercocks on Churches" (first quotations); George Washington Doane, quoted in Hills, *History of the Church in Burlington*, 457, 512–17 (last quotation).

7 For Reformation-based iconoclasm, see Duffy, *Stripping of the Altars*; Michalski, *Reformation and the Visual Arts*; and Dillenberger, *Visual Arts and Christianity in America*, 35–36. In 1643, England's Long Parliament ordered all crosses to be destroyed, with mixed results. See Tyack, *Cross in Ritual, Architecture, and Art*, 152.

8 "Methodist Church Architecture," December 1855, 501 (first quotations). The editor was endorsing the views presented in the Congregational Churches in the United States, *Book of Plans for Churches and Parsonages*, 11. Hopkins, *Essay on Gothic Architecture*, 41 (last quotation). See also Dexter, "Meeting-Houses." For the spread of spires and steeples, see Bushman, *Refinement of America*, 169–80, and Sweeney, "Meetinghouses, Town Houses, and Churches." For the elements of Protestant symbolism used in colonial and early national churches, see Upton, *Holy Things and Profane*; Benes, ed., *New England Meeting House and Church*; Ward, "In a Feasting Posture"; and Owen, "By Design."

9 R. A. Smith, *Smith's Illustrated Guide*, 51 (first quotation); R. A. Smith, *Philadelphia As It Is in 1852*, 299 (second quotation); Berg, *Trapezium* (third quotation). Many scholars have identified the lack of true iconoclasm among early American Protestants. See Ludwig, *Graven Images*; Deetz, *In Small Things Forgotten*; Sweeney, "Meetinghouses, Town Houses, and Churches"; Buggeln, *Temples of Grace*; Dillenberger, *Visual Arts and Christianity in America*; Combs, *Early Gravestone Art*; McDannell, *Material Christianity*, 67–131; and Hambrick-Stowe, *Practice of Piety*, esp. 197–241. The evidence presented in these studies confirms that, except for a handful of scattered appearances, symbolic crosses were not part of the Protestant lexicon until the mid-nineteenth century. For

one exceptional context, see Newman, "Reading the Bodies of Early American Seafarers."

10 "The Cross" (quotation).

11 Nevins, *Practical Thoughts*, 194–95 (first quotations); "Cross in Italy" (last quotation). An example of local attention to Catholic symbols can be found in Whitehead, *Directory of the Borough of Chester*, 33. For Flagg's *A Nun*, see John Davis, "Catholic Envy."

12 Review of Spring, *Attraction of the Cross*, 159.

13 Robins, "With the Nuns," 582 (first quotations); "Cross in Art" (last quotations).

14 W. Jos. Walters, "Catholic, Roman," in Rupp, *Original History of the Religious Denominations*, 154 (first quotation); Gibbons, *Faith of Our Fathers*, 19, 192–93, 202 (last quotations).

15 "Presbuteros," "Presbyterian Ritualism" (first quotation); "Freese," *Episcopalian*, quoted in "Last Gasp of the Anti-Catholic Faction," 850 (last quotation). One Episcopal bishop stated plainly, "The half-way step to image-worship is in the present reverence to the image of the Cross" (Charles McIlvaine, quoted in A Presbyterian, *"One Faith,"* 37).

16 "The Moral Influence of the Cross," 370 (first quotation); "On the Use of Crosses" (second quotation); Dunn, "Power of the Cross," 141 (last quotation). See also Spring, *Attraction of the Cross*, and "Cross Humbles But Elevates."

17 "Symbolism of the Cross" (first quotation); Short, "Symbolism of the Pre-Christian Cross," 612 (second quotation); "The Cross" (last quotations).

18 "Symbolism of the Cross," 659 (quotation); Tyack, *Cross in Ritual, Architecture, and Art*, 14–17. Examples of alternate cross designs were presented in Wills, *Ancient English Ecclesiastical Architecture*, plate 14.

19 Ingham, "Cross of Flowers," 266 (first quotation); R. A. Smith, *Smith's Illustrated Guide*, 80–81 (last quotation). See also McDannell, *Material Christianity*, 120–25. For an excellent example of a cross depicted in a rugged landscape scene, see Thomas Moran's *Mountain of the Holy Cross* (1875).

20 Varnum, "Chapter About Churches (Concluded)"; Wills, *Ancient English Ecclesiastical Architecture*; Stanton, *Gothic Revival*; Pierson, *American Buildings and Their Architects*, 2:152–58, 173–219.

21 Congregational Churches in the United States, *Book of Plans for Churches and Parsonages*, 3, 5, 11, 37–39.

22 George Adams, quoted in Pierson, *American Buildings and Their Architects*, 2:433–45, 480 (first quotation); review of Lyell, *Second Visit to the United States*, 337 (second quotations); Dexter, "Meeting-Houses," 207 (last quotation).

23 "The Cross" (first quotations); Ingham, "Cross of Flowers," 266–67 (last quotations). Endorsement for the Congregationalist *Book of Plans for Churches and Parsonages* can be found in "Methodist Church Architecture," December 1855, 497–98.

24 "Casa Wappy," 295; "Methodist Church Architecture," March 1856, 223; "Editor's Drawer," 677 (first quotations); Ingham, "Cross of Flowers"; "Photo of Mystic Methodist Church"; Howard, *Monumental City*, 36; Maxwell, "St. Paul's Methodist Episcopal Church, Cincinnati," 124 (last quotation).

25 For the Oxford Movement, see Chadwick, *Mind of the Oxford Movement*; Nockles, *Oxford Movement in Context*; Mullin, *Episcopal Vision/American Reality*, 149–77; and Stanton, *Gothic Revival*. For late-nineteenth-century "ritualism" and Anglo-Catholicism, see Holmes, *Brief History of the Episcopal Church*, esp. 103–12, and Chorley, *Men and Movements*. A fine example of an Episcopal debate over the use of the cross can be found in the pamphlet *Puseyite Developments*, 9.

26 Warren, *Causes and the Cure of Puseyism*, 169–70. In 1938, an Episcopal church historian recalled this change: "The use of a cross to mark church buildings . . . did not become general in the United States until after 1840, though a few hardy souls were bold enough to advocate it" earlier —in Trenton, New Jersey, and Poughkeepsie, New York. See Manross, *Episcopal Church in the United States*, 145.

27 Varnum, "Chapter about Churches (Concluded)"; Wills, *Ancient English Ecclesiastical Architecture*, 116–18; A Presbyterian, *"One Faith,"* 37; Vestry minutes, Church of the Ascension, Baltimore, Maryland; Patrick, "Ecclesiological Gothic," 137–38; Gibbons, *Faith of Our Fathers*, 204 (quotation); "Drawing of Church at St. Columba Mission, Gull Lake"; Scammon, "In and Around Astoria," 496.

28 A Presbyterian, *"One Faith,"* 37 (first quotation); Mines, *Presbyterian Clergyman Looking for the Church*, 504–11 (last quotations). See also Hoge, *Moses Drury Hoge*, 90; Melton, *Presbyterian Worship in America*, 61–70; and Presbytery of Chicago, "Report on the Architectural Setting."

29 Minutes of the Board of Trustees of the College of New Jersey, quoted in Greiff, *John Notman*, 30, 49, 125–26.

30 Wayland, *Notes on the Principles*, 153–57 (first quotations); "Church Ded-
    ication in Roxbury, Mass" (last quotation); "West Spruce St.
    Baptist Church"; *Baptist Home Missions in North America*, 168. By the twentieth
    century, Baptist acceptance of the cross had progressed to such a degree
    that Pastor Edwin A. Goldsworthy, in *Plain Thoughts On Worship*, pub-
    lished in 1936, declared the cross to be "the greatest religious symbol of
    man. In most churches the cross has been relegated to a place of mere
    decoration in the woodwork and windows. Can't we see how this great-
    est of all symbols is desecrated by any use which does not place it as the
    focus of attention for all who worship?" (75–78).

31 Withers, *Church Architecture*, xiv (first quotation); Prime, *Holy Cross*,
    137–38 (second quotation).

32 Strong, *Diary*, 38 (quotation). Strong recorded his comment in July
    1844.

33 *Puseyite Developments*, 9 (first quotation); Nevins, *Practical Thoughts*, 93
    (last quotation). For a few Protestant accusations of idolatry, see Benja-
    min M. Smith, *Popery Fulfilling Prophecy*, 28; Dowling, *History of Roman-
    ism*, 259; and Brownlee, *Letters in the Roman Catholic Controversy*, 282.

34 "Methodist Church Architecture," December 1855, 511–12 (quotation).
    The crucifix had appeared in a small number of Episcopal churches by
    the 1870s. At the General Conventions of 1871 and 1874, efforts arose to
    outlaw the use of the crucifix and other ceremonial items that had begun
    to creep into some parishes. See Chorley, *Men and Movements*, 376–92.
    Throughout the twentieth century, the crucifix made broader appear-
    ances in Protestant contexts, as in 1985 when a lone crucifix adorned
    the cover of the *American Baptist Quarterly* 4 (March 1985), without an
    editorial comment. For the role of Mary in Protestant households, see
    McDannell, *Christian Home in Victorian America*, 40–48, 128–45. The
    Wesleys' sculptured heads appeared on Christ's Church, Pittsburgh. For
    more on Protestantism and representations of the human form, see Mor-
    gan, ed., *Icons of American Protestantism*.

Chapter Four

1   "S," "Church Architecture in New-York," 139–40.

2   Ibid., 139 (first quotation); [Cleveland?] "American Architecture," 361,
    369 (second quotations); "Oxford Architecture," 119 (third quotation);
    "Architecture in the United States," 463 (fourth quotation); "New-York
    Church Architecture," 233–34 (fifth quotations); Varnum, "Chapter

About Churches" (sixth quotation); Wayland, *Notes on the Principles*, 156 (seventh quotation); Dexter, "Meeting-Houses," 194 (eighth quotation). In 1910, William F. Gray (*Philadelphia's Architecture*, 346) similarly observed of Philadelphia's architecture that in the nineteenth century, "a transition to Gothic motives in nearly all the churches built gradually took place."

3 "S," "Church Architecture in New-York," 141–42. The writer's identity is unknown, but it seems clear that he or she was not a Roman Catholic. Nor were the writer's comments motivated by a distaste for the Gothic; he or she admired the original medieval architecture and praised the builders' handiwork.

4 Few scholars have explored the Catholic associations of Gothic Revival architecture or the anti-Catholic context in which that architecture arose. Two short exceptions are Early, *Romanticism and American Architecture*, and McDannell, *Christian Home in Victorian America*. Phoebe Stanton, whose *Gothic Revival and American Church Architecture* remains the standard work on its topic, acknowledged some religious tension surrounding the style, but she denied that this tension would have any bearing on the style's use. See Stanton, *Gothic Revival*, xxii, 172, 213, 311. Comparable assumptions animated the work of Pierson, *American Buildings and Their Architects*, vol. 2, and Loth and Sadler, *Only Proper Style*. Other scholars have ignored or denied denominational associations entirely. An example can be found in Hoffecker, "Church Gothic" (223), in which Hoffecker claimed that a Methodist congregation in Wilmington employed the style "not for any specific symbolism reminiscent of medieval Christianity, but because it associated the style with grandeur, piety, and respectability." Most recently, Jeanne Halgren Kilde (*When Church Became Theatre*) has suggested that evangelicals in the 1830s embraced the Gothic as a denominationally neutral "Christian" style that could help bind politically divided parishioners together under a shared artistic theme.

5 Von Simson, *Gothic Cathedral*, 3–8. Von Simson offered an elegant definition of Gothic architecture that focused on the use of light and materials, but other definitions vary wildly. Kimball and Edgell, in *History of Architecture*, offered a relatively thorough definition: "Gothic is a system of vaults, supports, and buttresses, the supports being strong enough to bear the crushing weight of the vaults only, and the stability of the structure maintained chiefly by an equilibrium of counterthrusts" (277). In terms of timing, they wrote: "We may consider Gothic architecture that

style, specially marked by the general use of the pointed arch, which in all European countries succeeded the Romanesque style, and flourished until it was in turn superseded by the style of the Renaissance" (277–78). The Gothic gradually displayed an "emphasis on revealed structure," and it had an "aspiring quality" in its soaring expressions (281).

6 Jean Baptiste Molière wrote: "Le fade goût des monuments gothiques / Ces monstres odieux des siècles ignorants / Que de la barbarie ont vomis les torrents" (quoted and translated in Kimball and Edgell, *History of Architecture*, 275). See also Kenneth Clark, *Gothic Revival*, 7, and Gilchrist, *Romanticism and the Gothic Revival*, 22–24.

7 For the transfer of Catholic properties to the Anglican Church, see Duffy, *Stripping of the Altars*, and Phillips, *Reformation of Images*. For the evolution of Anglican church space and Anglicans' renovations of older Gothic structures, see Addleshaw and Etchells, *Architectural Setting of Anglican Worship*.

8 Walpole, quoted in Andrews, *American Gothic*, 8. An example of early Gothic Revival detailing intended for domestic settings can be found in Over, *Ornamental Architecture in the Gothic, Chinese, and Modern Taste*. As the title indicates, Over offered no special priority to the Gothic designs.

9 For America's earliest Gothic experiments, see Loth and Sadler, *Only Proper Style*, 11–41.

10 The debate over the "meetinghouse-to-church" transition is extensive. Key studies of late-eighteenth- and early-nineteenth-century meetinghouses include Dexter, "Meeting-Houses"; Place, "From Meeting House to Church in New England"; Pierson, *American Buildings and Their Architects*, vol. 1; Sweeney, "Meetinghouses, Town Houses, and Churches"; Buggeln, *Temples of Grace*; and Bushman, *Refinement of America*. Bushman's study is particularly relevant here, as he emphasized the role of competition in the evangelicals' changing architectural preferences.

11 Pierson, *American Buildings and Their Architects*, 2:113.

12 Joseph Clark, quoted in Lane, *Architecture of the Old South*, 166.

13 Presbytery of Chicago, "Report on the Architectural Setting," 4.

14 For Latrobe's statements and designs for the cathedral, see Kimball, "Latrobe's Designs," 542; Early, *Romanticism and American Architecture*, 40, 134; and Loth and Sadler, *Only Proper Style*, 29–31.

15 For St. Mary's chapel, see Pierson, *American Buildings and Their Architects*, 2:119, and Loth and Sadler, *Only Proper Style*, 33–34. The chapel's

Gothic design differentiated it from the campus's other boxy, institutional buildings, thereby reinforcing the devotional associations of the style. For the earlier St. Patrick's Cathedral, see Loth and Sadler, *Only Proper Style*, 34–35. For the Basilica of Notre Dame, see Toker, *Church of Notre-Dame*. For the later St. Patrick's Cathedral, see Pierson, *American Buildings and Their Architects*, 2:206–69.

16   Kevin F. Decker, "Grand and Godly Proportions," 19; Stanton, *Gothic Revival*, 225–52; Hampton, "German Gothic in the Midwest"; Howe, *Historical Collections of Ohio*, 204 (first quotation); "Edgefield Court-House, S.C.," 607 (last quotation). Likewise, in 1866, a correspondent described a view of Vicksburg, Mississippi, from the river: "On a neighboring eminence to the right rises with awe-inspiring solemnity the Catholic Church, built in chaste Gothic style, surmounted by numerous sky-piercing spires, and above which, standing out against the blue ether of space, is that emblem of suffering and mercy, the Cross" ("Vicksburg, Miss.," 218). For the church's Gothic patterns in Texas, see Cleary, "Texas Gothic, French Accent." Peter W. Williams (*Houses of God*, 16–18) described the Gothic as "the preeminent Catholic mode" in nineteenth-century New England. For southern churches, see Patrick, "Ecclesiological Gothic," 134–37.

17   Kevin F. Decker, "Grand and Godly Proportions," 22–23.

18   Pugin, *Contrasts*, 51 (first quotation); Pugin, *Apology for the Revival*, 4 (second quotation). For Pugin's life and influence, see Trappes-Lomax, *Pugin*, and Stanton, *Pugin*.

19   Giraud, "Christian Architecture," September 1843, 562 (first quotations); Giraud, "Pointed Style of Architecture," 602 (second quotations); Giraud, "Christian Architecture," October 1845, 627–31 (third quotations).

20   "Story of the Gothic Revival," 639, 640.

21   Spalding, *Miscellanea*, 86, 95; Hughes, quoted in Pierson, *American Buildings and Their Architects*, 2:209.

22   *Puseyite Developments*, 5.

23   McCulloh, *Analytical Investigations*, review in Bond, "M'Culloh on the Scriptures," 280–81.

24   "Church Architecture," 625, 636, 639 (first quotations); Thomas E. Peck, quoted in Melton, *Presbyterian Worship in America*, 69 (last quotations).

25   Edward N. Kirk, in a speech regarding Mount Vernon Church, published in the *Boston Daily Advertiser*, November 24, 1843, quoted in

Early, *Romanticism and American Architecture*, 121. The second quotation came from another article in the same issue, quoted in Early, *Romanticism and American Architecture*, 122. Similarly, in an 1850 *Christian Examiner* article, Thomas C. Clarke declared that if one Unitarian church in Boston, Gothic in style, had been designed for Catholic worship, it would have been flawless, since "Gothic cathedrals were perfectly suited to Catholic services" (Early, *Romanticism and American Architecture*, 121).

26 *Illustrations of Popery*, 29, 257–58.

27 Dexter, *Meeting-Houses*, 11, 16, 17, 20 (quotations). For other examples of this line of reasoning, see "Church Building," 3–4, 21–23, and Congregational Churches in the United States, *Book of Plans for Churches and Parsonages*.

28 Tiffany, *Expression in Church Architecture*, 14–15.

29 "Public Buildings" (first quotation); "Domestic notices. Design for a Rural Church," *The Horticulturist* 2 (March 1848): 433 (second quotation); "A Short Chapter on Country Churches," *The Horticulturist* 6 (January 1851): 9–12, quoted in Stanton, *Gothic Revival*, 312–13 (last quotations).

30 Long, "Gothic Architecture," 297, 303.

31 Hart, *Designs for Parish Churches*, quoted in Dexter, *Meeting-Houses*, 16 (first quotations); Wills, *Ancient English Ecclesiastical Architecture*, 9–10, 117 (second quotations). See Stanton, *Gothic Revival*, for a discussion of the Gothic's English associations.

32 Hopkins, *Essay on Gothic Architecture*, 3, 4, 9. See also Pierson, *American Buildings and Their Architects*, 2:170–71.

33 "Oxford Architecture," 128–29. For the view of Gothic as a more generic, "Christian" style, see Stanton, *Gothic Revival*, 9, 165–77, and Kilde, *When Church Became Theatre*, 56–83.

34 Horace B. Wallace, quoted in Early, *Romanticism and American Architecture*, 93. See also "Gothic Architecture and Natural Religion" and Unrau, *Looking at Architecture with Ruskin*.

35 Stanton, *Gothic Revival*, 240–43; Hunter, "Robert Cary Long, Jr."

36 Raguin, "Revivals, Revivalists," 325–27; Sturm and Chotas, *Stained Glass*, 41.

37 John Paul Decker, *Art and Architecture*, 6–7, 11.

38 Dexter, *Meeting-Houses*, 20 (first quotations); Tiffany, *Expression in Church Architecture*, 12–16 (last quotations). For an example of Meth-

odist classroom additions adjacent to the nave, see the plans of Broad-Street Methodist Episcopal Church, Newark, New Jersey, in "Methodist Church Architecture," March 1856.

39 "West Spruce St. Baptist Church."

40 John Paul Decker, *Art and Architecture*, 10.

41 Dana, ed., *United States Illustrated*, 1:157 (quotation).

42 For examples of twentieth-century debates over the propriety of Gothic, see Cram, *Significance of Gothic Art*, and Presbytery of Chicago, "Report on the Architectural Setting." For an example of the lingering necessity of Gothic features for a "churchly" look, see Bragg, *Wooden Churches*.

43 Beecher, *Works*, 2:419 (first quotation); Congregational Churches in the United States, *Proceedings of the General Convention*, 65–66 (last quotation). For Beecher's role in the burning of the Charlestown convent in 1834, see Shea, *History of the Catholic Church*, 3:473–80; Billington, *Protestant Crusade*, 71–76, in which Billington refuted Shea's claims for Beecher's direct responsibility; and Schultz, *Fire and Roses*. Beecher's speech in question can be found in Beecher, *Plea for the West*.

For the Hanover Street Congregational Church and its "strikingly similar" successor, the Bowdoin Street Congregational Church, dedicated on June 15, 1831, see Harding, *Certain Magnificence*, 306; Guernsey, "Lyman Beecher"; Willard, "Recent Church Architecture in Boston," 643 44; and Jenks, "Lowell Mason."

Chapter Five

1 For background on this parish, see Duke, *History of the Ginter Park Baptist Church*.

2 My descriptions are based on the service and program leaflet dated April 30, 2000.

3 Clinton Locke, quoted in Chorley, *Men and Movements*, 363.

4 Brownlee, *Letters in the Roman Catholic Controversy*, 264–65 (first quotations); Beman, *Letters to Rev. John Hughes*, 29 (second quotations); Kirwan, *Romanism at Home*, 53–57 (last quotations). Similar attacks were published in *Illustrations of Popery*, 29 and 257–59, in which the author discerned the unity of "Popery and Paganism" in the two systems' "erection of altars," their use of "vestments of white decorated with gold," and their general abuse of ritualistic "frippery." See also Haynes, *Baptist Denomination*, 55–56; Rufus Clark, *Popery and the United States*, 14–15;

and Van Dyke, *Popery, the Foe of the Church*, 52–53, 71–100. Almost all of these publications owed a debt to Conyers Middleton's influential *Letter from Rome* (1729).

5 For the contours of Protestant worship characteristics in colonial and early national America, see Bushman, *Refinement of America*, 169–80; Tucker, *American Methodist Worship*; Schmidt, *Holy Fairs*; Melton, *Presbyterian Worship in America*; Benes, ed., *New England Meeting House and Church*; Ward, "In a Feasting Posture"; Buggeln, *Temples of Grace*; Upton, *Holy Things and Profane*; Holmes, *Brief History of the Episcopal Church*; White, *Protestant Worship*; and Kilde, *When Church Became Theatre*. For a sense of the contrasts presented by Catholic worship, see Spalding, *Lectures on the Evidences of Catholicity*, 194–228; England and Rosati, *Ceremonial for the Use of the Catholic Churches*; and James F. White, *Roman Catholic Worship*.

6 Bradford, "Phoebe George Bradford Diaries," 347–48 (first quotation); Breckinridge, *Papism in the XIX. Century*, 56–65, 175–81 (second quotation); Tefft, "Day with the Catholics," 283 (third quotations). For the role of German immigrants in the rise in popularity of Christmas celebrations, see Schmidt, *Consumer Rites*, 122–59, and, for a nineteenth-century example, "Christmas Service in Bethlehem."

7 Dowling, *History of Romanism*, frontispiece; Barnum, *Romanism As It Is*, 422 and facing p. 544; "Romanism at Rome," 84 (last quotations). For Robert W. Weir's *Taking the Veil*, see John Davis, "Catholic Envy." See also Morgan, *Protestants and Pictures*.

8 Dix, "Ritualism," 293–94.

9 Tefft, "Day with the Catholics," 283 (quotation). Richard Bushman outlined these tastes in his study of the spread of gentility, *The Refinement of America*. And both Bushman and Leigh Eric Schmidt, in *Consumer Rites*, delineated the relationship between nineteenth-century church arts and commercial prosperity, though both downplayed the position of Roman Catholicism. See also Thomas, *Revivalism and Cultural Change*; Kilde, *When Church Became Theatre*; Douglas, *Feminization of American Culture*; and Colin Campbell, *Romantic Ethic*.

10 "Church Building," 7–8.

11 Frank Fields Ellinwood, *Dedication Sermon*, 10–11.

12 "Methodist Church Architecture," February 1856, 123–24. A portion of this article was also quoted in the Episcopal pamphlet *Plea for the Use of the Fine Arts*, 7.

13 Magoun, "Architecture and Christian Principle," 379 (first quotations); Wightman, "Fundamental Law of Christian Worship," 194–95 (last quotations).

14 "Church Dedication" (first quotation); Woolson, "Peter, the Parson," 601 (second quotation); Jones, *Arranging Church Flowers*, 1, 22 (last quotations). Similarly, in 1844, a contributor to New York's *Living Age* reviewed an English book on church needlework and found the work "apparently intended for Protestant ladies." The book contained designs and directions for producing vestments, altar cloths, and other coverings—"in short, all the information necessary to guide the taste of ladies desirous of contributing to the embellishment of the altar by their handiwork" ("Miss Lambert," *Church Needlework*). For explorations of women's roles in Protestant worship, see Procter-Smith and Walton, eds., *Women at Worship*, and Walton, "Missing Element of Women's Experience."

15 For a discussion of early organs in New England's Congregational churches, see "Church Reminiscences." For the varieties of Protestant church music, see Stevenson, *Protestant Church Music in America*; Etherington, *Protestant Worship Music*; and Sherwood, "'Buds the Infant Mind.'"

16 "Church Reminiscences," 125 (first quotation); "Romanism at Rome," 91 (second quotation); F. F. H., "Sacred Music," 412 (third quotation); Tefft, "Day with the Catholics," 283 (last quotations). For Catholic church music in America, see Hume, *Catholic Church Music*, and Grimes, *How Shall We Sing in a Foreign Land?*

17 John Fanning Watson, *Annals of Philadelphia and Pennsylvania*, 1:457–60 (first quotations); "*Concert of Sacred Music*," *Philadelphia Daily Sun*, February 12, 1847 (second quotation); Blake, "Christmas Music in America" (last quotations). See also Hastings, "Instruments in Church Music," and Gould, *Church Music in America*.

18 "Presbuteros," "Presbyterian Ritualism" (first quotations); Wayland, *Notes on the Principles*, 151–52 (last quotations).

19 *Nickerson's Illustrated Church Musical and School Directory of New York and Brooklyn* (1895), quoted in Leonard Ellinwood, *History of American Church Music*, 78–79; General Assembly of the Presbyterian Church in the United States of America, quoted in Melton, *Presbyterian Worship in America*, 129 (first quotation); General Assembly of the Presbyterian Church in the United States of America, *Hymnal*, 85–86 (last quotation).

20 Osgood, "Easter Flowers" (first quotations); "Easter Sunday" (second quotations); C. W. E., "Our Monthly Gossip," 414 (last quotations). The spread of Christmas, Easter, and other celebrations is detailed in Schmidt, *Consumer Rites*. See also "Editor's Easy Chair," June 1882, 146–47. For an early rejection of these innovations in worship, see "A Presbyterian," *Man's Feasts and Fasts*.

21 A Presbyterian, *Apostacy of Mr. Newman*, 2, 3 (first quotations); Warren, *Causes and the Cure of Puseyism*, 149 (last quotations). That same decade, New Jersey's "Presbyterian" issued another pamphlet critiquing the recent adoption of such "ridiculous Papal mummeries" as the use of "Lighted Candles in the Church"; "Peculiar Decorations on Feast Days," which included "altar coverings and pulpit hangings . . . or the natural flowers of the season woven into wreaths, or placed . . . upon the altar"; and "Bowings, Genuflections, &c." (A Presbyterian, *"One Faith,"* 40).

22 Spencer, "Visit to St. Alban's, New York," 416–18.

23 Ibid., 418–20. One year earlier, a Baptist observer declared, "The Episcopal Chapel of St. Albans in New York is a bubble on the wave which indicates the direction of the tide in this country. . . . [Activities] are there exhibited in a style so Romish, that to the beholder nothing seems to be wanting to complete the illusion that he is gazing on papal mummeries in a European cathedral, except the majesty of grand architecture, the gleam of silver censers, and the hazy perfume of sacred smoke" (Wightman, "The Fundamental Law of Christian Worship," 194). Another review and debate over St. Alban's services can be found in Paletta, "Ritualism." See also Bacon, "Roman Philosopher." For official debates over Episcopal "ritualism," see Chorley, *Men and Movements*. For a creative example of Episcopal conservatism, see a story recounted by E. E. Beardsley in Cameron, *Connecticut Churchmanship*, selection 5, in which one minister's surplice "strangely disappeared from the Vestry-room and could not afterwards be found."

24 "Presbuteros," "Presbyterian Ritualism" (first quotation); "Ecclesiastical Furniture," 247 (second quotations); Ex-clergyman, *Review of Bishop Ives' "Trials of a Mind,"* 18–19 (last quotations). See also Giffin, "More Liturgy or More Life," and Norwood, *Story of American Methodism*, 325–28.

25 Barnes, *Christian Sanctuary*, 19–20.

26 Osgood, "Easter Flowers," 190, 194 (first quotations); "Flower-Arranging," 445 (second quotations); "Methodist Episcopal Church: Orange City, Florida"; "Union Baptist Church, Mystic Connecticut."

See also Conway, "Stolen Flowers," 612, and Schmidt, *Consumer Rites*, 192–237. For Methodist altar guild activity, see Arnett and Clark, *Methodist Altars*.

27 Prime, *Holy Cross*, 132–34.

28 Jones, *Arranging Church Flowers*, vii–viii, 22 (first quotations); Milhouse, *Christian Worship in Symbol and Ritual*, 87 (last quotations); Arnett and Clark, *Methodist Altars*, 3. For other mid-twentieth-century altar guidebooks, see McClinton, *Flower Arrangement in the Church*; Mullins, *Flowers and Symbols for the Christian Year*; and Leach, *Use of Candles in Christian Fellowship*.

29 John Fanning Watson, *Annals of Philadelphia and Pennsylvania*, 1:457–60 (first quotation); Nygaard and Miller, *Importance of Appropriate Pulpit Attire*, 2–7 (second quotations). The authors also referenced the commonality of robed choirs and processionals. Hickman, *United Methodist Altars*, 46–49. See also "Editor's Easy Chair," November 1868, and Milhouse, *Christian Worship in Symbol and Ritual*, 90. For another reference to the early Protestant traditions of black suits and parsons' gray, see "Clerical Manners and Habits," 513.

30 Leonard Ellinwood, *History of American Church Music*, 76–86; Krehbiel, "Surpliced Choirs in New York"; "Vesting of Choirs" (first quotations); "Surpliced Choirs," 708, 710 (last quotations).

31 Methodist Episcopal Church, *Doctrines and Discipline*, 106, 112–13, 120 (first quotation); "A Presbyterian," "Posture in Public Prayer" (second quotations); General Assembly of the Presbyterian Church U.S.A., quoted in Todd, *Posture in Prayer*, 1 (third quotations); Wayland, *Notes on the Principles*, 159 (fourth quotations); *Baptist Praise Book*, 24 (last quotation); "Ecclesiastical Furniture," 247. See also Mines, *Presbyterian Clergyman Looking for the Church*, 112–14. The activities at camp meetings and revivals offered exceptions to Protestants' traditional reverential reserve, as attendees made all sorts of movements, including kneeling.

32 Melton, *Presbyterian Worship in America*, 91 (quotation). For the Episcopal schism over ritualism, see Guelzo, *For the Union of Evangelical Christendom*, and Chorley, *Men and Movements*. In 1871, the Episcopal bishop of Ohio brought a minister to trial over the latter's refusal to disband his church's robed choir and halt their processions. See Ellinwood, *History of American Church Music*, 84. For a recent example of the lingering tensions surrounding Protestant worship materials, see Webber, "Worship Perspectives."

33 "New-York Church Architecture," 234.

34 Sholl, *Working Designs for Ten Catholic Churches*, 6 (first quotation); "Protesting Christians," 173–74 (second quotations). For the grandiose architectural goals of Hughes and others, see Pierson, *American Buildings and Their Architects*, vol. 2; Kevin F. Decker, "Grand and Godly Proportions"; and Oliveri, "Building a Baroque Catholicism."

Epilogue

1 Joseph Wuest, quoted in Dolan, *Catholic Revivalism*, 87; Brownson, "Protestant Revivals and Catholic Retreats." Dolan's work endeavors to show how Catholic revivals were distinct from Protestant revivals and how they both drew from European precedents.

2 Giffin, "More Liturgy or More Life," 73, 74, 78.

3 Gilchrist, *Romanticism and the Gothic Revival*; "Crosses on Protestant Places of Worship," 251–53 (quotations).

4 Sturm and Chotas, *Stained Glass*, 14, 69; Coffin, *Riverside Church in the City of New York*; Johnson, *Radiance of Chartres*, 67–68.

Bibliography

Selected Primary Sources

"Action and Reaction Between America and Romanism." *Church Review* 3 (July 1850): 268–75.

Adams Family Papers: An Electronic Archive. Massachusetts Historical Society. <http://www.masshist.org/digitaladams/>.

Address of the Catholic Lay Citizens of the City and County of Philadelphia, to Their Fellow-Citizens: In Reply to the Presentment of the Grand Jury of the Court of Quarter Sessions of May Term 1844, in Regard to the Causes of the Late Riots in Philadelphia. Philadelphia: M. Fithian, 1844.

Allen, Alexander V. G. *Phillips Brooks, 1835–1893: Memories of His Life, With Extracts from his Letters and Note-books*. New York: E. P. Dutton, 1907.

"Architecture in the United States." *North American Review* 58 (April 1844): 436–80.

"At the Church Door." *Catholic World* 10 (February 1870): 651–55.

Bacon, L. "A Roman Philosopher, A Review of an Article on 'Conversion' in the 'Catholic World.'" *New Englander and Yale Review* 26 (January 1867): 114–48.

Baptist Home Missions in North America; Including a Full Report of the Proceedings and Addresses of the Jubilee Meeting, and a Historical Sketch of the American Baptist Home Mission Society, Historical Tables, Etc., 1832–1882. New York: Baptist Home Mission Rooms, 1883.

The Baptist Praise Book. Chicago: A. S. Barnes and Company, 1872.

Barnes, Albert. *The Christian Sanctuary: A Sermon Preached at the Dedication of the Central Presbyterian Church, Wilmington, Delaware, November 10, 1857*. Philadelphia: Henry B. Ashmead, 1858.

Barnum, Samuel W. *Romanism As It Is: An Exposition of the Roman Catholic System, For the Use of the American People; Embracing a Full Account of Its Origin and Development at Rome and from Rome, Its Distinctive Features in Theory and Practice, its Characteristic Tendencies and Aims, Its Statistical and Moral Position, and Its Special Relations to American Institutions and Liberties; the Whole Drawn from Official and Authentic Sources, and Enriched with Numerous Illustrations, Documentary, Historical, Descriptive,*

Anecdotical, and Pictorial: Together with a . . . Complete Index. Hartford: Connecticut Publishing Co., 1871.

Beecher, Lyman. *Autobiography, Correspondence, etc. of Lyman Beecher*. 2 vols. Edited by Charles Beecher. New York: Harper, 1865.

———. *A Plea for the West*. Cincinnati: Truman and Smith, 1835.

———. *Works*. 3 vols. Boston: Jewett, 1852–53.

Beman, Nathan S. S. *Letters to Rev. John Hughes, D.D., Papal Archbishop of New York, in Review of His Sermon, Preached in St. Patrick's Cathedral, June 29, 1851*. Troy, NY: L. Willard, 1851.

Bennett, C. W. "Catholicism and Protestantism as Patrons of Christian Art." *Methodist Quarterly Review* 59 (January 1877): 79–99.

Berg, Joseph F. *Trapezium; or, Law and Liberty Versus Despotism and Anarchy, A Vindication of Protestantism from Papal Assailants, and Infidel Advocates*. Philadelphia: E. S. Jones, 1851.

"Bishop Doane and the Oxford Tracts." *Princeton Review* 13 (July 1841): 450–62.

Blake, A. B. "Christmas Music in America." *Harper's New Monthly Magazine* 58 (April 1879): 735–40.

Boardman, Henry A. "Is There Any Ground to Apprehend the Extensive and Dangerous Prevalence of Romanism in the United States?" 1841. In *Anti-Catholicism in America, 1841–1851: Three Sermons*. New York: Arno Press, 1977.

Bond, T. E., Jr. "M'Culloh on the Scriptures." *Methodist Quarterly Review* 35 (April 1853): 256–81.

Bradford, Phoebe George. "Phoebe George Bradford Diaries." Edited by W. Emerson Wilson. *Delaware History* 16 (1975): 337–57.

Breckinridge, Robert J. *Papism in the XIX. Century, in the United States: Being, Select Contributions to the Papal Controversy, During 1835–40*. Baltimore: D. Owen, 1841.

Brownlee, W. C. *Letters in the Roman Catholic Controversy*. 2nd ed. New York: Published by the author, 1834.

Brownson, Orestes. "Protestant Revivals and Catholic Retreats." *Brownson's Quarterly Review* 3 (July 1858): 289.

Burnett, Peter Hardeman. *The Path Which Led a Protestant Lawyer to the Catholic Church*. New York: D. Appleton and Co., 1860.

"California." *New Englander and Yale Review* 8 (November 1850): 585–98.

"Casa Wappy." *National Magazine* 7 (October 1855): 293–95.

"Catholic Choirs and Choir Music in Philadelphia." *Records of the American Catholic Historical Society of Philadelphia* 2 (1886–88): 115–26.

"The Chamber of Imagery in the Church of Rome." *Presbyterian Critic and Monthly Review* 1 (September 1855): 403–11.

"Christmas Service in Bethlehem." *New York Observer* 36 (January 28, 1858).

"Church Architecture." *Princeton Review* 27 (October 1855): 625–49.

Church of the Ascension, Baltimore, Maryland. MSA SC 2467, Church Records, Maryland State Archives, Annapolis, Maryland.

"Church Building." *New Englander and Yale Review* 6 (January 1848): 1–24.

"Church Dedication." *New York Observer* 39 (September 19, 1861).

"Church Dedication in Roxbury, Mass." *New York Observer* 31 (August 4, 1853).

"Church Reminiscences." *The New-England Magazine* 9 (August 1835): 123–28.

Clark, Rufus W. *Popery and the United States, Embracing an Account of Papal Operations in Our Country, With a View of the Dangers Which Threaten Our Institutions.* Boston: J. V. Bean and Co., 1847.

Clarke, Richard H. "Our Converts." *American Catholic Quarterly Review* 18 (1893): 539–61; 19 (1894): 112–38.

"Clerical Manners and Habits." *North American Review* 28 (April 1829): 503–22.

[Cleveland, Henry Russell?]. "American Architecture." *North American Review* 43 (October 1836): 361–69.

Cobbin, Ingram. *The Book of Popery: A Manual for Protestants Descriptive of the Origin, Progress, Doctrines, Rites, and Ceremonies of the Papal Church.* Philadelphia: Presbyterian Board of Publication, 1840.

Comes, John Theodore. *Catholic Art and Architecture.* Pittsburgh: n.p., 1920.

Congregational Churches in the United States. *A Book of Plans for Churches and Parsonages.* New York: D. Burgess, 1853.

———. *Proceedings of the General Convention of Congregational Ministers and Delegates in the United States, held at Albany, N.Y., on the 5th, 6th, 7th and 8th of October, 1852.* New York: S. W. Benedict, 1852.

Conway, M. D. "Stolen Flowers." *Harper's New Monthly Magazine* 43 (September 1871): 610–12.

"The Cross." *Christian Recorder* 1 (December 14, 1861).

"Crosses and Weathercocks on Churches." *Episcopal Watchman* 1 (April 1827): 14.

"Crosses on Protestant Places of Worship." *Canadian Examiner.* Reprinted in *Religious Monitor and Evangelical Repository* 17 (November 1840): 251–56.

"The Cross Humbles But Elevates." *New York Observer* 29 (January 9, 1851).

"The Cross in Art." *Ladies' Repository: A Monthly Periodical, Devoted to Literature, Arts, and Religion* 33 (April 1873): 307–8.

"The Cross in Italy." *Presbyterian Magazine* 2 (February 1852): 92.

"C. W. E." "Our Monthly Gossip: Customs and Traditions of Easter." *Lippincott's Magazine of Popular Literature and Science* 7 (April 1884): 414–17.

Dana, Charles A., ed. *The United States Illustrated; in Views of City and Country, With Descriptive and Historical Articles.* 2 vols. New York: H. J. Meyer, 1853.

Dexter, H. M. "Meeting-Houses: Considered Historically and Suggestively." *Congregational Quarterly* 1 (April 1859): 186–214.

———. *Meeting-Houses: Considered Historically and Suggestively.* Boston: J. E. Tilton, 1859.

"Difficulties of the Cross." *Presbyterian Magazine* 3 (September 1853): 438.

Dix, Morgan. "Ritualism." *The Galaxy* 4 (July 1867): 285–94.

Doane, George Washington. *The Life and Writings of George Washington Doane.* 4 vols. Edited by William Croswell Doane. New York: D. Appleton and Co., 1860–61.

"Domestic." *United States Catholic Magazine and Monthly Review* 4 (September 1845): 608.

Dowling, John. *The History of Romanism: From the Earliest Corruptions of Christianity to the Present Time: With Full Chronological Table, Analytical and Alphabetical Indexes and Glossary: Illustrated By Numerous Accurate and Highly Finished Engravings of its Ceremonies, Superstitions, Persecutions, and Historical Incidents.* 11th ed. New York: Edward Walker, 1846.

"Drawing of Church at St. Columba Mission, Gull Lake." 1854. Location no. E97.7r7, negative no. 10716. Minnesota Historical Society, St. Paul, Minnesota.

Dunn, Lewis R. "Power of the Cross." *Ladies' Repository: A Monthly Periodical, Devoted to Literature, Arts, and Religion* 8 (May 1848): 140–41.

"Easter Sunday." *New York Observer* 39 (April 4, 1861).

"Ecclesiastical Furniture." *The Manufacturer and Builder* 1 (August 1869): 247–48.

"Edgefield Court-House, S.C." *Debow's Review, Agricultural, Commercial, Industrial Progress and Resources* 27 (November 1859): 606–8.

"Editor's Drawer." *Harper's New Monthly Magazine* 32 (April 1866): 671–80.

"Editor's Easy Chair." *Harper's New Monthly Magazine* 37 (November 1868): 849–53.

"Editor's Easy Chair." *Harper's New Monthly Magazine* 50 (January 1875): 281–86.

"Editor's Easy Chair." *Harper's New Monthly Magazine* 65 (June 1882): 145–56.

Egan, Maurice Francis. *Glories of the Catholic Church in Art, Architecture and History. Comprising 256 Superb Photographic Views, with Graphic Commentary, Legend and Description, by Eminent Catholic Writers.* Chicago: D. H. McBride, 1895.

Ellinwood, Frank Fields. *Dedication Sermon, Church of the Mountain, Delaware Water-Gap, Pa, August 29, 1854.* Philadelphia: Isaac Ashmead, 1854.

E[llis], G[eorge] E. "The Artistic and Romantic View of the Church of the Middle Ages." *Christian Examiner and Religious Miscellany* 46 (May 1849): 345–83.

England, John, and Joseph Rosati. *Ceremonial for the Use of the Catholic Churches in the United States of America: Published by Order of the First Council of Baltimore. . . .* 2nd rev. ed. Baltimore: J. Murphy and Co., 1852.

Ex-Clergyman. *A Review of Bishop Ives' "Trials of a Mind, In Its Progress to Catholicism."* Philadelphia: T. Curtis, 1855.

F. F. H. "Sacred Music." *Christian Examiner* 45 (November 1848): 406–12.

"Flower-Arranging." *Continental Monthly: Devoted to Literature and National Policy* 2 (October 1862): 444–48.

Frederic, Harold. *The Damnation of Theron Ware, or, Illumination.* New York: Stone and Kimball, 1896.

The Full Particulars of the Late Riots, With a View of the Burning of the Catholic Churches, St. Michaels and St. Augustines. Philadelphia: n.p., [1844].

General Assembly of the Presbyterian Church in the United States of America. *The Hymnal.* 1933. Reprint, Philadelphia: Presbyterian Board of Christian Education; imprinted for the First Presbyterian Church, Huntington, West Virginia, 1948.

Gibbons, James. *The Faith of Our Fathers: Being a Plain Exposition and Vindication of the Church Founded by Our Lord Jesus Christ.* Baltimore: John Murphy and Co., 1877.

Giffin, C. M. "More Liturgy or More Life." *Methodist Quarterly Review* 84 (January 1902): 71–79.

Giraud, T. E. "Christian Architecture." *United States Catholic Magazine and Monthly Review* 2 (September 1843): 562–64.

———. "Christian Architecture." *United States Catholic Magazine and Monthly Review* 4 (October 1845): 627–31.

———. "Pointed Style of Architecture." *United States Catholic Magazine and Monthly Review* 3 (September 1844): 599–603.

Goldsworthy, Edwin A. *Plain Thoughts on Worship*. New York: Willet, Clark and Co., 1936.

"Gothic Architecture and Natural Religion." *Southern Literary Messenger* 32 (January 1861): 63–65.

Gould, Nathaniel D. *Church Music in America, Comprising its History and its Peculiarities at Different Periods, with Cursory Remarks on its Legitimate Use and Its Abuse; with Notices of the Schools, Composers, Teachers, and Societies*. Boston: A. N. Johnson, 1853.

"Grounds of Hope and Fear Respecting Romanism in Our Country." *American Protestant Magazine* 1 (April 1846): 326–29.

Guernsey, A. H. "Lyman Beecher." *Harper's New Monthly Magazine* 30 (May 1865): 697–711.

Hart, Joseph Coleman. *Designs for Parish Churches, in the Three Styles of English Church Architecture: With an Analysis of Each Style: A Review of the Nomenclature of the Periods of English Gothic Architecture, and Some Remarks Introductory to Church Building: Exemplified in a Series of Over One Hundred Illustrations*. New York: Dana and Company, 1857.

Hastings, Thomas. "Instruments in Church Music. No. 1." *New York Observer* 25 (April 10, 1847).

Hawthorne, Nathaniel. "The Artist of the Beautiful." In *Mosses from an Old Manse*. New York: Wiley and Putnam, 1846.

Haynes, D. C. *The Baptist Denomination: Its History, Doctrines, and Ordinances; Its Polity, Persecutions, and Martyrs; Facts and Statistics of Its Missionary Institutions, Schools of Learning, etc.; the Indebtedness of the World to Baptists, and Their Duty to the World*. New York: Sheldon, Blakeman and Co., 1856.

[Henderson, Thulia Susannah]. *The Head and the Heart Enlisted Against Popery, Under the Banner of Christian Truth: A Prize Essay, Designed for Sabbath-school, Teachers and Scholars*. Richmond, VA: Presbyterian Committee of Publication, 1867.

Herbert, Lady. "The Story of a Conversion." *Catholic World* 53 (April 1891): 7–14.

Hewit, Augustine F. "How I Became a Catholic." *Catholic World* 46 (October 1887): 32–43.

Hogan, William. *A Synopsis of Popery: As It Was and As It Is*. Boston: Redding, 1845.

Hoge, Peyton Harrison. *Moses Drury Hoge: Life and Letters*. Richmond, VA: Presbyterian Committee of Publication, 1899.

Hopkins, John Henry. *Essay on Gothic Architecture, With Various Plans and Drawings for Churches: Designed Chiefly for the Use of the Clergy*. Burlington, VT: Smith and Harrington, 1836.

"How Account for the Success of Romanism." *The American Protestant* 1 (December 1845): 193–95.

Howard, George W. *The Monumental City: Its Past History and Present Resources*. Baltimore: J. D. Ehlers, 1873.

Howe, Henry. *Historical Collections of Ohio; Containing a Collection of the Most Interesting Facts, Traditions, Biographical Sketches, Anecdotes, etc. Relating to Its General and Local History: With Descriptions of Its Counties, Principal Towns and Villages*. Cincinnati: Derby, Bradley and Co., 1848.

Huntington, Joshua. *Gropings After Truth: A Life Journey from New England Congregationalism to the One Catholic and Apostolic Church*. New York: The Catholic Publication Society, 1868.

"Idolatry—Its Origin and Effects." *National Magazine* 8 (February 1856): 162–65.

Illustrations of Popery; the "Mystery of Iniquity" Unveiled: in its "Damnable Heresies, Lying Wonders, and Strong Delusion." With the Sanguinary Persecutions of the "Woman Drunk With the Blood of the Saints." New York: J. P. Callender, 1838.

Ingham, Mary Janes. "The Cross of Flowers." *Ladies' Repository: A Monthly Periodical, Devoted to Literature, Arts, and Religion* 27 (May 1867): 266–69.

Jenks, Francis H. "Lowell Mason." *New England Magazine* 17 (January 1895): 651–68.

Jobson, Frederick J. *America, and American Methodism*. London: J. S. Virtue, 1857.

Johnston, James F. W. *Notes on North America, Agricultural, Economical, and Social*. Boston: C. C. Little and J. Brown, 1851.

Kirwan, [Nicholas Murray]. *Romanism at Home: Letters to the Hon. Roger B. Taney*. New York: Harper, 1852.

Krehbiel, H. E. "Surpliced Choirs in New York." *Harper's New Monthly Magazine* 77 (June 1888): 65–75.

"The Last Gasp of the Anti-Catholic Faction." *Catholic World* 7 (September 1868): 848–55.

Lattimore, S. A. "Recollections of Summer Rambles." *Ladies' Repository: A Monthly Periodical, Devoted to Literature, Arts, and Religion* 12 (February 1852): 45–48.

"A Letter from Bishop Young." *Spirit of Missions* 32 (November 1868): 799–802.

"Local Affairs." *Public Ledger* 17 (May 9, 1844).

Long, R. C. "Gothic Architecture—New Church." *United States Catholic Magazine and Monthly Review* 2 (May 1843): 297–304.

Magoun, George F. "Architecture and Christian Principle." *Congregational Quarterly* 1 (October 1859): 373–85.

Markley, J. E. "Memorandum Book 1850–52." Winterthur Library, Winterthur, Delaware.

Maxwell, S. D. "St. Paul's Methodist Episcopal Church, Cincinnati." *Ladies' Repository: A Monthly Periodical, Devoted to Literature, Arts, and Religion* 31 (February 1871): 122–26.

McCulloh, J. H. *Analytical Investigations Concerning the Credibility of the Scriptures, and of the Religious System Inculcated in Them: Together With a Historical Exhibition of Human Conduct During the Several Dispensations Under Which Mankind Have Been Placed By Their Creator*. Baltimore: James S. Waters, 1852.

McLeod, John N. *Popery in the United States*. N.p., 1848.

"Methodist Church Architecture." *National Magazine* 7 (December 1855): 497–512.

"Methodist Church Architecture, Second Article." *National Magazine* 8 (January 1856): 77–79.

"Methodist Church Architecture, Third Article." *National Magazine* 8 (February 1856): 121–25.

"Methodist Church Architecture." *National Magazine* 8 (March 1856): 220–25.

Methodist Episcopal Church. *Doctrines and Discipline of the Methodist Episcopal Church*. Cincinnati: Swormsteat and Poe, 1854.

"Methodist Episcopal Church: Orange City, Florida" [1880s], image PR07914, Florida Photographic Collection, Florida State Archives, Tallahassee, Florida.

Metropolitan Catholic Almanac and Laity's Directory, for the Year of our Lord 1853. Baltimore: Fielding Lucas, 1852.

Mickle, Isaac. *A Gentleman of Much Promise: The Diary of Isaac Mickle, 1837–*

1845. 2 vols. Edited by Philip English Mackey. Philadelphia: University of
   Pennsylvania Press, 1977.
Miller, Samuel. *The Dangers of Education in Roman Catholic Seminaries:
   A Sermon, Delivered by Request, Before the Synod of Philadelphia, in the City
   of Baltimore, October 31, 1837, and Afterwards the City of New York,
   November 26, 1837*. Baltimore: Matchett and Neilson, 1838.
Mines, Flavel S. *A Presbyterian Clergyman Looking for the Church. By One of
   Three Hundred Sixth and Seventh Thousand*. New York: Gen. Protestant
   Episcopal Sunday School Union, 1853.
Moore, T. V. "The Gospel and the Female Sex." *Presbyterian Magazine*
   2 (July 1852): 300–303.
"The Moral Influence of the Cross." *Princeton Review* 7 (July 1835): 367–77.
Morse, Samuel F. B. *Foreign Conspiracy Against the Liberties of the United
   States*. New York: Leavitt, Lord, and Co., 1835.
Nevins, William. *Practical Thoughts: Thoughts on Popery*. New York:
   American Tract Society, 1836.
"The New Catholic Cathedral, Cincinnati." *United States Catholic Magazine
   and Monthly Review* 6 (January 1847): 1.
"New-York Church Architecture." *Putnam's Monthly* 2 (September 1853):
   233–48.
"The Office and Influence of Clothes." *North American Review* 104 (January
   1867): 156–75.
"On the Use of Crosses." *New York Observer* 20 (December 3, 1842).
Osgood, Samuel. "Easter Flowers." *Harper's New Monthly Magazine* 27
   (July 1863): 189–94.
"Our Earliest Printed Church History of the United States." *Catholic
   Historical Review* 6 (October 1920): 343–57.
Over, Charles. *Ornamental Architecture in the Gothic, Chinese, and Modern
   Taste: Being Above Fifty Intire New Designs of Plans, Sections, Elevations,
   &c. (Many of Which May be Executed With Roots of Trees) for Gardens,
   Parks, Forests, Woods, Canals, &c.: The Whole Neatly Engrav'd on Fifty Four
   Copper-plates*. London: Robert Sayer, 1758.
"Oxford Architecture." *Princeton Review* 16 (January 1844): 119–29.
Paletta. "Ritualism." *Watson's Art Journal* 7 (August 3, 1867): 230.
Parton, James. "Our Roman Catholic Brethren." *Atlantic Monthly* 21 (April
   1868): 432–52.
"Photo of Mystic Methodist Church decorated for U.S. Centennial," 1876.
   Accession number 1975.294.440, Mystic Seaport, Mystic, Connecticut.
   Photograph by Edwin Scholfield.

"Plan for a Country Church." *Catholic World* 7 (April 1868): 135–38.

A Plea for the Use of the Fine Arts in the Decoration of Churches. New York: John F. Trow, 1857.

"Popery in Britain." *Christian Recorder* 2 (March 15, 1862).

"*Popery in Wisconsin.*" *American Protestant Magazine* 1 (August 1845): 92.

"Presbuteros." "Presbyterian Ritualism." *New York Observer* 45 (July 18, 1867).

A Presbyterian [Cortlandt van Rensselaer?]. *The Apostacy of Mr. Newman, and Some Traces of Newmania on New Jersey Soil.* Burlington, NJ: n.p., 1845.

"A Presbyterian" [Cortlandt van Rensselaer?]. *Man's Feasts and Fasts in God's Church. A New-Year's Gift; Being a Review of "The Rector's Christmas Offering."* Burlington, NJ: J. L. Powell, 1842.

A Presbyterian [Cortlandt van Rensselaer?]. *"One Faith": or, Bishop Doane vs. Bishop M'Ilvaine on Oxford Theology; Exhibited in Extracts from the Writings of the Diocesans of New Jersey and of Ohio.* Burlington, NJ: J. L. Powell, 1843.

"A Presbyterian." "The Posture in Public Prayer." *New York Observer* 24 (January 31, 1846).

Presbytery of Chicago. "A Report on the Architectural Setting of Presbyterian Worship." Chicago: n.p., 1955.

Prime, W. C. *Holy Cross: A History of the Invention, Preservation, and Disappearance of the Wood Known as the True Cross.* New York: Anson D. F. Randolph and Co., 1877.

"Progress of Popery." *Zion's Herald and Wesleyan Journal* 18 (January 1847): 7.

"Progress of Popery in Great Britain." *New York Observer* 11 (March 23, 1833).

"Progress of Popery in the United States." *Quarterly Review of the American Protestant Association* 2 (April 1845): 198–200.

"Progress of the Roman Catholics in the United States." *Episcopal Watchman* 7 (October 12, 1833).

"Protesting Christians." *Catholic World* 29 (May 1879): 169–80.

"Public Buildings." *The New York Mirror* 7 (May 15, 1830): 353–54.

Pugin, A. Welby. *An Apology for the Revival of Christian Architecture in England.* London: J. Weale, 1843.

———. *Contrasts; or, A Parallel Between the Noble Edifices of the Middle Ages, and Corresponding Buildings of the Present Day: Shewing the Present Decay of Taste.* London: Charles Dolman, 1841.

————. *The True Principles of Pointed or Christian Architecture: Set Forth in Two Lectures Delivered at St. Marie's Oscott.* London, 1841. Reprint, New York: St. Martin's Press, 1973.

Puseyite Developments, or Notices of the New York Ecclesiologists. Dedicated to their Patron, the Right Rev. Bishop Ives, of North Carolina. New York: Berford and Co., 1850.

Rameur, E. "The Progress of the Church." *Catholic World* 1 (April 1865): 1–19.

"Rapid Increase of Romanism in the United States." *The Daily Sun* [Philadelphia] 8 (February 15, 1847).

Review of *The Attraction of the Cross, Designed to Illustrate the Leading Truths, Hopes, and Obligations of Christianity*, by Gardiner Spring. *Princeton Review* 18 (January 1846): 158–75.

Review of *Church Needlework: With Practical Remarks on its Arrangement and Preparation*, by "Miss Lambert." *The Living Age* 1 (June 1, 1844): 130.

Review of *A Second Visit to the United States of North America*, by Sir Charles Lyell. *North American Review* 69 (October 1849): 325–53.

Robins, C. E. "With the Nuns." *Putnam's Monthly*, n.s., 2 (November 1868): 575–85.

"Roman Catholic Cathedral of the Assumption, 435 S. Fifth St., Louisville, Jefferson County, KY." Historic American Buildings Survey, Library of Congress, Washington, DC.

"Roman Catholics." *Zion's Herald and Wesleyan Journal* 19 (March 1, 1848).

"Roman Catholic Statistics of the U.S." *American Protestant Magazine* 1 (February 1846): 262–64.

"Romanism at Rome." *Princeton Review* 41 (January 1869): 83–103.

"Romanism in Cincinnati." *Zion's Herald and Wesleyan Journal* 20 (January 31, 1849).

"Romanism in England." *The American Protestant* 4 (November 1848): 185.

"Romanists and the Roman Catholic Controversy." *New Englander and Yale Review* 2 (April 1844): 233–56.

"Romanizing Tendency." *National Era* 7 (June 16, 1853): 94.

Rupp, Daniel I., ed. *An Original History of the Religious Denominations at Present Existing in the United States.* Philadelphia: J. Y. Humphreys, 1844.

"S." "Church Architecture in New-York." *United States Democratic Review* 20 (February 1847): 139–44.

St. John's Manual, a Guide to the Public Worship and Services of the Catholic Church, and a Collection of Devotions for the Private Use of the Faithful. New York: T. W. Strong, 1856.

"St. Patrick's Cathedral, in New York." *Harper's Weekly* 13 (December 18, 1869): 808, 812.

The Satanic Plot; or, Awful Crimes of Popery in High and Low Places, by a Know Nothing. Boston: N. B. Parsons, 1855.

Scammon, C. M. "In and Around Astoria." *Overland Monthly and Out West Magazine* 3 (December 1869): 495–99.

Schmucker, S. S. *The American Lutheran Church, Historically, Doctrinally and Practically Delineated, in Several Occasional Discourses.* Philadelphia: E. W. Miller, 1852.

Seton, Elizabeth Ann. *Elizabeth Seton: Selected Writings.* Edited by Ellin Kelly and Annabelle Melville. New York: Paulist Press, 1987.

Sholl, Charles. *Working Designs for Ten Catholic Churches: Containing All Dimensions, Details, and Specifications Necessary for the Proper Execution of "Each Work" to Completion: By an Ecclesiastical Architect.* New York: D. and J. Sadlier, 1869.

Short, John T. "Symbolism of the Pre-Christian Cross." *Methodist Quarterly Review* 58 (October 1876): 612–28.

Smith, Benjamin M. *Popery Fulfilling Prophecy: A Sermon Preached Before the Synod of Virginia, October 18th, 1850.* Philadelphia: Presbyterian Board of Publication, 1850.

Smith, R. A. *Philadelphia As It Is In 1852: Being a Correct Guide to All the Public Buildings; Literary, Scientific, and Benevolent Institutions; and Places of Amusement; Remarkable Objects; Manufacturies; Commercial Warehouses; and Wholesale and Retail Stores in Philadelphia and its Vicinity.* . . . Philadelphia: Lindsay and Blakiston, 1852.

———. *Smith's Illustrated Guide to and through Laurel Hill Cemetery, With a Glance at Celebrated Tombs and Burying Places, Ancient and Modern, an Historical Sketch of the Cemeteries of Philadelphia, an Essay on Monumental Architecture, and a Tour up the Schuylkill.* Philadelphia: W. P. Hazard, 1852.

"Some Conversions." *Catholic World* 57 (September 1893): 816–20.

Spalding, M. J. *Lectures on the Evidences of Catholicity; Delivered in the Cathedral of Louisville.* 2nd ed. Louisville, KY: Webb and Levering, 1857.

———. *Miscellanea: Comprising Reviews, Lectures, and Essays, on Historical, Theological and Miscellaneous Subjects.* 6th rev. ed. Baltimore: John Murphy and Co., 1875.

Spencer, J. A. "A Visit to St. Alban's, New York." *Putnam's Magazine*, n.s., 1 (April 1868): 416–20.

Spring, Gardiner. *The Attraction of the Cross, Designed to Illustrate the Leading*

Truths, Obligations and Hopes of Christianity. New York: M. W. Dodd, 1846.

Steen, Mary. "Journal," entry for November 22, 1848, Winterthur Library, Winterthur, Delaware.

"The Story of the Gothic Revival." *Catholic World* 25 (August 1877): 639–51.

Strong, George Templeton. *The Diary of George Templeton Strong.* Edited by Allan Nevins and Milton Halsey Thomas. Abridged by Thomas J. Pressly. Seattle: University of Washington Press, 1988.

"Summary of Religious News." *New York Observer* 24 (January 31, 1846).

"Surpliced Choirs." *Catholic World* 47 (August 1888): 708–10.

"Symbolism of the Cross." *Harper's Weekly* 15 (July 15, 1871): 659.

Tefft, [Benjamin F.] "A Day with the Catholics." *Ladies' Repository: A Monthly Periodical, Devoted to Literature, Arts, and Religion* 7 (September 1847): 281–83.

Tiffany, Charles Comfort. *Expression in Church Architecture: A Paper Read Before the Church Conference in the Chapel of the Church of the Incarnation, New York, Lent, 1875.* New York: T. Whittaker, 1875.

Todd, Isaac. *The Posture in Prayer, or God to be Worshipped with the Body as Well as the Mind.* Philadelphia: Presbyterian Board of Publication, 1851.

The Truth Unveiled; or, A Calm and Impartial Exposition of the Origin and Immediate Cause of the Terrible Riots in Philadelphia, on May 6th, 7th, and 8th, A.D. 1844, by a Protestant and Native Philadelphian. Philadelphia: M. Fithian, 1844.

"Photo of Union Baptist Church Interior, with Floral Arrangements," circa 1875. Accession number 1975.294.439. Mystic Seaport, Mystic, Connecticut. Photograph by Edwin Scholfield.

Van Dyke, Joseph S. *Popery, the Foe of the Church, and of the Republic.* Philadelphia: Peoples Publishing Co., 1872.

Varnum, Joseph S., Jr. "A Chapter about Churches." *New York Observer* 25 (April 24, 1847).

———. "A Chapter about Churches (Concluded)." *New York Observer* 25 (May 1, 1847).

"The Vesting of Choirs—How it Came into Vogue in Old Trinity." *Brooklyn Eagle* 52 (March 13, 1892): 16.

"Vicksburg, Miss." *Debow's Review, Agricultural, Commercial, Industrial Progress and Resources* 2 (August 1866): 218.

Walker, James. "Reaction in Favor of the Roman Catholics. A Discourse Delivered Before the University in Cambridge, at the Dudleian Lecture, May 10, 1837." *Christian Examiner* 23 (September 1837): 1–29.

Walworth, C. L. "Reminiscences of a Catholic Crisis in England Fifty Years Ago." *Catholic World* 69 (September 1899): 814–16.

Walworth, Clarence E. *The Oxford Movement in America; or, Glimpses of Life in an Anglican Seminary.* 1895. Reprint, New York: United States Catholic Historical Society, 1974.

Warren, Ira. *The Causes and the Cure of Puseyism; or, The Elementary Principles of Roman Error Detected in the Liturgy, Offices, Homilies, and Usages of the Episcopal Churches of England and America; With a Proposed Remedy.* Boston: Crocker and Brewster, 1847.

Watson, John Fanning. *Annals of Philadelphia and Pennsylvania, In the Olden Time: Being a Collection of Memoirs, Anecdotes, and Incidents of the City and its Inhabitants, and of the Earliest Settlements of the Inland Part of Pennsylvania, From the Day. . . .* 2 vols. Philadelphia: Carey and Hart, 1845.

Wayland, Francis. *Notes on the Principles and Practices of Baptist Churches.* 1857. Reprint, New York: Arno Press, 1980.

Welby, Adlard. *A Visit to North America and the English Settlements in Illinois, With a Winter Residence at Philadelphia; Solely to Ascertain the Actual Prospects of the Emigrating Agriculturist, Mechanic, and Commercial Speculator.* London: J. Drury, 1821.

"West Spruce St. Baptist Church, Philadelphia." *Scientific American* 20 (January 23, 1869): 53.

Whitehead, William. *Directory of the Borough of Chester, for the Years 1859–60, Containing a Concise History of the Borough. . . .* West Chester, PA: E. F. James, 1859.

Wightman, J. Colver. "The Fundamental Law of Christian Worship." *Baptist Quarterly* 1 (April 1867): 191–215.

Willard, A. R. "Recent Church Architecture in Boston." *New England Magazine* 7 (February 1890): 641–62.

Wills, Frank. *Ancient English Ecclesiastical Architecture and Its Principles, Applied to the Wants of the Church at the Present Day.* New York: Stanford and Swords, 1850.

Withers, Frederick Clarke. *Church Architecture: Plans, Elevations, and Views of Twenty-one Churches and Two School-houses, Photo-lithographed from Original Drawings: With Numerous Illustrations Shewing Details of Construction, Church Fittings, etc.* New York: A. J. Bicknell, 1873.

Woolson, Constance Fenimore. "Peter, the Parson." *Scribners Monthly* 8 (September 1874): 600–610.

Young, Alfred. *Catholic and Protestant Countries Compared in Civilization,*

Popular Happiness, General Intelligence, and Morality. New York: The Catholic Book Exchange, 1895.

Secondary Sources

Addleshaw, G. W. O., and Frederick Etchells. *The Architectural Setting of Anglican Worship; An Inquiry into the Arrangements for Public Worship in the Church of England from the Reformation to the Present Day*. London: Faber and Faber, 1948.

Ahlstrom, Sydney E. *A Religious History of the American People*. New Haven: Yale University Press, 1972.

Aldrich, Megan. *A. W. N. Pugin: Master of Gothic Revival*. Edited by Paul Atterbury. New Haven: Published for the Bard Graduate Center for Studies in the Decorative Arts, New York, by Yale University Press, 1995.

Allitt, Patrick. *Catholic Converts: British and American Intellectuals Turn to Rome*. Ithaca, NY: Cornell University Press, 1997.

Anderson, William, and Clive Hicks. *The Rise of the Gothic*. Salem, NH: Salem House, 1985.

Andrews, Wayne. *American Gothic: Its Origins, Its Trials, Its Triumphs*. New York: Random House, 1975.

Arnett, Dessie Ash, and Lenace Robinette Clark. *Methodist Altars, New Edition*. Charleston, WV: D. A. Arnett, 1961.

Baker, Paul R. *The Fortunate Pilgrims: Americans in Italy, 1800–1860*. Cambridge, MA: Harvard University Press, 1964.

Beals, Carleton. *Brass-Knuckle Crusade: The Great Know-Nothing Conspiracy: 1820–1860*. New York: Hastings House, 1960.

Bell, Catherine. *Ritual Theory, Ritual Practice*. New York: Oxford University Press, 1992.

Bellah, Robert N., and Frederick E. Greenspahn, eds. *Uncivil Religion: Interreligious Hostility in America*. New York: Crossroad, 1987.

Bendroth, Margaret. "Rum, Romanism, and Evangelism: Protestants and Catholics in Late-Nineteenth-Century Boston." *Church History* 68 (September 1999): 627–47.

Benes, Peter, ed. *New England Meeting House and Church: 1630–1850*. Dublin, NH: Dublin Seminar for New England Folklife, 1979.

Bennett, William Harper. *Catholic Footsteps in Old New York: A Chronicle of Catholicity in the City of New York From 1524 to 1808*. New York: Schwartz, Kirwin and Fauss, 1909.

Berger, Teresa. *Women's Ways of Worship: Gender Analysis and Liturgical History*. Collegeville, MN: Liturgical Press, 1999.

Billington, Ray Allen. *The Protestant Crusade: 1800–1860*. New York: Macmillan, 1938.

———. "Tentative Bibliography of Anti-Catholic Propaganda in the United States (1800–1860)." *Catholic Historical Review* 18 (January 1933): 492–513.

Boylan, Anne M. *Sunday School: The Formation of an American Institution, 1790–1880*. New Haven: Yale University Press, 1988.

Bradshaw, Paul F., and Lawrence A. Hoffman, eds. *The Changing Face of Jewish and Christian Worship in North America*. Notre Dame: University of Notre Dame Press, 1991.

Bragg, Rick. *Wooden Churches: A Celebration*. Chapel Hill, NC: Algonquin Books of Chapel Hill, 1999.

Buggeln, Gretchen Townsend. *Temples of Grace: The Material Transformation of Connecticut's Churches, 1790–1840*. Hanover, CT: University Press of New England, 2003.

Bushman, Richard L. *The Refinement of America: Persons, Houses, Cities*. New York: Random House, 1992.

Butler, Jon. *Awash in a Sea of Faith: Christianizing the American People*. Cambridge, MA: Harvard University Press, 1990.

———. "Historiographical Heresy: Catholicism as a Model for American Religious History." In *Belief in History: Innovative Approaches to European and American Religion*, edited by Thomas A. Kselman, 286–309. Notre Dame: University of Notre Dame Press, 1991.

Cameron, Kenneth Walter. *Connecticut Churchmanship; Records and Historical Papers Concerning the Anglican Church in Connecticut in the Eighteenth and Early Nineteenth Centuries*. Hartford: Transcendental Books, 1969.

Campbell, Colin. *The Romantic Ethic and the Spirit of Modern Consumerism*. New York: B. Blackwell, 1987.

Campbell, Debra. "Catholicism from Independence to World War I." In *Encyclopedia of the American Religious Experience*, edited by Charles H. Lippy and Peter W. Williams, 1:357–73. New York: Scribner, 1988.

Carey, Patrick W. *People, Priests and Prelates: Ecclesiastical Democracy and the Tensions of Trusteeism*. Notre Dame: University of Notre Dame Press, 1987.

Cashdollar, Charles D. *A Spiritual Home: Life in British and American*

Reformed Congregations, 1830–1915. University Park: Pennsylvania State University Press, 2000.

Chadwick, Owen. *The Mind of the Oxford Movement*. Stanford: Stanford University Press, 1960.

————. *The Reformation*. London: Hodder and Stoughton, 1965.

Chidester, David, and Edwart T. Linenthal. *American Sacred Space*. Bloomington: Indiana University Press, 1995.

Chinnici, Joseph P., O.F.M. *Living Stones: The History and Structure of Catholic Spiritual Life in the United States*. New York: Macmillan, 1989.

Chorley, E. Clowes. *Men and Movements in the American Episcopal Church*. New York: Scribner, 1946.

Clark, Kenneth. *The Gothic Revival, an Essay in the History of Taste*. London: Constable and Co., ltd., 1928.

Cleary, Richard. "Texas Gothic, French Accent: The Architecture of the Roman Catholic Church in Antebellum Texas." Paper presented at the 55th Annual Meeting of the Society of Architectural Historians, Richmond, VA, April 17–21, 2002.

Coffey, Rachel. "Negotiating Tradition and Technology: Benziger Brothers' Trade Catalogues of Church Goods, 1879–1937." M.A. thesis, University of Delaware, 2001.

Coffin, William, Jr. *The Riverside Church in the City of New York*. New York: Sterling Roman Press, 1978.

Combs, Diana Williams. *Early Gravestone Art in Georgia and South Carolina*. Athens: University of Georgia Press, 1986.

Conkin, Paul K. *The Uneasy Center: Reformed Christianity in Antebellum America*. Chapel Hill: University of North Carolina Press, 1995.

Cram, Ralph Adams. "Gothic Architecture." Transcribed by Michael C. Tinkler in *The Catholic Encyclopedia* 6. <http://www.newadvent.org>.

————. *My Life in Architecture*. Boston: Little, Brown, and Company, 1936.

————. *The Significance of Gothic Art*. Boston: Marshall Jones Company, 1918.

Crews, Clyde F. *Presence and Possibility: Louisville Catholicism and its Cathedral: An Historical Sketch of the Louisville Catholic Experience as Seen Through the Cathedral of the Assumption*. Louisville, KY: n.p., 1973.

Curtis, Georgina Pell, ed. *Some Roads to Rome in America; Being Personal Records of Conversions to the Catholic Church*. St. Louis, MO: Freiburg Baden, B. Herder, 1910.

Davis, David Brion. "Some Themes of Counter-Subversion: An Analysis of

Anti-Masonic, Anti-Catholic and Anti-Mormon Literature." *Mississippi Valley Historical Review* 47 (September 1960): 205–24.

Davis, John. "Catholic Envy: The Visual Culture of Protestant Desire." In *The Visual Culture of American Religions*, edited by David Morgan and Sally Promey, 105–28. Berkeley: University of California Press, 2001.

Davis, Lawrence B. *Immigrants, Baptists, and the Protestant Mind in America*. Urbana: University of Illinois Press, 1973.

Decker, John Paul. *The Art and Architecture of the First Presbyterian Church in Philadelphia*. Philadelphia: J. P. Decker, 2001.

Decker, Kevin F. "Grand and Godly Proportions: Roman Catholic Cathedral Churches of the Northeast, 1840–1900." Ph.D. dissertation, State University of New York at Albany, 2000.

Deetz, James. *In Small Things Forgotten: The Archaeology of Early American Life*. Garden City, NY: Anchor Press/Doubleday, 1977.

Dillenberger, John. *The Visual Arts and Christianity in America: The Colonial Period Through the Nineteenth Century*. Chico, CA: Scholars Press, 1984.

Dolan, Jay P. *The American Catholic Experience: A History from Colonial Times to the Present*. Garden City, NY: Doubleday, 1985.

———. *Catholic Revivalism: The American Experience, 1830–1900*. Notre Dame: University of Notre Dame Press, 1978.

———. *The Immigrant Church: New York's Irish and German Catholics, 1815–1865*. Baltimore: Johns Hopkins University Press, 1975.

Dorgan, Howard. *Giving Glory to God in Appalachia: Worship Practices of Six Baptist Subdenominations*. Knoxville: University of Tennessee Press, 1987.

Dorsey, John, and James D. Dilts, eds. *A Guide to Baltimore Architecture*. 3rd ed. Centreville, MD: Tidewater Publishers, 1997.

Douglas, Ann. *The Feminization of American Culture*. New York: Knopf, 1977.

Downs, Arthur Channing, Jr. "America's First 'Medieval' Churches." *Historical Magazine of the Protestant Episcopal Church* 45 (June 1972): 165–76.

Drummond, Andrew Landale. *The Church Architecture of Protestantism, an Historical and Constructive Study*. Edinburgh: T. and T. Clark, 1934.

Drury, Marjule Anne. "Anti-Catholicism in Germany, Britain, and the United States: A Review and Critique of Recent Scholarship." *Church History* 70 (March 2001): 98–131.

Duffy, Eamon. *The Stripping of the Altars: Traditional Religion in England, 1400–1580*. New Haven: Yale University Press, 1992.

Duke, Jane Taylor. *History of the Ginter Park Baptist Church, Richmond,*

Virginia, Published for the Twenty-Fifth Anniversary. Richmond: n.p., 1941.

Early, James. *Romanticism and American Architecture*. New York: A. S. Barnes, 1965.

Ellinwood, Leonard. *The History of American Church Music*. New York: Morehouse-Gorham Co., 1953.

Ellis, John Tracy. *American Catholicism*. Chicago: University of Chicago Press, 1956.

Etherington, Charles L. *Protestant Worship Music: Its History and Practice*. New York: Holt, Rinehart and Winston, 1962.

Farnsworth, Jean M. "An American Bias for Foreign Stained Glass." *Nineteenth Century Studies* 17 (1997): 15–20.

Farnsworth, Jean M., Carmen R Croce, and Joseph F. Chorpenning, eds. *Stained Glass in Catholic Philadelphia*. Philadelphia: St. Joseph's University Press, 2002.

Feldberg, Michael. *The Philadelphia Riots of 1844: A Study of Ethnic Conflict*. Westport, CT: Greenwood Press, 1975.

Field, William Noe. "Ecclesiastical Architecture in the United States." *Journal of Texas Catholic History and Culture* 2 (1991): 9–14.

Finke, Roger, and Rodney Starke. *The Churching of America, 1776–1990: Winners and Losers in Our Religious Economy*. New Brunswick, NJ: Rutgers University Press, 1992.

Finley, Gregg. "Stained Glass and Stone Tracery: The Gothic Revival and the Shaping of Canadian Sensibilities." *British Journal of Canadian Studies* 5 (1990): 78–98.

Finney, Paul Corby, ed. *Seeing Beyond the Word: Visual Arts and the Calvinist Tradition*. Grand Rapids, MI: Eerdmans, 1999.

Fleming, Daniel J. "Religious Symbols Crossing Cultural Boundaries." In *Religious Symbolism*, edited by F. Ernest Johnson, 81–106. Port Washington, NY: Kennikat Press, 1969.

Fox, Stephen. "Nicholas Joseph Clayton as a Catholic Architect." *The Journal of Texas Catholic History and Culture* 2 (1991): 54–77.

Franchot, Jenny. *Roads to Rome: The Antebellum Protestant Encounter with Catholicism*. Berkeley: University of California Press, 1994.

Frey, Sylvia R., and Betty Wood. *Come Shouting to Zion: African American Protestantism in the American South and British Caribbean to 1830*. Chapel Hill: University of North Carolina Press, 1998.

Garber, Paul Neff. *The Methodist Meeting House*. New York: Board of Missions and Church Extension, 1941.

Garrett, James Leo. *Baptists and Roman Catholicism*. Nashville, TN: Broadman Press, 1965.

Garrigan, Kristine Ottesen. *Ruskin on Architecture: His Thought and Influence*. Madison: University of Wisconsin Press, 1973.

Gaustad, Edwin S. *Historical Atlas of Religion in America*. New York: Harper and Row, 1976.

Gaustad, Edwin Scott, and Philip L. Barlow, with the special assistance of Richard W. Dishno. *New Historical Atlas of Religion in America*. New York: Oxford University Press, 2001.

Gerber, David A. "Ambivalent Anti-Catholicism: Buffalo's American Protestant Elite Faces the Challenge of the Catholic Church, 1850–1860." *Civil War History* 30 (June 1984): 120–43.

Gilchrist, Agnes Addison. *Romanticism and the Gothic Revival*. New York: R. R. Smith, 1938.

Goen, C. C. *Broken Churches, Broken Nation: Denominational Schisms and the Coming of the American Civil War*. Macon, GA: Mercer University Press, 1985.

Gray, William F. *Philadelphia's Architecture*. Philadelphia: The Society, 1915.

Greiff, Constance M. *John Notman, Architect, 1810–1865*. Philadelphia: Athenaeum of Philadelphia, 1979.

Grimes, Robert R. *How Shall We Sing in a Foreign Land? Music of Irish-Catholic Immigrants in the Antebellum United States*. Notre Dame: University of Notre Dame Press, 1996.

Guelzo, Allen C. *For the Union of Evangelical Christendom: The Irony of the Reformed Episcopalians*. University Park: Pennsylvania State University Press, 1994.

———. "Ritual, Romanism, and Rebellion: The Disappearance of the Evangelical Episcopalians, 1853–1873." *Anglican and Episcopal History* 62 (December 1993): 551–77.

Gundersen, Joan R. "Rural Gothic: Episcopal Churches on the Minnesota Frontier." *Minnesota History* 50 (Fall 1987): 258–68.

Hall, James. *Dictionary of Subjects and Symbols in Art*. London: J. Murray, 1974.

Hambrick-Stowe, Charles E. *The Practice of Piety: Puritan Devotional Disciplines in Seventeenth-Century New England*. Chapel Hill: University of North Carolina Press, 1982.

Hamburger, Philip. *Separation of Church and State*. Cambridge, MA: Harvard University Press, 2002.

Hampton, Roy A., III. "German Gothic in the Midwest: The Parish

Churches of Franz Georg Himpler and Adolphus Druiding." *U.S. Catholic Historian* 15 (Winter 1997): 51–74.

Handy, Robert T. *A Christian America: Protestant Hopes and Historical Realities*. New York: Oxford University Press, 1971.

Harding, Vincent. *A Certain Magnificence: Lyman Beecher and the Transformation of American Protestantism, 1775–1863*. Brooklyn, NY: Carlson Pub., 1991.

Hatch, Nathan O. *The Democratization of American Christianity*. New Haven: Yale University Press, 1989.

Heyrman, Christine Leigh. *Southern Cross: The Beginnings of the Bible Belt*. New York: Knopf, 1997.

Hickman, Hoyt L. *United Methodist Altars: A Guide for the Local Church*. Nashville, TN: Abingdon Press, 1984.

Higham, John. *Strangers in the Land: Patterns in American Nativism, 1860–1925*. New Brunswick, NJ: Rutgers University Press, 1955.

Hills, George Morgan. *History of the Church in Burlington, New Jersey; Comprising the Facts and Incidents of Nearly Two Hundred Years, From Original, Contemporaneous Sources*. Trenton, NJ: W. S. Sharp, 1876.

Hoffecker, Carol E. "Church Gothic: A Case Study of Revival Architecture in Wilmington, Delaware." *Winterthur Portfolio* 8 (1973): 215–32.

Hoffman, Lawrence A., and Janet R. Walton. *Sacred Sound and Social Change: Liturgical Music in Jewish and Christian Experience*. Notre Dame: University of Notre Dame Press, 1992.

Holmes, David L. *A Brief History of the Episcopal Church*. Valley Forge, PA: Trinity Press International, 1993.

Howe, Katherine S., and David B. Warren. *The Gothic Revival Style in America, 1830–1870*. Houston, TX: Museum of Fine Arts, 1976.

Hults, Linda C. "Pilgrim's Progress in the West: Moran's 'The Mountain of the Holy Cross.'" *American Art* 5 (Winter/Spring 1991): 68–85.

Hume, Paul. *Catholic Church Music*. New York: Dodd, Mead, 1960.

Hunter, Wilbur H., Jr. "Robert Cary Long, Jr., and the Battle of the Styles." *Journal of the Society of Architectural Historians* 16 (March 1957): 28–30.

Johnson, F. Ernest, ed. *Religious Symbolism*. Jewish Theological Seminary of America, Religion and Civilization Series. Port Washington, NY: Kennikat Press, 1969.

Johnson, James Rosser. *The Radiance of Chartres: Studies in the Early Stained Glass of the Cathedral*. New York: Random House, 1965.

Jones, Ina. *Arranging Church Flowers*. Dallas: B. Upshaw, 1950.

Kane, Paula M. *Separatism and Subculture: Boston Catholicism, 1900–1920*. Chapel Hill: University of North Carolina Press, 1994.

Kasson, John F. *Rudeness and Civility: Manners in Nineteenth-Century Urban America*. New York: Hill and Wang, 1990.

Kervick, Francis William Wynn. *Architects in America of Catholic Tradition*. Rutland, VT: C. E. Tuttle Co., 1962.

Kilde, Jeanne Halgren. *When Church Became Theatre: The Transformation of Evangelical Architecture and Worship in Nineteenth-Century America*. New York: Oxford University Press, 2002.

Kimball, Fiske. "Latrobe's Designs for the Cathedral of Baltimore." *Architectural Record* 42 (December 1917): 540–50.

Kimball, Fiske, and George Harold Edgell. *A History of Architecture*. New York: Harper, 1918.

Lane, Mills. *Architecture of the Old South: Maryland*. Rev. ed. Savannah, GA: Beehive Press, 1996.

Lanier, Gabrielle M., and Bernard L. Herman. *Everyday Architecture of the Mid-Atlantic: Looking at Buildings and Landscapes*. Baltimore: Johns Hopkins University Press, 1997.

Leach, William H. *The Use of Candles in Christian Fellowship*. New York: Goodenough and Woglom Co., 1940.

Lears, T. J. Jackson. *No Place of Grace: Antimodernism and the Transformation of American Culture, 1880–1920*. New York: Pantheon Books, 1981.

LeBeau, Bryan. "'Saving the West from the Pope': Anti-Catholic Propaganda and the Settlement of the Mississippi River Valley." *American Studies International* 32 (Spring 1991): 101–14.

Linden-Ward, Blanche. *Silent City on a Hill: Landscapes of Memory and Boston's Mount Auburn Cemetery*. Columbus: Ohio State University Press, 1989.

Little, Bryan. *Catholic Churches Since 1623: A Study of Roman Catholic Churches in England and Wales from Penal Times to the Present Decade*. London: Robert Hale, Ltd., 1966.

Lord, Robert Howard, John E. Sexton, and Edward T. Harrington. *History of the Archdiocese of Boston in the Various Stages of its Development, 1604 to 1943*. 3 vols. New York: Sheed and Ward, 1944.

Loth, Calder, and Julius Trousdale Sadler Jr. *The Only Proper Style: Gothic Architecture in America*. Boston: New York Graphic Society, 1975.

Ludwig, Allan I. *Graven Images: New England Stonecarving and Its Symbols, 1650–1815*. Middletown, CT: Wesleyan University Press, 1966.

Manross, William Wilson. *The Episcopal Church in the United States, 1800–*

1840: A Study in Church Life. New York: Columbia University Press, 1938.

Martin, Ann Smart, and J. Ritchie Garrison. *American Material Culture: The Shape of the Field*. Winterthur, DE: Henry Francis du Pont Winterthur Museum; Knoxville, TN: Distributed by University of Tennessee Press, 1997.

Matovina, Timothy M. "Sacred Place and Collective Memory: San Fernando Cathedral, San Antonio, Texas." *U.S. Catholic Historian* 15 (Winter 1997): 33–50.

McCarthy, Michael J. *The Origins of the Gothic Revival*. New Haven: Published for the Paul Mellon Centre for Studies in British Art by Yale University Press, 1987.

McClinton, Katharine Morrison. *Flower Arrangement in the Church*. New York: Morehouse-Gorham Co., 1949.

McDannell, Colleen. *The Christian Home in Victorian America, 1840–1900*. Religion in North America Series. Bloomington: Indiana University Press, 1986.

————. *Material Christianity: Religion and Popular Culture in America*. New Haven: Yale University Press, 1995.

Memorial Volume of the Centenary of St. Mary's Seminary of St. Sulpice, Baltimore, Md. Baltimore: John Murphy, 1891.

Melton, Julius. *Presbyterian Worship in America: Changing Patterns Since 1787*. Richmond, VA: John Knox Press, 1967.

Michalski, Sergiusz. *The Reformation and the Visual Arts: The Protestant Image Question in Western and Eastern Europe*. New York: Routledge, 1993.

Milhouse, Paul W. *Christian Worship in Symbol and Ritual*. Harrisburg, PA: Evangelical Press, 1953.

Milspaw, Yvonne J. "Pioneer Churches in Central Pennsylvania: Plain Walls and Little Angels." *Pioneer America Society Transactions* 3 (1980): 57–75.

Morgan, David. *Protestants and Pictures: Religion, Visual Culture and the Age of American Mass Production*. New York: Oxford University Press, 1999.

————. *Visual Piety: A History and Theory of Popular Religious Images*. Berkeley: University of California Press, 1998.

————, ed. *Icons of American Protestantism: The Art of Warner Sallman*. New Haven: Yale University Press, 1996.

Morgan, David, and Sally Promey, eds. *The Visual Culture of American Religions*. Berkeley: University of California Press, 2001.

Mullin, Robert Bruce. *Episcopal Vision/American Reality: High Church*

Theology and Social Thought in Evangelical America. New Haven: Yale University Press, 1986.

Mullins, Ruth E. *Flowers and Symbols for the Christian Year*. New York: Hearthside Press, 1967.

Newman, Simon P. "Reading the Bodies of Early American Seafarers." *William and Mary Quarterly*, 3d ser., 55 (January 1998): 59–82.

Nockles, Peter Benedict. *The Oxford Movement in Context, Anglican High Churchmanship, 1760–1857*. New York: Cambridge University Press, 1994.

Noll, Mark A., David W. Bebbington, and George A. Rawlyk, eds. *Evangelicalism: Comparative Studies of Popular Protestantism in North America, the British Isles, and Beyond, 1700–1990*. New York: Oxford University Press, 1994.

Norwood, Frederick A. *The Story of American Methodism: A History of the United Methodists and Their Relations*. Nashville: Abingdon Press, 1974.

Nygaard, Norman E., and Virginia G. Miller. *The Importance of Appropriate Pulpit Attire*. Culver City, CA: Murray and Gee, 1955.

O'Connell, J. B. *Church Building and Furnishing: The Church's Way, A Study in Liturgical Law*. Notre Dame: University of Notre Dame Press, 1955.

Oliveri, Gregory William. "Building a Baroque Catholicism: The Philadelphia Churches of Edwin Forrest Durang." Master's thesis, University of Delaware, 1999.

Orsi, Robert A. *The Madonna of 115th Street: Faith and Community in Italian Harlem, 1880–1950*. New Haven: Yale University Press, 1985.

Owen, Christopher H. "By Design: The Social Meaning of Methodist Church Architecture in Nineteenth-Century Georgia." *Georgia Historical Quarterly* 75 (Summer 1991): 223–35.

Pagliarini, Marie Anne. "The Pure American Woman and the Wicked Catholic Priest: An Analysis of Anti-Catholic Literature in Antebellum America." *Religion and American Culture* 9 (Winter 1999): 97–128.

Patrick, James. "Ecclesiological Gothic in the Antebellum South." *Winterthur Portfolio* 15 (Summer 1980): 117–38.

Peterson, Fred W. *Building Community, Keeping the Faith: German Catholic Vernacular Architecture in a Rural Minnesota Parish*. St. Paul: Minnesota Historical Society Press, 1998.

Philadelphia Art Alliance. *Philadelphia Architecture in the Nineteenth Century*. Edited by Theo B. White. Philadelphia: Published for the Philadelphia Art Alliance by the University of Pennsylvania Press, 1953.

Phillips, John. *The Reformation of Images: Destruction of Art in England, 1535–1660*. Berkeley: University of California Press, 1973.

Pierson, William H., Jr. *American Buildings and Their Architects*. Vol. 1, *The Colonial and Neoclassical Styles*. Garden City, NY: Doubleday, 1970.

———. *American Buildings and Their Architects*. Vol. 2, *Technology and the Picturesque, the Corporate and the Early Gothic Styles*. Garden City, NY: Doubleday and Company, 1978.

Place, Charles. "From Meeting House to Church in New England." *Old Time New England* 13 (October 1922): 69–77.

Platt, Colin. *The Parish Churches of Medieval England*. London: Secker and Warburg, 1981.

Pocius, Gerald L., ed. *Living in a Material World: Canadian and American Approaches to Material Culture*. St. John's, Newfoundland: Institute of Social and Economic Research, Memorial University of Newfoundland, 1991.

Praetzellis, Adrian, and Mary Praetzellis, eds. "Archaeologists as Storytellers." *Historical Archaeology* 32 (1998).

Procter-Smith, Marjorie, and Janet R. Walton, eds. *Women at Worship: Interpretations of North American Diversity*. Louisville, KY: Westminster/J. Knox Press, 1993.

Prown, Jules David. "Style as Evidence." *Winterthur Portfolio* 15 (Autumn 1980): 197–210.

Raguin, Virginia Chieffo. *Glory in Glass: Stained Glass in the United States: Origins, Variety, and Preservation*. New York: American Bible Society, 1998.

———. "Revivals, Revivalists, and Architectural Stained Glass." *Journal of the Society of Architectural Historians* 49 (September 1990): 310–29.

Raguin, Virginia Chieffo, and Mary Ann Powers. *Sacred Spaces: Building and Remembering Sites of Worship in the Nineteenth Century*. Worcester, MA: Iris and B. Gerald Cantor Art Gallery, College of the Holy Cross, 2002.

Reed, Henry Hope, Jr. "In the Shadow of St. Barbara and St. Thomas, Catholic Architecture in America." *Thought: Fordham University Quarterly* 31 (Autumn 1956): 326–49.

Restad, Penne L. *Christmas in America*. New York: Oxford University Press, 1995.

Richardson, Douglas Scott. *Gothic Revival Architecture in Ireland*. Outstanding Dissertations in the Fine Arts. New York: Garland Publishing, 1983.

Rose, Anne C. *Beloved Strangers: Interfaith Families in Nineteenth-Century America*. Cambridge, MA: Harvard University Press, 2001.

Rose, Michael S. *Ugly As Sin: Why They Changed Our Churches from Sacred Places to Meeting Spaces and How We Can Change Them Back Again*. Manchester, NH: Sophia Institute Press, 2001.

Rosenthal, Bernard, and Paul E. Szarmach, eds. *Medievalism in American Culture*. Binghamton: Center for Medieval and Early Renaissance Studies, State University of New York at Binghamton, 1989.

Roy, Jody M. *Rhetorical Campaigns of the 19th-Century Anti-Catholics and Catholics in America*. Lewiston, NY: Edwin Mellen Press, 2000.

Schapiro, Meyer. *Theory and Philosophy of Art: Style, Artist, Society*. New York: George Braziller, 1994.

Schmidt, Leigh Eric. *Consumer Rites: The Buying and Selling of American Holidays*. Princeton, NJ: Princeton University Press, 1995.

———. *Holy Fairs: Scottish Communions and American Revivals in the Early Modern Period*. Princeton: Princeton University Press, 1989.

Schneider, A. Gregory. *The Way of the Cross Leads Home: The Domestication of American Methodism*. Bloomington: Indiana University Press, 1993.

Schultz, Nancy Lusignan. *Fire and Roses: The Burning of the Charlestown Convent, 1834*. New York: Free Press, 2000.

Schuyler, David. *Apostle of Taste: Andrew Jackson Downing, 1815–1852*. Baltimore: Johns Hopkins University Press, 1996.

Shaughnessy, Gerald. *Has the Immigrant Kept the Faith? A Study of Immigration and Catholic Growth in the United States, 1790–1920*. New York: Macmillan, 1925.

Shea, John Gilmary. *A History of the Catholic Church Within the Limits of the United States, From the First Attempted Colonization to the Present Time*. 4 vols. New York: J. G. Shea, 1886–92.

Shelley, Donald A. *Lewis Miller, Sketches and Chronicles: The Reflections of a Nineteenth Century Pennsylvania German Folk Artist*. York, PA: Historical Society of York County, 1966.

Sherwood, Gayle. "'Buds the Infant Mind': Charles Ives's *The Celestial Country* and American Protestant Choral Traditions." *19th-Century Music* 23 (Fall 1999): 163–89.

Smith, John Talbot. *The Catholic Church in New York: A History of the New York Diocese From Its Establishment in 1808 to the Present Time*. 2 vols. New York: Hall and Locke Co., 1905.

Smith, Ryan K. "Carpenter Gothic: The Voices of Episcopal Churches on the St. Johns River." *El Escribano* 32 (1995): 65–90.

———. "The Cross: Church Symbol and Contest in Nineteenth-Century America." *Church History* 70 (December 2001): 705–34.

Spalding, Thomas W. *The Premier See: A History of the Archdiocese of Baltimore, 1789-1989.* Baltimore: Johns Hopkins University Press, 1989.

Springer, Annemarie. *Nineteenth Century German-American Church Artists.* <http://www.ulib.iupui.edu/kade/springer/index.html>.

Stanton, Phoebe B. *The Gothic Revival and American Church Architecture: An Episode in Taste, 1840-1856.* Baltimore: Johns Hopkins University Press, 1968.

———. *Pugin.* New York: Viking Press, 1971-72.

Stein, Roger B. *John Ruskin and Aesthetic Thought in America.* Cambridge, MA: Harvard University Press, 1967.

Stevenson, Robert. *Protestant Church Music in America: A Short Survey of Men and Movements from 1564 to the Present.* New York: W. W. Norton, 1966.

The Story of St. Joseph's Proto-Cathedral and Its Paintings. N.p., 1930s.

Sturm, James L., and James Chotas. *Stained Glass from Medieval Times to the Present: Treasures to Be Seen in New York.* New York: E. P. Dutton, Inc., 1982.

Sweeney, Kevin M. "Meetinghouses, Town Houses, and Churches: Changing Perceptions of Sacred and Secular Space in Southern New England, 1720-1850." *Winterthur Portfolio* 28 (Spring 1993): 59-93.

Taves, Ann. *The Household of Faith: Roman Catholic Devotions in Mid-Nineteenth-Century America.* Notre Dame: University of Notre Dame Press, 1986.

Thomas, George M. *Revivalism and Cultural Change: Christianity, Nation Building, and the Market in the Nineteenth-Century United States.* Chicago: University of Chicago Press, 1989.

Toker, Franklin. *The Church of Notre-Dame in Montreal: An Architectural History.* Montreal: McGill-Queen's University Press, 1970.

Townsend, Gretchen Carol. "Protestant Material Culture and Community in Connecticut, 1785-1840." Ph.D. dissertation, Yale University, 1995.

Trappes-Lomax, Michael. *Pugin, a Medieval Victorian.* London: Sheed and Ward, 1932.

Tucker, Karen B. Westerfield. *American Methodist Worship.* New York: Oxford University Press, 2000.

Tyack, Geo. S. *The Cross in Ritual, Architecture, and Art.* London: W. Andrews, 1900.

Unrau, John. *Looking at Architecture with Ruskin.* Toronto: University of Toronto Press, 1978.

Upjohn, Everard Miller. *Richard Upjohn, Architect and Churchman*. New York: Columbia University Press, 1939.

Upton, Dell. *Holy Things and Profane: Anglican Parish Churches in Colonial Virginia*. Cambridge, MA: M.I.T. Press, 1986.

Vance, William L. *America's Rome*. 2 vols. New Haven: Yale University Press, 1989.

Van Trump, James D. "The Romanesque Revival in Pittsburgh." *Journal of the Society of Architectural Historians* 16 (October 1957): 22–29.

Von Simson, Otto Georg. *The Gothic Cathedral: Origins of Gothic Architecture and the Medieval Concept of Order*. 3d ed. Princeton, NJ: Princeton University Press, 1988.

Walton, Janet. "The Missing Element of Women's Experience." In *The Changing Face of Jewish and Christian Worship in North America*, edited by Paul F. Bradshaw and Lawrence A. Hoffman, 199–217. Notre Dame: University of Notre Dame Press, 1991.

Ward, Barbara McLean. "In a Feasting Posture: Communion Vessels and Community Values in Seventeenth- and Eighteenth-Century New England." *Winterthur Portfolio* 23 (Spring 1988): 1–24.

Watson, Goodwin. "A Psychologist's View of Religious Symbols." In *Religious Symbolism*, edited by F. Ernest Johnson, 117–27. Port Washington, NY: Kennikat Press, 1969.

Webber, Robert. "Worship Perspectives." *Worship Leader Magazine*, May/June 2000.

Weber, Edward Joseph. *Catholic Church Buildings, Their Planning and Furnishing*. New York: J. F. Wagner; London: B. Herder, 1927.

Westfall, William. *Two Worlds: The Protestant Culture of Nineteenth-Century Ontario*. Kingston, Ontario: McGill-Queen's University Press, 1989.

Whiffen, Marcus. *American Architecture Since 1780: A Guide to the Styles*. Rev. ed. Cambridge, MA: M.I.T. Press, 1992.

White, James F. *The Cambridge Movement: The Ecclesiologists and the Gothic Revival*. New York: Cambridge University Press, 1979.

———. *Christian Worship in North America, A Retrospective: 1955–1995*. Collegeville, MN: The Liturgical Press, 1997.

———. *Protestant Worship: Traditions in Transition*. Louisville, KY: Westminster/John Knox Press, 1989.

———. *Roman Catholic Worship: Trent to Today*. New York: Paulist Press, 1995.

White, L. Michael. *Building God's House in the Roman World: Architectural Adaptation Among Pagans, Jews, and Christians*. Baltimore: Johns

Hopkins University Press, for the American Schools of Oriental Research, 1990.

Wilkinson, Stephanie. "A Novel Defense: Fictional Defenses of American Catholicism: 1829–1869." Ph.D. dissertation, University of Virginia, 1997.

Williams, Peter W. *Houses of God: Region, Religion, and Architecture in the United States.* Urbana: University of Illinois Press, 1997.

Wilson, Christopher. *The Gothic Cathedral: the Architecture of the Great Church, 1130–1530.* New York: Thames and Hudson, 1992.

Wolffe, John. "Anti-Catholicism and Evangelical Identity in Britain and the United States, 1830–1860." In *Evangelicalism: Comparative Studies of Popular Protestantism in North America, the British Isles, and Beyond, 1700–1990,* edited by Mark A. Noll, David W. Bebbington, and George A. Rawlyk, 179–97. New York: Oxford University Press, 1994.

———. *The Protestant Crusade in Great Britain, 1829–1860.* New York: Oxford University Press, 1991.

Wolniewicz, Richard. "Comparative Ethnic Church Architecture." *Polish American Studies* 54 (1997): 53–73.

Index

The letter *i* following a page number denotes an illustration; the letter *t* denotes a table.

78*i*, 173 (n. 30); and the Gothic
Revival, 84, 114, 120*i*, 161–62;
earlier worship practices of, 88,
125; church naming traditions of,
109; adoption of Roman Catholic worship practices, 119–23,
132, 134, 137, 138, 139, 149–52,
150*i*
Basilica of Notre Dame, Montreal,
Canada. *See* Cathedral of Notre
Dame, Montreal, Canada
Beecher, Catherine, 157
Beecher, Lyman, 9, 22, 116–17,
116*i*
Blacks. *See* African Americans
Boston, Massachusetts, 38, 45, 52,
54, 74, 101, 111, 116–17, 116*i*, 141
Bowdoin Street Congregational
Church, Boston, Massachusetts,
178 (n. 43)
Brainerd, Elizabeth Washburn, 48
Broad-Street Methodist Episcopal
Church, Newark, New Jersey, 73*i*,
110, 177–78 (n. 38)
Brook Farm, 48
Brooklyn, New York, 138, 149
Brownlee, W. C., 124
Brownson, Orestes, 48
Brunswick, Maine, 70
Buffalo, New York, 8, 110, 150
Burlington, New Jersey, 51–52,
66–67, 75, 113*i*

California, 52
Calvin, John, 6
Cambridge Camden Society, 2, 4
Cambridgeport, Massachusetts, 70
Camden, New Jersey, 38
Canada, 160

Candles: use of in worship, 18, 27–
44 passim, 121–34 passim, 141–42,
143, 147, 181 (n. 21)
Carroll, John, 91–92, 97
Cathedral of the Assumption, Baltimore, Maryland, 40–41, 124
Cathedral of the Assumption,
Louisville, Kentucky, 26, 28–30,
29*i*, 30*i*, 33
Cathedral of the Immaculate Conception, Albany, New York, 40
Cathedral of Notre Dame, Montreal, Canada, 40–41, 92
Cathedral of Saint John and Saint
Finibar, Charleston, South Carolina, 94
Cathedral of St. Peter in Chains,
Cincinnati, Ohio, 31, 35–37
Catholic Emancipation Act of 1829,
24
Catholics. *See* Roman Catholics
Catholic Telegraph, 25
Catholic World, 44, 47, 48, 97, 150,
155–56
Charleston, South Carolina, 39, 94
Charlestown, Massachusetts, 70
Chartres, France, cathedral at, 161
Cheverus, Jean de, 38
Chicago, Illinois, 90
Choirs. *See* Music
Christian Examiner, 18, 24, 135–36
Christian Recorder, 24, 61, 70–71
Christmas, 45, 126, 138–39
Christ's Church, Pittsburgh, Pennsylvania, 110, 173 (n. 34)
Church of the Ascension, Baltimore, Maryland, 75
Church of the Assumption, Philadelphia, Pennsylvania, 109

as observers of Roman Catholicism, 22, 24, 35–37, 40, 41, 46, 47; conversions to Roman Catholicism, 48, 168 (n. 36); adoption of Roman Catholic worship practices, 49, 134–56 passim, 146*i*, 148*i*, 158–59; use of the cross and other religious symbols among, 57, 58, 59, 67, 70–72, 73*i*, 81; on the cross as church symbol, 62, 65–66; earlier worship practices of, 88, 125, 131–32, 151, 157; and the Gothic Revival, 99–100, 114; church naming traditions of, 109–10

Metropolitan Catholic Almanac and Laity's Directory, 22–23
Middle Ages, 62, 86–98 passim
Middleton, Conyers, 179 (n. 4)
Milledgeville, Georgia, 88
Molière, Jean Baptiste, 86, 175 (n. 6)
Montreal, Canada, 40–41, 47, 92
Moran, Thomas, 171 (n. 19)
Moravians, 58, 164 (n. 11)
Moriarty, Thomas, 48
Morrisville, Pennsylvania, 134
Morse, Samuel F. B., 22
Murray, Nicholas, 124
Music: use of in Protestant worship, 9, 120–22, 125, 131–56 passim, 159; Protestant choirs, 13, 49, 100, 121–22, 125, 133–56 passim, 150*i*, 159; Lutheran traditions, 13, 135; use of in Roman Catholic worship, 35–37, 40, 45, 135–37, 157; Roman Catholic choirs, 39, 40, 94–95, 135–36. *See also* Organs, pipe
Mystic, Connecticut, 72, 145

Mystic Methodist Church, Mystic, Connecticut, 72

National Magazine, 46, 71, 81, 131
Nativism, 1, 64–65, 161. *See also* Anti-Catholicism
Newark, New Jersey, 71, 73*i*, 110
Newburyport, Rhode Island, 109
New Englander and Yale Review, 129–30
New Jersey, 140
Newman, John Henry, 48–49, 140
New Orleans, Louisiana, 14–15, 19, 94
New York City, New York: Roman Catholic churches in, 19, 40–43, 42*i*, 45, 92–93, 98, 109; Protestant churches in, 53, 68, 74, 84, 88, 96–97, 115, 161–62; Protestant conference in, 103–4; anti-Catholicism in, 124; art galleries in, 127; Protestant worship in, 128, 137, 138, 141–42, 149–50; furniture company in, 144*i*
New York Ecclesiological Society, 99
New York Mirror, 104
New York Observer, 24, 25, 64, 65, 66, 134, 137, 139, 142, 151
New York Times, 43
Norfolk, Virginia, 109
North American Review, 83, 84
North Bergen, New Jersey, 75
Notman, John, 76

Orange City, Florida, 145, 146*i*, 156
Organs, pipe: usage by denomination, 8, 49, 135; architecturally placed in Roman Catholic

churches, 28; use of in Roman Catholic worship, 36, 40; criticism of, 100, 137, 153; architecturally placed in Protestant churches, 112; use of in Protestant worship, 121, 141. *See also* Music

Oxford Movement, 72, 139–40

Palatka, Florida, 25, 110
Pentecostal groups, 148
Philadelphia, Pennsylvania: Roman Catholic churches in, 1–2, 15, 39, 40, 109, 174 (n. 2); anti-Catholicism in, 1–2, 3*i*, 22, 46, 70–71; Protestant churches in, 2, 4–5, 4*i*, 34–35, 77, 110, 111, 114, 174 (n. 2); Laurel Hill Cemetery in, 60, 67; secular buildings in, 88; church music in, 136
Pittsburgh, Pennsylvania, 81, 93, 109, 110
Poughkeepsie, New York, 172 (n. 26)
Presbyterian Critic and Monthly Review, 45–46
Presbyterian Magazine, 61
Presbyterians, 11–12; church construction rates of, 20*t*, 21; as observers of Roman Catholic expansion, 23, 24, 37–38, 41; concern regarding conversions to Roman Catholicism, 45–46, 168 (n. 36); adoption of Roman Catholic worship practices, 49, 134–54 passim; on the cross as church symbol, 51–53, 61, 62, 77; use of the cross and other religious symbols among, 57, 58, 59*i*, 60, 75–76; and the Gothic

Revival, 83, 85, 90, 100–101, 101*i*, 107–8, 110, 114–15; earlier worship practices of, 88–89, 124, 125, 130–31; church naming traditions of, 109; and representations of the human form, 111; on Anglican ritualism, 140, 142
Princeton, New Jersey, 76
Princeton Review, 83–84, 100, 135
Processions, 124, 125, 133, 140, 141–42, 148–50, 152, 154, 159
Protestant Episcopal Church. *See* Episcopalians
Protestants: and anti-Catholicism, 2, 5, 6, 8, 10, 12–13, 15, 17, 43, 52–54, 102, 124, 156, 160–61; and appropriation of Roman Catholic church art, 5, 6, 10–12, 15, 17–18, 49–50, 57–58, 65, 85, 106, 123, 128–29, 133–35, 152–55, 158–61; and the Reformation, 6–7, 58, 87; historians' treatment of, 7; nature of church architecture, 8–9, 15, 18, 21, 26–27, 33, 129–33, 152–53, 157–58; "meetinghouse-to-church" transition in early America, 8–9, 88–90; characteristics of denominations, 11–13, 79; as tourists at Roman Catholic churches, 14–15, 21, 33–43; conversions to Roman Catholicism, 18, 44–49, 58; observation of Roman Catholic expansion, 22–26; and church symbolism, 52–82; and the Gothic Revival, 68, 83–86, 90, 98–117, 160; church naming traditions of, 109–10; worship practices of, 119–56; musical traditions, 135, 136–38, 149–50; and

St. Peter's Catholic Church, Memphis, Tennessee, 94

St. Philip de Neri Catholic Church, Philadelphia, Pennsylvania, 2

St. Philomena's Catholic Church, Pittsburgh, Pennsylvania, 109

St. Thomas's Episcopal Church, Brooklyn, New York, 149

Salem, New Jersey, 75

Second Presbyterian Church, Baltimore, Maryland, 109

Second Presbyterian Church, Philadelphia, Pennsylvania, 111, 114–15

Second Presbyterian Church, St. Louis, Missouri, 59*i*

Seton, Elizabeth Ann, 45, 48

Sholl, Charles, 31, 32*i*, 155

Smith, Al, 161

Society of Friends. *See* Quakers

Southport, Wisconsin, 25

Spalding, Martin, 26–29, 31, 97–98

Stained glass, 6; Protestant use of, 2, 68, 74, 77, 81, 84, 111, 114, 120–21, 161–62; and the Gothic Revival, 2, 68, 83, 87, 93, 108, 111, 114, 161–62; Roman Catholic use of, 35, 46, 93, 95; representations of the human form in, 81, 111

Stearns, Sarah F., 48

Stone, Charles P., 48

Storer, Horatio Robinson, 48

Stowe, Harriet Beecher, 157

Strawberry Hill, 87

Strickland, William, 88

Stuart, Gilbert, 38

Tefft, Benjamin F., 35–37

Tennessee, 75

Texas, 94

Tiffany, Charles Comfort, 103–4

Trenton, New Jersey, 172 (n. 26)

Trinity Episcopal Church, New Haven, Connecticut, 109–10

Trinity Episcopal Church, New York City, New York, 53, 74, 88, 96–97, 115, 149–50

Tryon, Sarah Josephine, 48

Union Baptist Church, Mystic, Connecticut, 145

Unitarians, 48, 165 (n. 16), 168 (n. 36)

United Kingdom. *See* Great Britain

United States Catholic Magazine, 96–97, 105

United States Democratic Review, 83–84, 86, 115

Universalists, 48

Upjohn, Richard, 53, 70, 72, 74, 96, 115

Utica, New York, 38

Vestments: and the clergy, 6, 54, 124, 125, 126, 140–42, 147–49, 154, 169 (n. 2), 178 (n. 4); and church choirs, 121, 122, 127, 149–50, 150*i*, 159; preparation of, 133–34, 143, 180 (n. 14), 181 (n. 23)

Vicksburg, Mississippi, 176 (n. 16)

Virginia, 145–47, 153–54

Wadsworth, Daniel, 88

Walpole, Horace, 87

Washington, George, 34

Washington, D.C., 25

Washington, Ohio, 93–94

Weir, Robert W., 127